Theory and Practice of Decision Making in Regulation, Diagnostics and Reliability of Machines

Theory and Practice of Decision Making in Regulation, Diagnostics and Reliability of Machines provides a guide to decision-making in the areas of regulation, diagnostics and reliability of machines. Outlining the theoretical foundations that support decision-making processes and applying them to practical examples, the book provides insight and direction to enable informed decisions leading to optimum system operation.

It is difficult to achieve suitable safety and cost-efficiency without decision-making processes in place. Tackling this head-on, this book discusses theoretical foundations of decision-making and how this can impact diagnostics and the reliability of machines. Discussing cybernetics, artificial intelligence, engine control, machine diagnostics and reliability, the book uses practical examples such as turbine blades of aircraft engines and vehicles such as cars and buses.

This book will be of interest to students and industry professionals in the fields of mechanical, aerospace and automotive engineering, enabling readers to make informed decisions in their field of work.

Theory and Practice of Decision Making in Regulation, Diagnostics and Reliability of Machines

Paweł Lindstedt, Rafał Grądzki and Karol Golak

CRC Press
Taylor & Francis Group
Boca Raton London New York

CRC Press is an imprint of the
Taylor & Francis Group, an **informa** business

Designed cover image: Shutterstock

First edition published 2025
by CRC Press
2385 NW Executive Center Drive, Suite 320, Boca Raton FL 33431

and by CRC Press
4 Park Square, Milton Park, Abingdon, Oxon, OX14 4RN

CRC Press is an imprint of Taylor & Francis Group, LLC

© 2025 Paweł Lindstedt, Rafał Grądzki and Karol Golak

ISBN: 978-1-032-63841-6 (hbk)
ISBN: 978-1-032-63842-3 (pbk)
ISBN: 978-1-032-63844-7 (ebk)

DOI: 10.1201/9781032638447

Typeset in Times
by Apex CoVantage, LLC

Contents

Preface... ix
Author Biographies... xi
Introduction... xiii

Chapter 1 Elements of Applied Cybernetics: Theoretical Foundations of
Decision-Making.. 1

    1.1   Introduction 1
    1.2   The System and Its Environment....................................... 1
          1.2.1   The Concept of System and Environment............... 1
          1.2.2   Deterministic Systems... 4
          1.2.3   Probabilistic Systems 9
          1.2.4   System Failure.. 29
          1.2.5   Structure of Systems and System Coupling 41
          1.2.6   The Essence of Regulation and Control 45
          1.2.7   Basic Regulation Pattern: Balance and
                    Stability of Systems, Signal Dating,
                    Proprietary and Feed Components in Systems....... 48
          1.2.8   A Cybernetic Approach to Economic Systems:
                    Keynes Multiplier and Its Importance in
                    System Analysis 57
          1.2.9   Operation of Systems Under Mutual Conflict
                    Conditions: Game with Nature—the Minimax
                    and Maxmini Strategies... 58
          1.2.10 Risks in Decision-Making Processes 61
          1.2.11 Large Systems: Control Tasks in a Large
                    System—Monte Carlo Method 63
          1.2.12 Large Systems: Operational Research.................... 72
    1.3   Selected Elements of Information Theory........................... 78
          1.3.1   System Interactions 78
          1.3.2   Types of Information 79
          1.3.3   Information/Energy Relations in Systems............. 80
          1.3.4   Transmission of Information: Maxwell's
                    Demon 82
    1.4   Summary.. 89
    References 90

Chapter 2 Cybernetic Operating System... 92

    2.1   Introduction 92
    2.2   Elements of a Cybernetic Operating System of a
          Technical Object 92

2.3   Diagnostics in Cybernetic Operating Systems of
       Objects and Its Relations with Reliability and
       Regulation 96
2.4   Regulation in Operating Systems of Objects and Its
       Relations with Reliability and Diagnostics 100
2.5   Reliability in Operating Systems of Objects and Its
       Relations with Diagnostics and Regulation 103
2.6   Summary 104
References 105

Chapter 3 Decision Support in Turbine Jet Engine Control 107

3.1   Introduction 107
3.2   Description of the Turbine Jet Engine and Its
       Environment 108
3.3   Problems of Jet Engine Operation During Ground and
       Flight Tests 112
3.4   Simulation Testing of Turbine Jet Engines from Signal
       w on the Ground and from Signal z in Flight 113
3.5   Assessment Method for the Turbine Jet Engine
       Performance in Flight Based on the Engine's Ground
       Tests 119
       3.5.1   Theoretical Foundations 119
       3.5.2   Verification of the Operating Status of a
                Turbine Jet Engine on the Ground from Signal
                w and in Flight from Signal z Based on the
                Response from Signal w 122
3.6   Theoretical Foundations for Generating Modified
       Signals Which Describe Engine Inputs and Outputs 126
3.7   Assessment of the Regulation Quality of a Turbine Jet
       Engine in Flight Based on Its Ground Tests 128
3.8   Testing the Effect of Input and Output Changes on the
       Characteristics of a Turbine Jet Engine 131
       3.8.1   Test Program 131
       3.8.2   Test Results 133
3.9   Summary 142
References 144

Chapter 4 Decision Support in Machine Diagnostics 146

4.1   Introduction 146
4.2   Diagnostic Object, Diagnostic Signal 147
4.3   Theoretical Foundations of Object Diagnostic Models
       with Environment Elimination 149
       4.3.1   Model A^2_{T12T01} 149
       4.3.2   Model φ_{T12T01} 151

4.4   Determination of Model Parameters from
       Experimental Tests 153
4.5   Graphic Technical Status Portraits for Blades 162
4.6   Non-Parametric Method of Blade Technical Status
       Assessment 164
4.7   Summary 174
References 175

Chapter 5   Test Method for Reliability of a Bus in Various Operating
               Conditions 178

5.1   Introduction 178
5.2   Theoretical Foundation for Parametric and Transient
       Failure Identification from Equations of Interaction 179
5.3   In-Service Testing of Buses 183
5.4   Method for Conversions of Operating Data (Number
       of Failures, Set Size, and Failure Instance) into
       Reliability Parameters 201
5.5   Summary 208
References 209

Monograph Conclusion 213
Index 215

Preface

The modern world includes a very large number of interrelated engineered objects (their assemblies and components) and biological objects (their organs and parts). This reality requires people, and especially the services specialising in the operation and maintenance of these objects, to act rationally and regulate, diagnose, and test the reliability and safety of the object by following the principles of decision support theory.

Observations of these interdependent activities—which exist very close to one another—have facilitated the formulation of the following basic requirements, directly derived from practice and which, as it turns out, are absolutely necessary for a synthetic and unambiguous assessment of the state of fitness of any engineered (or biological) object under consideration:

- The object must be regulated (according to the principles of automation).
- The object must be diagnosed (according to the principles of diagnostics).
- The object must be safe and reliable (these properties are defined according to the theory of reliability and safety).

Current operating practice does not fail to confirm the well-known fact that regulation, diagnostics, and reliability of objects are processes performed in separation from one another and that the decisions made in any of the three areas are autonomous. This condition is difficult to accept and has continued up to the present. The most likely cause of the condition is the large disparities between theory and practice of basic automation engineering, principles of diagnostics, and the theory of reliability. There is an obvious need to coordinate the decisions which have been developed in these three areas. It is confirmed by the sequence of events often encountered in real life, such that the decision to perform regulation (automation) is caused by a change of the technical status (a.k.a. condition) (diagnostics), which—in extreme cases—is identified as a failure of the object in question (reliability).

It turns out that the rationale for a coordination of operating decisions in the areas of regulation, diagnostics, and reliability can be the fact that in the process of operating an object, realistically, there is only one measurable piece of information available about the object and that the information can be used many times and processed in different ways into decisions according to different needs resulting from the object's current state of fitness. Information like this can be used to validate the following: the regulation status of an object (according to automation principles), the technical status of an object (according to diagnostic principles), and the reliability status of an object (according to the theory of reliability).

This leads to the conclusion that in the process of operating engineered objects, there is an ever growing importance of full coordination between the decisions applicable to regulation, diagnostic, and reliability activities to ensure the suitable safety of engineered objects in operation. It can be expected that the result of this rational action will be an optimal system of operation of objects "according to the technical status" (with the system being cost-efficient, effective, and efficient), where the system ensures proper regulation of the objects, their correct technical status, and their required reliability status. Without support for the decision-making practice, it is difficult or even often impossible to achieve such a goal.

This condition has been the cause of the continuous development of the science of decision theory.

Author Biographies

Paweł Lindstedt PhD Eng. was born in 1942 in Grabów Kościerski. He is a graduate of the Military University of Technology in Warsaw. He served for many years as a professor at the Air Force Institute of Technology (ITWL) in Warsaw, in the Department of Aircraft Engines. He was also a professor at the Bialystok University of Technology from 1998 to 2014 and at the Bydgoszcz University of Technology. He is now retired. His scientific disciplines include automation and robotics, diagnostics, and the reliability of machines. His specialization is in applied automation, diagnostics, and the reliability of machines. Throughout his career, he has promoted eight PhDs in engineering sciences and supervised over 120 Master Engineers of Science. He has served as a reviewer for numerous doctoral and post-doctoral theses and has managed more than ten research and scientific projects. He is the author of more than 200 books and papers on applied automation, diagnostics, and machine reliability.

Rafał Grądzki PhD Eng. was born in 1984 in Mońki. He is a graduate of the Bialystok University of Technology in the field of automation and robotics, specializing in information systems (2008). He obtained his PhD in Mechanical Engineering with a specialization in Technical Diagnostics in 2012. Since 2011, he has been an employee of the Faculty of Mechanical Engineering at the Bialystok University of Technology. From 2011 to 2012, he worked as an assistant at the Department of Production Engineering. From 2012 to 2020, he served as an assistant professor at the Department of Automation and Robotics. From 2020 to 2023, he continued his role as an assistant professor at the Department of Automation and Robotics. Since 2023, he has been an assistant professor at the Department of Dynamic Systems. He has so far supervised approximately 100 master's/graduate students at Bialystok University of Technology. He is the author of papers on automation, diagnostics, machine reliability, and robotics.

Karol Golak PhD Eng. was born in 1984 in Białystok. He completed his master's degree at Bialystok University of Technology in 2008 with a degree in automation and robotics, specialising in information systems. In the same year, he also graduated from the University of Bialystok with a degree in management. In 2016, he obtained a PhD in Mechanical Engineering, specialising in Technical Diagnostics. Since 2014, he has been employed at the Faculty of Mechanical Engineering at the Bialystok University of Technology, in the Department of Materials and Production Engineering. To date, he has supervised the promotion of dozens of master's graduate students at the Bialystok University of Technology. He is the author of numerous papers on automation, diagnostics, machine reliability, and tribology.

Introduction

Decision support theory is an ever-evolving field of knowledge that has existed since time immemorial (2000 BC in China). It has a critical impact on improving and streamlining the processes of operation and maintenance of engineered objects (like air planes, helicopters, or aircraft engines). It provides substantive and practical requirements and principles (guidelines) for making reasonably founded decisions, which are the foundation of optimising the human actions (so they become safe, reliable, cost-efficient, and multi-directional) in the modern world.

The decision support theory is based on the continuous acquisition and processing of information concerning various physical and chemical phenomena, socio-technical systems, and production (manufacturing) processes using specialised measurement systems and computing machines (computers), which—for example—can be expert and cognitive systems.

The essence of decision-making has become the focus of many theories and scientific disciplines which describe the formation and execution of decisions from different perspectives and in different systems. Decision-making is the focus of several scientific disciplines, such as operational research, optimisation theory, control theory, game theory, artificial intelligence theory, organisation and management theory, and the theory of operation. Each decision stems from an analysis and synthesis of the multifaceted relationships occurring between matter, energy, and information in different systems as these systems move and develop. Note that from the perspective of cybernetics, the movement of a system is performed in Newtonian (real) time and the development of a system occurs in Bergsonian time (the time of evolution). What is investigated are the changes in the status (the quality of functioning) of the system of interest. Optimal decisions are adapted to these changes in order to achieve the desired operational, economic, social, and natural (environmental) objectives.

Interdisciplinary knowledge is required to make a decision (by the decision-maker). It is important to understand that decisions (both right and wrong) have a significant impact on the functioning of a system, a machine, or an organism, as applicable. There are many examples that only the correct decisions lead to the correct operation of a process system. Systems are very diverse. Hence, they can include:

- a helmsman who steers the boat along a specific route;
- a driver driving the car so that he or she avoids obstacles and reaches his or her destination;
- an operator who controls the operation of the turbine generator at a power plant;
- a manager who directs the work of the entire power plant so that the team of personnel and the machines working there perform specified functions as efficiently as possible;

- an operator, or a technical device, which regulates the temperature in an industrial oven according to a preset programme in the function of changing ambient temperature;
- the relevant physiological mechanisms controlling metabolism of matter and energy in the living organism;
- the doctor in charge of the patient's therapy, appropriately administering the medicines or therapeutic procedures;
- a computer that controls a motor vehicle assembly process which involves human operators and robots;
- the commander in chief of the staff and the army;
- the managing director of the corporate board and the production site.

The common feature of these systems is that they always include a decision-maker, a decision, and a decision object, which together form a decision system subject to the laws of cybernetics.

1 Elements of Applied Cybernetics
Theoretical Foundations of Decision-Making

1.1 INTRODUCTION

The term "cybernetics" derives from three Greek words: "kybernes" for "helmsman", "governor" as in "regulator", and "governor" as in "managing authority". The word "cybernetics" was already used by Plato to denote the art of management. The first modern definition of cybernetics is found in the title of Norbert Wiener's book: *Cybernetics, or Control and Communication in the Animal and the Machine*. Objects, arrangements, and inanimate and animate systems are the object of study in cybernetics from the point of view of their organised functioning, an activity associated with control, regulation, or management. Cybernetics therefore provides a new picture of the reality around us, in which—in addition to the matter and energy we have perceived so far—a third component appears: information. It has been recognised that information is a component of exceptional importance because it is the only link between a given system and its outside world and between the individual elements in the system of interest. Information facilitates studying systems not only during their motion (in Newtonian time) but also during their development (in Bergsonian time) using an appropriate mathematical description.

Mathematical, statistical, mechanical, electrical, economic, and other models are built to reproduce the operation of an object that is the basis for decision-making.

1.2 THE SYSTEM AND ITS ENVIRONMENT

1.2.1 THE CONCEPT OF SYSTEM AND ENVIRONMENT

A system operates in an environment. A system in its environment consists of a great many elements that interact and are interdependent. The interaction of elements means that, for example, an object interacts with a regulator and the regulator interacts with the object [1–3]. Interdependence means that a pilot can create new conditions for the flight of the aircraft and thus generate new properties of the aircraft, and thus new requirements for the pilot's interaction with the aircraft are determined. In a whole set of elements (the system and its environment), there

DOI: 10.1201/9781032638447-1

1

are elements more concentrated in space and time, and these are called systems (or arrangements); the remaining elements of the set are called the environment. A system and its environment are shown in Figure 1.1.

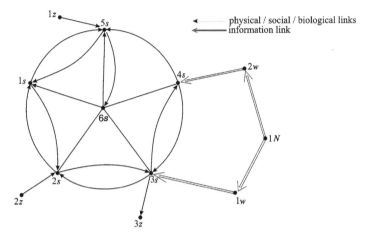

FIGURE 1.1 Elements of a system and its environment.

Figure 1.1 shows the following:

- Items 1s to 6s are strongly related. Their strong relationship is mechanical, electrical, economic, chemical, social, and/or biological in nature. They form an inseparable whole.
- Items 1z to 3z are independent. They are interrelated only by the system. They can be elements of other functioning systems. They are interfering elements in the system. They can be of different physical nature. They can also act on elements of other systems.
- Items 1w to 2w are independent. They are linked only by the arrangement. They can be decision-makers who input information into the system to improve its organisation, order, and governance.
- Item 1N—it is independent. It is linked by items 1w and 2w and the system. It is the top-level decision-maker. It inputs information into the system from a higher level of the hierarchical system.

Typical examples of systems in their environment are shown in Figures 1.2 and 1.3.

Only signals are important in the decision-making process. They contain information about the dynamics of the system and its relationship to the environment. System elements "*M*" and "*D*" are reduced to the functions they perform. For "*M*", this could be the function of object "*S*", while for "*D*", it could be the function of regulator "*R*". Then the regulating system shown in Figure 1.3 takes the form of the graph in Figure 1.4.

The signal flow graph in Figure 1.4 corresponds closely to the system shown in Figure 1.3. It can be easily reduced to its classical form; see Figure 1.5 [3–5].

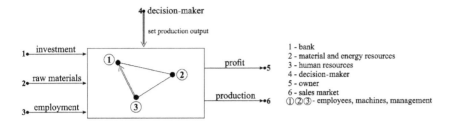

FIGURE 1.2 Block diagram of a production system in an environment; 1—bank; 2—material and energy resources; 3—human resources; 4—decision-maker; 5—owner; 6—sales market; ●—strongly linked elements; ○—elements linked by arrangement; ==> physical link; →information link.

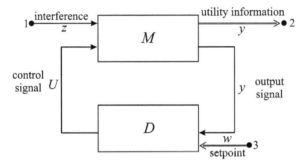

FIGURE 1.3 Block diagram of a regulating system. *M*—machine (object); *D*—decision-maker (regulator); •1, •2, •3—elements of the environment; ==> physical link, →information link.

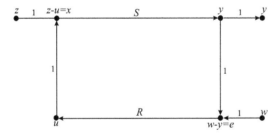

FIGURE 1.4 Signal flow graph. *S*—object model; *R*—regulator model; *x*—input signal for the object; *e*—regulation offset signal.

It is directly evident from Figure 1.5 that the flow of signals in the system depends (and obviously) on models "*S*" and "*R*", and not only, because it also depends on an additional model, *R•S*, which is the product of "*S*" and "*R*". For the graph of flow from "*z*", the following stands:

$$y = zS - yRS \tag{1.1}$$

a)   b)

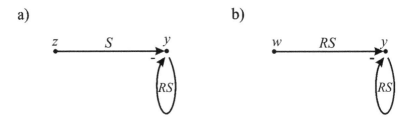

FIGURE 1.5 Signal flow graph: the (a) flow from signal "z" to "y" and (b) from signal "w" to "y".

and further, the transmittance:

$$H_z = \frac{y}{z} = \frac{S}{1+RS} \tag{1.2}$$

while from the flow from w, the following applies:

$$y = wRS - yRS \tag{1.3}$$

and further, the transmittance:

$$H_w = \frac{y}{w} = \frac{RS}{1+RS} \tag{1.4}$$

The RS product is used to study the stability of systems.
    Whenever:

$RS < 1$ — the system is stable;

$|S| < \dfrac{1}{|R|}$ — the system is stable, whereas $\dfrac{1}{|R|}$ is the critical graph [1, 4, 6].

Generally speaking, all systems can be divided into two classes. There are deterministic systems and probabilistic systems.

1.2.2 Deterministic Systems

A deterministic system is a system in which all its elements and the whole system can be described mathematically by algebraic, integral, or differential equations. The output signal is "y", and the input signal is "x" (alternatively, "z" or "w"). Also the "y" and "x" signals are uniquely determined and described [1, 3, 7, 8].

• The model of object "S" (Figures 1.3 and 1.4) can be a differential equation:

$$a_n y^n + \ldots + a_2 \ddot{y} + a_1 \dot{y} + a_0 y = b_m x^m + \ldots + b_2 \ddot{x} + b_1 \dot{x} + b_0 x \tag{1.5}$$

There can also be an operator equation, which is derived from the differential equation by applying the Laplace transform:

$$a_n s^n Y + ... + a_2 s^2 Y + a_1 sY + a_0 Y = b_m s^m X + ... + b_2 s^2 X + b_1 sX + b_0 X \quad (1.6)$$

with:

Y— transform of the output signal;
X— transform of the input signal;
s— complex variable (equivalent to time "t" or frequency "ω").

Here,

$$Y = Y(s) = \mathcal{L}y = \mathcal{L}y(t) \quad (1.7)$$

$$sY = \mathcal{L}\dot{y} \quad (1.8)$$

$$s^2 Y = \mathcal{L}\ddot{y} \quad (1.9)$$

$$\frac{1}{s}Y = \mathcal{L}\int ydt \quad (1.10)$$

The symbol $\mathcal{L}$ used in the equations denotes the Laplace transform operation.

What is taken advantage of here is that there are possibilities to make a transformation by applying a special operation of integrating any function x(t), y(t) of variable "t", called the original, into another function, X(s), Y(s) of a new complex variable "s" called the transform [1, 5]; as such, for example, given a signal x(t) and applying the Laplace transform, the result is a transform of input signal X(s), which can be expressed as follows:

$$\mathcal{L}x(t) = \int_0^\infty x(t)e^{-st}dt = X(s) \quad (1.11)$$

The basic model of object "S" is the transmittance:

$$S(s) = \frac{Y(s)}{X(s)} = \frac{b_m s^m + ... + b_2 s^2 + b_1 s + b_0}{a_n s^n + ... + a_2 s^2 + a_1 s + a_0} \quad (1.12)$$

Examples of object models can be simple transmittances:

$$S(s) = k; \quad S(s) = \frac{k}{Ts+1}; \quad S(s) = \frac{ke^{-sT_0}}{Ts+1}; \quad (1.13)$$

$$S(s) = \frac{k}{s}; \quad S(s) = \frac{k}{s(Ts+1)}; \quad S(s) = \frac{ke^{-sT_0}}{s(Ts+1)}; \quad (1.14)$$

with:

> k— amplification factor;
> T— object's time constant;
> T_0— delay time constant.

As can be seen from Formulas 1.13 and 1.14, objects can be divided into two groups: objects without integration (static) and objects with integration, $\dfrac{1}{s}$ — equation (1.10) (astatic).

- The regulator model can be the following equation [1, 4, 5, 9]:

$$u(t) = k_R e(t) + k_R T_D \dot{e} + k_R \frac{1}{T_I} \int edt \qquad (1.15)$$

with:

> $u(t)$— control signal;
> $e(t)$— offset signal (Figures 1.3 and 1.4);
> k_R— factor of proportionality;
> T_D— time constants of differentiation action;
> T_I— time constants of integration.

The operator form of equation (1.15) (after applying the Laplace transform— see Formulas 1.7, 1.8, 1.10) is an algebraic expression:

$$U(s) = k_R E(s) + k_R T_D sE(s) + \frac{k_R}{T_I s} E(s) \qquad (1.16)$$

The regulator transmittance is:

$$R(s) = \frac{U(s)}{E(s)} = k_R \left(1 + T_D s + \frac{1}{T_I s}\right) \qquad (1.17)$$

with:

> k_R, T_D, T_I— regulator settings. They can be changed (set) as required:
> $k_R = 0$ to ∞, $T_D = 0$ to ∞, $T_I = \infty$ to 0.

The following types of regulator apply here:

$R(s) = k_R$ — proportional controller, or P controller

$R(s) = k_R T_D s$ — differential controller, or D controller

$$R(s) = k_R \frac{1}{T_I s} \quad \text{— integral controller, or } I \text{ controller}$$

$$R(s) = k_R (1 + T_D s + \frac{1}{T_I s}) \quad \text{— proportional-integral-differential controller, or}$$
PID regulator.

P controllers are most popular (due to their simplicity of construction and operation), along with PID controllers (due to their versatility).

Half (fractional) order controllers are of particular importance: $R(s) = \sqrt{\pi} s^{\frac{1}{2}}$ and $R(s) = \frac{\pi}{2} s^{-\frac{1}{2}}$; these controllers feature time $\hat{t} = \sqrt{t}$ [10].

- A deterministic system is described by transmittances (Figures 1.3 and 1.4).

$$H_z = \frac{Y}{Z} = \frac{S}{1 + RS} \quad \text{– interference transmittance;}$$

$$H_w = \frac{Y}{W} = \frac{RS}{1 + RS} \quad \text{– follow-up transmittance.}$$

which take the following operator form:

$$H_z(s) = \frac{Y(s)}{Z(s)} = \frac{b_m s^m + \ldots + b_2 s^2 + b_1 s + b_0}{a_n s^n + \ldots + a_2 s^2 + a_1 s + a_0} \tag{1.18}$$

$$H_w(s) = \frac{Y(s)}{W(s)} = \frac{c_m s^m + \ldots + c_2 s^2 + c_1 s + c_0}{a_n s^n + \ldots + a_2 s^2 + a_1 s + a_0} \tag{1.19}$$

Signals $z(t)$ and $w(t)$ are determined and explicitly expressed [1, 4, 5, 9]. These are assumed to be:

- pulse $\delta(t) = \begin{cases} 0 \text{ for } t \neq 0 \\ \infty \text{ for } t = 0 \end{cases}$; its transform is $\mathcal{L}\,\delta(t) = 1$;

- step $1(t) = \begin{cases} 0 \text{ for } t < 0 \\ 1 \text{ for } t \geq 0 \end{cases}$; its transform is $\mathcal{L}\,1(t) = \frac{1}{s}$;

- velocity step $z(t) = t$ for $t \geq 0$; its transform is $\mathcal{L}\,t = \frac{1}{s^2}$;

- harmonic function

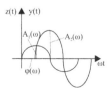

$$x(t) = A_1(\omega)\sin \omega t;$$

$$y(t) = A_2(\omega)\sin \omega t + \varphi(\omega).$$

The relationships between output signal y(t)and input signal x(t) are examined (the input signal can also be z(t) or w(t)).
The answer is determined:

- pulsed:

$$Y(s) = H(s)X(s) = H(s)\cdot 1 \xrightarrow{\mathcal{L}^{-1}} y(t) = g(t) \tag{1.20}$$

- stepped:

$$Y(s) = H(s)X(s) = H(s)\cdot\frac{1}{s} \xrightarrow{\mathcal{L}^{-1}} y(t) = h(t) \tag{1.21}$$

- to a velocity step:

$$Y(s) = H(s)X(s) = H(s)\cdot\frac{1}{s^2} \xrightarrow{\mathcal{L}^{-1}} y(t) \tag{1.22}$$

- to harmonic functions:

$$H(s) = \frac{Y(s)}{X(s)} \tag{1.23}$$

with H(s) is the operator transmittance of the system.
Hence, after substituting s = jω:

$$H(j\omega) = \frac{Y(j\omega)}{X(j\omega)} = P(\omega) + jQ(\omega) \tag{1.24}$$

with:

H(jω)— the spectral transmittance of the system;
P(ω)— the real part of the spectral transmittance;
Q(jω)— the imaginary part of the spectral transmittance.

The following is determined:

$$A(\omega) = \sqrt{P^2(\omega) + Q^2(\omega)} = \frac{A_2(\omega)}{A_1(\omega)} - \text{amplitude gain} \tag{1.25}$$

$$\varphi(\omega) = arctg\,\frac{P(\omega)}{Q(\omega)} - \text{phase shift} \tag{1.26}$$

The determined A(ω) and φ(ω) facilitate a unique determination of the output harmonic function relative to the input harmonic function [1, 7].

The description of the system in the form of operator transmittance $G(s)$ and spectral transmittance $G(j\omega)$ allow to study the stability and quality of the system. Hurwitz and Nyquist criteria are applied for testing stability [1, 4, 5, 7].

There are close relationships between frequency responses (with the variable being "ω") and time responses (with the variable being "t"). There is step response and pulse response):

$$g(t) = \frac{2}{\pi} \int_0^\infty P(\omega) \cos \omega t \, d\omega \qquad (1.27)$$

$$h(t) = \frac{2}{\pi} \int_0^\infty P(\omega) \frac{\sin \omega t}{\omega} \, d\omega \qquad (1.28)$$

Hence, the priority role of spectral transmittance in the description of arrangements and systems.

It was found that the dynamics of a process depend on the process itself and the environment in which the process occurred [1, 4–6, 11].

In a simplified way, the following can be expressed:

$$\dot{y} = ay + bx \qquad (1.29)$$

The solution of this equation is the phase trajectory with Lyapunov functions.

Very often the relations between output signal "y" and input signal "x" are described with coupled equations of state [1, 2, 12, 13]:

$$\begin{aligned} \dot{y} &= a_y y + b_x x \\ \dot{x} &= a_x x + b_y y \end{aligned} \qquad (1.30)$$

with: a, a_y, a_x— parameters of state;
b, b_x, b_y— parameters of environmental effects.

A system of coupled equations (equations of interaction) can describe the relationship between the technical status a_y and the operating status a_x of an object, as well as the energy state defined with Lyapunov functions [2, 6, 14, 15].

1.2.3 PROBABILISTIC SYSTEMS

A selection of knowledge from three areas of mathematics, namely probability calculus, mathematical statistics, and stochastic processes, which are required in engineering practice to describe random (chance) phenomena, when taken together are referred to by the common term "probabilistics". Thus, probabilistic systems are those systems that can be described using probability calculus, mathematical statistics, and the theory of stochastic processes, that is, according to probabilistic laws, which are based on the fact that the behaviour of a system and its elements can only be predicted with a certain probability and only at a strictly defined time.

Probability calculus allows the analytical study of random (chance) phenomena by assigning to them appropriate probabilities of occurrence under certain environmental conditions of the system.

Mathematical statistics allows the study of globally captured random phenomena by studying their fragments (or samples).

Stochastic processes involve the study of random phenomena in relation to time, that is, the study of the probability of a phenomenon over time.

In a mathematical description of a probabilistic control system, there is a high degree of uncertainty associated with the existence of various random signals and with the lack of understanding of the exact mathematical expression of the system elements and the system as a whole. This makes the description of probabilistic systems complicated (difficult or intricate) and complex (because of many different dependencies, a large number of elements, and numerous links).

1.2.3.1 Elements of the Probability Calculus

A. Random events and probabilities [16–19].

- Probability $P(A)$ of event A (according to Laplace's definition) is the ratio of the number of "m" cases favouring event A to the number of all n possible cases. Hence,

$$P(A) = \frac{m}{n} \tag{1.31}$$

- The axioms of probability calculus are:

   1. Probability $P(A)$ of event A satisfies the inequality:

$$0 \leq P(A) \leq 1 \tag{1.32}$$

   2. Probability $P(E)$ of certain event E is equal to 1:

$$P(E) = 1 \tag{1.33}$$

   3. The probability of the sum of events is equal to the sum of the probabilities of those events:

$$P(A_1 + A_2 + \ldots + A_n) = P(A_1) + P(A_2) + \ldots + P(A_n) \tag{1.34}$$

The following theorems are formulated on the basis of the axioms from the probability calculus:

   1. If the number of random events, A_1, A_2, . . ., and A_n exhausts the set of all events, then:

$$P(\sum_{1}^{n} A_i) = 1 \qquad (1.35)$$

2. The sum of the probabilities of random event $A \rightarrow P(A)$ and its opposite event $\bar{A} \rightarrow P(\bar{A})$ is equal to 1:

$$P(A) + P(\bar{A}) = 1 \qquad (1.36)$$

3. Probability $P(U)$ of impossible event U is equal to 0:

$$P(U) = 0 \qquad (1.37)$$

- The frequency of a random event $v(E) = 1$ is the ratio of the number of m experiments during which event A occurred to the number of all n experiments:

$$v(A) = \frac{m}{n} \qquad (1.38)$$

The relationship between probability $P(A)$ and frequency $v(A)$ can be expressed with the formula:

$$P(A) = \lim_{n \to \infty} v(A) = \lim_{n \to \infty} \frac{m}{n} \qquad (1.39)$$

In practical terms, the following is given:

$$v(A) - P(A) < \varepsilon \qquad (1.40)$$

where error ε is an arbitrarily small number greater than 0.

- Conditional probability $P(A|B)$ is called the probability of occurrence of event A, conditional on the occurrence of event B. The conditional probability is calculated from the formula:

$$P(A \mid B) = \frac{P(AB)}{P(B)} \qquad (1.41)$$

$$P(B \mid A) = \frac{P(AB)}{P(A)} \qquad (1.42)$$

These relationships are due to the fact that

$$\frac{N_{AB}}{N_B} = \frac{N_{AB}}{N} : \frac{N_B}{N} \qquad (1.43)$$

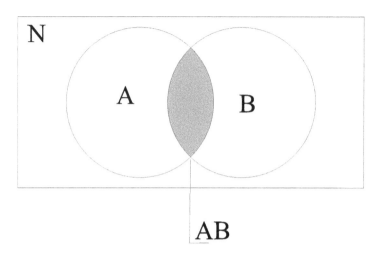

FIGURE 1.6 Geometric interpretation of the product of events.

with:

N_{AB}— the number of events AB in set B, and also in the whole set $A + B$;
N_B— the number of events B in set N;
N— the number of all possible events;

as illustrated in this figure.

- The probability of the product of events follows from the conditional probability (Figure 1.6).

From the conditional probability formulae, the following is given:

$$P(A\ B) = P(A \mid B)P(B) \qquad (1.44)$$

$$P(A\ B) = P(B \mid A)P(A) \qquad (1.45)$$

If events A and B are independent, then:

$$P(A \mid B) = P(A) \qquad (1.46)$$

$$P(B \mid A) = P(B) \qquad (1.47)$$

Considering the foregoing, the following is given:

$$P(A\ B) = P(A)P(B) \qquad (1.48)$$

The formula for total (complete) probability follows from a generalisation of the formulas for the sum and product of probabilities. This formula has the following form:

$$P(A)=\sum_{i=1}^{n}P(H_i)P(A\mid H_i)\tag{1.49}$$

with:

$P(A)$— the total probability of the event;
$P(H_i)$— the probability of a total system of events H_1, H_2, etc.
$P(A\mid H_i)$— the conditional probability of occurrence of A conditioned by the occurrence of H_1, H_2, etc.

- Bayes' formula applies to conditional probabilities (Formulas 1.41 and 1.42).

The conditional probability of any event H_i—assuming that event A has occurred— is calculated from the formula:

$$P(H_i\mid A)=\frac{P(H_i)P(A\mid H_i)}{\sum_{i=1}^{n}P(H_i)P(A\mid H_i)}\tag{1.50}$$

with:

$P(H_i\mid A)$— the probability of occurrence of H_i, conditioned that A occurs;
P(Hi)— the probability of a total system of events H_1, H_2, etc.;
P(A | Hi)— the probability of event A occurring, provided event H_i occurs.

B.   Random variables and distributions.

- A random variable is a quantity that, as a result of an experiment, takes a finite number of different values with positive probabilities and is denoted by X.
- The realisation of random variable X is a set of values of the random variable in a given experiment and denoted by $\{x_i\}$.
- Step random variable X (Figure 1.7) is a variable satisfying the condition:

$$P(X=x_i)>0\tag{1.51}$$

where $P(X=x_i)$ is the probability that random variable X takes the value x_i. Random variable X is definite if:

1.   All the numerical values of x_i that the random variable can take and probabilities p_i of these values occurring are known.

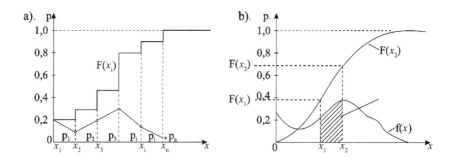

FIGURE 1.7 (a) Distribution functions of a step random variable and (b) of a continuous random variable (for (a))—values of p_i for the given x_i are known, and for (b) $f(x)$ is known.

2. The dependence of probability p_i on x_i of random variable X is known, and the dependence is known as the probability distribution $P(X = x_i) = p_i$ of random variable X.

• A continuous random variable is random variable X (Figure 1.7) which has a limit:

$$\lim_{\Delta x \to \infty} \frac{P\{x < X < x + \Delta x\}}{\Delta x} = f(x) \tag{1.52}$$

and the limit is at each point in interval (a, b) of random variable X.

• The distribution function of a random variable is the probability of an event that random variable X takes values less than or equal to an assumed (fixed) value of x:

$$F(x) = P(X \le x) \tag{1.53}$$

The general properties of the distribution function are as follows:

1. If $x_2 > x_1$, then $F(x_2) \ge F(x_1)$
2. Since $F(x)$ is a probability, then $0 \le F(x) \le 1$
3. If $x = -\infty$, then $F(-\infty) = 0$
4. If $x = +\infty$, then $F(+\infty) = 1$

The distribution function for a step random variable and a continuous random variable are shown in Figure 1.7 [18].

The probability density of continuous random variable X is:

$$f(x) = F(x) = \lim_{\Delta x \to \infty} \frac{F(x + \Delta x) - F(x)}{\Delta x} \tag{1.54}$$

The general properties of probability density are as follows:

1. $f(x) = F'(x)$ — is a distribution function derivative
2. $f(x)$ — is a non-negative function
3. $\int_{-\infty}^{\infty} f(x)\, dx = 1$
4. Knowing the probability density function, the probability that random variable X will take values between α and β can be calculated:

$$P(\alpha < X < \beta) = \int_{\alpha}^{\beta} f(x) dx \tag{1.55}$$

5. Knowing the probability density function, the distribution function can be calculated at a given point of x_i:

$$F(x) = \int_{-\infty}^{x_i} f(x) dx \tag{1.56}$$

- The expected value of a step random variable is calculated from the formula:

$$E(X) = m = \sum_i x_i p_i \tag{1.57}$$

while for a continuous random variable, this formula is used:

$$E(X) = m = \int_{-\infty}^{\infty} f(x)\, dx \tag{1.58}$$

with:

x_i— the value of a step random variable;
p_i— the probabilities corresponding to the values of x_i (Figure 1.7a);
$f(x)$— the probability density of random variable X (Figure 1.7b);
m— the expected value of the random variable.

- The variance of a random variable is calculated from the formulas which follow:
  - for a step random variable:

$$\sigma^2 = \sum_i (x_i - m)^2 p_i \tag{1.59}$$

- for continuous random variable x:

$$\sigma^2 = \int_{-\infty}^{\infty} (x-m)^2 f(x)\, dx \qquad (1.60)$$

- The standard deviation of a random variable is calculated from the formula:

$$\sigma = \sqrt{\sigma^2} \qquad (1.61)$$

It is the positive square root of variance (spread).

- Probability distributions of random variables are functions that represent the relationship between the values of a random variable (which can be a step or a continuous variable) and the probabilities of occurrence of those values:
  1. In technical applications for a step random variable, the binomial (Bernoulli) distribution is most commonly used. It allows describing events which occur with probability p and which do not occur with probability $1\text{-}p$

Probability $P(X = x_i)$ is calculated from the formula:

$$P(X = x_i) = \frac{n!}{x_i(n-x_i)!} p^{x_i} (1-p)^{n-x_i} \qquad (1.62)$$

with:

$P(X = x_i)$— the probability that random variable X takes the value x_i;
n— the total number of measurements, experiments, checks, tests, etc.
x_i— the consecutive values of the random variable from within 0 to n;
p— the probability of the event ($p=1/2$ for a coin toss; $p=1/6$ for a dice roll);
$n!$— the product of real numbers from within 1 to n (for $n=3$, it is $3!=1\cdot2\cdot3=6$);
$0!=1$.

  2. When studying measurement errors, target hits, or scatter of product dimensions, normal (Gaussian) distribution is most often used. It allows describing probability density $f(x)$ and the distribution function $F(x)$ with these formulas:

$$f(x) = \frac{1}{\sigma\sqrt{2\pi}} e^{-\frac{(x-m)^2}{2\sigma^2}} \qquad (1.63)$$

$$F(x) = \frac{1}{\sigma\sqrt{2\pi}} \int_{-\infty}^{x} e^{-\frac{(x-m)^2}{2\sigma^2}}\, dx \qquad (1.64)$$

with:

x— the continuous variable of random variable X in the interval of $-\infty$ to $+\infty$;
m— the expected value of random variable X;
σ— standard deviation.

1.2.3.2   Elements of Mathematical Statistics

A. Outline of basic concepts and formulas of mathematical statistics [16, 18–20]

Mathematical statistics deals with inferences concerning a general population on the basis of tests performed on a random sample from the general population. The conclusions obtained are valid if the sample is like the general population, that is, when the sample is representative of that population. The foundation of mathematical statistics is the probability calculus.

A statistic is a parameter of a random sample from the general population. The basic statistics include the mean value within the sample, the variance within the sample, and the standard deviation within the sample.

They are calculated from these formulas:

$$\overline{X} = \frac{1}{n} \sum_{i=1}^{n} x_i \tag{1.65}$$

$$s^2 = \frac{1}{n} \sum_{i=1}^{n} (x_i - \overline{x})^2 \tag{1.66}$$

$$s = \sqrt{s^2} \tag{1.67}$$

with:

$\overline{X}$— the mean value in the sample;
n— sample size;
x_i— the result of the test of the subsequent element;
s^2— sample variance;
s— standard deviation of the sample.

• Student's t-statistic is calculated from this formula [17, 21]:

$$t = \frac{\overline{X} - m}{s} \sqrt{n} \tag{1.68}$$

with:

$\overline{X}$— the mean value in the sample;
n— sample size;

m— the expected value (Formula 1.57) (the general population average);
s— standard deviation of the sample.

The consistency t-statistic assesses whether the difference between $\overline{X}$ and m is significant (substantial). This relation is correct if [18, 21]:

$$t_{obl} < t_{kr} \qquad (1.69)$$

with:

t_{obl}— computational statistics;
t_{kr}— the critical statistic is given in Table 1.1.

TABLE 1.1
Student's Critical t_{kr}-Value [21], Where u—Confidence; $a = 1 - u$—
Significance (Type 1 Error—See Figure 1.8)

Value of t for confidence intervals $u = 1 - a$	95%	97.5%	99%	99.5%
Critical value of $|t|$ for $a =$	0.05	0.25	0.01	0.005
number of degrees of freedom = sample size				
1	6.31	12.71	31.82	63.66
2	2.92	4.30	6.96	9.92
3	2.35	3.18	4.54	5.84
4	2.13	2.78	3.75	4.60
5	2.02	2.57	3.36	4.03
6	1.94	2.45	3.14	3.71
7	1.89	2.36	3.00	3.50
8	1.86	2.31	2.90	3.36
9	1.83	2.26	2.82	3.25
10	1.81	2.23	2.76	3.17
12	1.78	2.18	2.68	3.05
14	1.76	2.14	2.62	2.98
16	1.75	2.12	2.58	2.92
18	1.73	2.10	2.55	2.88
20	1.72	2.09	2.53	2.85
30	1.70	2.04	2.46	2.75
50	1.68	2.01	2.40	2.68
∞	1.64	1.96	2.33	2.58

- Statistic χ^2 (chi-square) is calculated from this formula [18, 19]:

$$\chi^2 = \sum_{i=1}^{l} \frac{(n_i - np_i)^2}{np_i} \qquad (1.70)$$

$$np_i = n \int_{x_i}^{x_{i+1}} f(x)dx \qquad (1.71)$$

with:

$f(x)$— the density of theoretical distribution;
x_i, $x_i + 1$— the limits of the ith interval;
n_i— the number of values of the random variable, observed in each interval
$$\sum_{i=1}^{l} n_i = n;$$
l— the number of intervals.

The probability that the assumed theoretical distribution will be close to the empirical distribution when the following applies [22] is:

$$\chi_{obl} < \chi_{kr} \qquad (1.72)$$

or when accuracy factor H is:

$$H = \frac{\chi_{obl}}{l-1} \qquad (1.73)$$

or Romanowski's consistency factor R is:

$$R = \frac{|\chi_{obl} - k|}{\sqrt{2k}} < 3 \qquad (1.74)$$

with:

χ_{obl}— the computational statistic;
χ_{kr}— the critical statistic given in Table 1.2 [21]
$K = l - 1$.

- The Kolmogorov λ-statistic is calculated from Formula 1.75 [18]:

$$\lambda = D \max \sqrt{n} \qquad (1.75)$$

TABLE 1.2
Critical Values of χ^2 for $\alpha = 0.05$ [21]

Number of degrees of freedom = sample size	Critical value
1	3.841
2	5.991
3	7.815
4	9.488
5	11.070
6	12.592
7	14.067
8	15.507
9	16.919
10	18.307

with:

Dmax— the maximum difference between the theoretical distribution function $F(x) = \int_{-\infty}^{x} f(x)dx$ and the empirical distribution function: $F(x_i)$, that is: $D\max = |F(x_i) - F(x)|$;

n— sample size.

The empirical (calculated) distribution will be consistent with the theoretical (assumed) distribution if:

$\lambda \leq 1$ means optimum consistency;
$\lambda \leq 1,5$ means satisfactory consistency.

B. Statistical hypotheses, estimation, and estimators.

- A null hypothesis, H_0, is a confident assumption (and one fully justified, based on probability) that is subject to testing.
    - A parametric hypothesis concerns the unknown values of the parameters of the distributions of sets.
    - A non-parametric hypothesis concerns the unknown shapes of the functions of the distributions of sets.
- An alternative hypothesis, H_1, is any hypothesis different from hypothesis H_0. For a parametric hypothesis, the following can be expressed:

$$H_1 = \theta - H_0 \tag{1.76}$$

with: θ — the set of all possible parameter values of a known form of distribution (e.g. a normal/Gaussian distribution).

The same is true for a non-parametric hypothesis—then, one operates with the distribution functions of a random variable.

- Type 1 error and type 2 error.

  1. A type 1 error is made when a null hypothesis, H_0, is rejected even when it is true.
  2. A type 2 error is made when a null hypothesis, H_0, is accepted even when it is false. This error is tested using an alternative hypothesis, H_1.
  3. The level of significance and α is the predetermined probability of rejecting a verified hypothesis H_0, assuming that the hypothesis is true. Normally, α takes 0.01, 0.05, or 0.1. Taking $\alpha = 0.01$ practically means that once in a hundred cases, hypothesis H_0 will be wrongly rejected. Significance level α is also a type I error.
  4. The power of a test, according to the definition, is $1-\beta$, where β is a type 2 error. It is a function of the parameter value adopted in alternative hypothesis H_1 relative to null hypothesis H_0 (Figure 1.8).

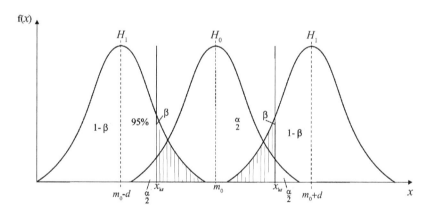

FIGURE 1.8 Type 1 and 2 errors; $f(x)$—the probability density of random variable X value in a Gaussian distribution; m_0—the expected random variable value of null hypothesis H_0 (e.g. $m_0 = 3$); $m_0 \pm d$—the expected random variable value of alternative hypothesis H_1 (e.g. $m_1 = 3 \pm 0.1$); x_{kr}—the critical value, driven from the assumed value of significance level α (for $\alpha = 0.05$, the critical value is x_{kr} for which $x_{kr} = m_0 \pm 1,96\sigma / \sqrt{n}$, equivalent to that the surface area below the curve of $f(x)$ is divided into three parts at the ratios of $95\% + 2.5\% + 2.5\%$; $\alpha = \alpha/2 + \alpha/2$—type 1 error (significance level); β—type 2 error; $1 - \beta$—the power of the test.

A type 1 error can be reduced arbitrarily (e.g. from 5% to 1%), and if so, x_{kr} moves away from m_0, which increases the type 2 error, meaning that the power of the test is reduced. Type 1 and 2 errors shall be small, which can be achieved by increasing the sample size.

C. Parametric and non-parametric estimation

- Estimation (per the estimation theory) is an assessment (statistical evaluation) of the parameters of a set of events based on the study of the statistics of the samples from the same set. When the parameters of this set are estimated, it is a parametric estimation. When the functional form of the distribution of the set is estimated (distribution function and density), it is a non-parametric estimation.

In a parametric estimation, the estimation is performed in two variants:

1. By providing a single number corresponding to the assumed value of the parameter — this is a point estimation.
2. By defining an interval within which the true value of the parameter falls — this is an interval estimation.

In a non-parametric estimation, the functional form of the distribution function is estimated (i.e. predicted). It is when interval estimation is used. A certain band is specified in which the true distribution fits with a predetermined probability.

- Estimator is a statistic used for the estimation of the parameters of a random variable. The basic parameters of a step random variable x_i are, for example:

$$m = \sum_i^\infty x_i p_i - \text{expected value (Formula 1.57)}$$

$$\sigma^2 = \sum_i^\infty (x_i - m)^2 p_i - \text{variance of random variable (Formula 1.59)}$$

These parameters cannot be determined experimentally because they require an infinite number of "i" observations. Estimators of the parameters are therefore determined:

$$\bar{x} = m^* = \frac{1}{n}\sum_{i=1}^n x_i = \sum_{i=1}^n x_i p_i - \text{sample average} \qquad (1.77)$$

$$s^2 = \sigma^{2*} = \frac{1}{n}\sum(x_i - \bar{x})^2 = \sum_{i=1}^{n}(x_i - \bar{x})^2\, p_i \quad \text{— sample variance} \quad (1.78)$$

Estimators m^*, σ^{2*} of parameters m and σ^2 of random variable x_i are the statistics $\bar{x}$ and s^2 of a sample with a finite number of observations $i = n$.

When assessing the quality or "goodness" of a given estimator, three main characteristics are considered:

1. It is preferable that the expected value of the estimator is equal to the value of the parameter:

$$E(m^*) = m \qquad (1.79)$$

If the condition is satisfied, the estimator is said to be unbiased. The difference:

$E(m^*) - m = $ estimator bias

2. It is preferable that the mean squared error of the chosen estimator is less than the error for all other possible estimators, that is:

$$E[(m_w^* - m)^2] \le E[(m_i^* - m)^2] \qquad (1.80)$$

with:

m_w^* — the chosen estimator;
m_i^* — any other estimator.

If this condition is satisfied, the given estimator is said to be the most efficient of all possible estimators.

3. It is preferable that the estimator should approach the value of the parameter being estimated with the probability approaching unity:

$$\lim_{n\to\infty} P\big[\big|(m^x - m)\big| \le \varepsilon\big] = 1 \qquad (1.81)$$

or which is equivalent to:

$$\lim_{n\to\infty} E(m^* - m)^2 = 0 \qquad (1.82)$$

where ε is any low positive number.

If this condition is satisfied, the estimator is said to be consistent and converging with the estimated parameter.

4. The estimators should be unbiased and efficient, that is, have a low variance and small bias [20, 21]

$$m^* = \overline{x} = \frac{1}{n}\sum_{i=1}^{n} x_i \text{ — unbiased estimator} \tag{1.83}$$

$$\delta^{2*} = s^2 = \frac{1}{n}\sum_{i=1}^{n}(x_i - \overline{x})^2 \text{ — biased estimator} \tag{1.84}$$

$$\delta^{2*} = s^2 = \frac{1}{n-1}\sum_{i=1}^{n}(x_i - \overline{x})^2 \text{ — unbiased estimator} \tag{1.85}$$

1.2.3.3 Elements of Stochastic Processes

A. Introductory remarks: Basic concepts

- Theories of stochastic processes facilitate creating models which describe random (chance) phenomena with links to time — $X(x_i, t_i)$, $X_t(x_i)$. Thus, stochastic models describe random processes using random variable $X(x_i)$ in close relation to non-random time t. The realisation of random variable $Xt(xi)$ *is the*realisation of all the values of variable x_i at time t_i. An example of random function $X_t(x_i)$ of a stochastic process is a family of single trends of $X_i(t)$ — Figure 1.9.

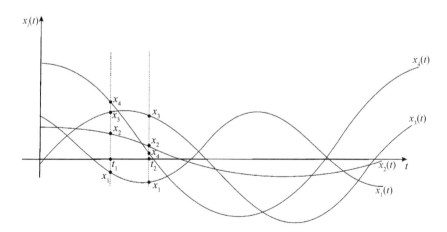

FIGURE 1.9 Realisation of the random function $X_t(x_i)$ of a stochastic process. It can be seen in Figure 1.9 that for each instant t_i (i = 1, 2, 3, etc.) *of the realisation of* $X_i(t)(i = 1, 2, 3,$ etc.) a specific value x_i of random variable $X(x_i, t_i)$, $X_t(x_i)$ is derived.

- Examples of stochastic processes are momentary changes of the following in time: pressure, temperature measured in specific places in Poland, the number of inhabitants of Poland, the number of road accidents in a selected province of the country, the number of sick people in Warsaw, the number of times mains power, water, or sewage systems failed, the price of a product in free market sales, or the level of radio frequency noise. There are always different values of x_i at different times t_i. The variability of a phenomenon at the present moment, for example, t_1, does not allow a determination of the phenomenon at the next moment, for example, t_2—Figure 1.9. One can only speak of the probability that a random variable, $X(x t_i)$, takes a value from a certain interval of x_i values defined by the probability distribution of a stochastic process.
- The statistical characteristics of the stochastic process $x(x t_i)$ are:

1. The density of the stochastic process, f_n:

   - $$f_n(t_1,t_2...t_n,x_1,x_2....x_n) = \frac{\vartheta^n F_n(t_1,t_2...t_n,x_1,x_2....x_n)}{\vartheta x_1 \vartheta x_2...\vartheta x_n} \tag{1.86}$$

   - $f_1(t_1,x_1)$ for the process value of x_1 in instant t_1 — the process is mono-dimensional
   - $f_2(t_1,t_2,x_1,x_2)$ — the process is two-dimensional
   - F_n — the distribution of the stochastic process.

2. The expected value of the stochastic process $X(xiti)$

$$E\left[X(x_i t_i)\right] = \int_{-\infty}^{\infty} x_1 f_1(x_1,t_i)dx_1 = m_x(t_i) \tag{1.87}$$

A multidimensional stochastic process can be reduced to a set of one-dimensional stochastic processes.

3. The variance of the stochastic process, var $X(x t_i)$

$$\text{var}\left[X(x_i t_i)\right] = E\{X(x_i,t_i) - E[X(x_i,t_i)]^2\} = \sigma_x^2(t_i) \tag{1.88}$$

4. The self-correlation function

$$K_{XX}(t_1,t_2) = E\{X(t_1,x_i) - E[X(t_i,x_i)]\} \cdot E\{X(t_2,x_i) - E[X(t_i,x_i)]\} =$$
$$= \int_{-\infty}^{\infty}\int_{-\infty}^{\infty}[x_1 - m_x(t_1)][x_2 - m_x(t_2)]f(x_1,t_1;x_2,t_2)dx_1 dx_2 = K_{xx}(\tau) \tag{1.89}$$

with: $\tau = t_2 - t_1$

5. The cross-correlation function

$$K_{XY}(t_1,t_2) = E\{X(t_1,x_i) - E[X(t_i,x_i)]\} \cdot E\{Y(t_2,y_i) - E[Y(t_i,y_i)]\} =$$
$$= \int_{-\infty}^{\infty}\int_{-\infty}^{\infty}[x_1 - m_x(t_1)][y_2 - m_y(t_2)]f(x_1,t_1;y_2,t_2)dxdy = K_{XY}(\tau) \tag{1.90}$$

B. Basic stochastic processes

- Stationary processes are those processes whose probabilistic relationships do not change with a time shift of τ:

$$P\{X(t) < y\} = P\{X(t + \tau) < y\} \tag{1.91}$$

The joint distribution of random variables $X(t_1)$, $X(t_2)$ is the same as the joint distribution of random variables $X(t_1 + \tau)$, $X(t_2 + \tau)$, etc.
  The expected value $E[X(t)] = m$ does not depend on t.
  The correlation function depends only on the time distance of t_2 from t_1, that is, on τ.

- Ergodic processes are those for which the expected value calculated after a set X_i is equal to the mean calculated after time t_i. Thus, a single trend can be analysed (e.g. 1 — Figure 1.9) over a sufficiently long time (e.g. $t_i = 20$ s) and evaluate all $X_i(t)$ of trends (e.g. 4 — Figure 1.9) on this basis. Practically, ergodicity is assumed to occur when $K_{xx}(\tau)=>0$ with $|\tau| \to \infty$.
- Normal process. Wiener process [17].

A normal process is a stochastic process characterised by that all random variables have a normal (Gaussian) distribution. When the average value $m = 0$ and variance $s^2 = ct(c > 0)$, such a normal process is called a Wiener process. The probability density of the random variable of the Wiener process is:

$$f_n(t_1, t_2 \ldots t_n, x_1, x_2 \ldots x_n) =$$

$$\frac{1}{\sqrt{2\pi t_1}} \exp\left(-\frac{x_1^2}{2t_1}\right) \prod_{i=2}^{n} \frac{1}{\sqrt{2\pi(t_i - t_{i-1})}} \exp\left[-\frac{(x_i - x_{i-1})^2}{2(t_i - t_{i-1})}\right] \tag{1.92}$$

When describing such processes, one can only speak of the probability that random variable $X(t_0 + \Delta t)$ will take a value from the interval defined by the probability distribution of the stochastic process.

- Markov's processes [17] are models of phenomena in which knowledge of the state at a given instant t_0 fully determines the probabilistic relations for future instants and possible information about the previous behaviour of the system (up to instant t_0) does not bring new information. Markov's processes are based on the assumption that the past of a system is forgotten. The analytical apparatus for studying Markov's processes is partial differential equations. Diffusion processes are examples of Markov's processes. Their defining characteristic is that the probability of large changes occurring in a short period of time is very low. The conditional distribution is assumed to be like so:

$$F(t_{n+1}, x_{n+1}, t_n, x_n) = F(t_{n+1}, x_{n+1} | t_1, t_2 \ldots t_n, x_1, x_2 \ldots x_n) \tag{1.93}$$

The conditional density of process g for $n + 1$ is:

$$g(t_1, x_1, t_2, x_2) = \frac{\vartheta}{\vartheta x_2} F(t_2, x_2 | t_1, x_1) \tag{1.94}$$

when function "g" satisfies the equations:

$$\frac{\vartheta}{\vartheta t_1} g(t_1, x_1, t_2, x_2) + a_1(t_1, x_1) \frac{\vartheta}{\vartheta x_1} g(t_1, x_1, t_2, x_2) + $$
$$+ \frac{1}{2} a_2(t_1, x_1) \frac{\vartheta^2}{\vartheta^2 x_1} g(t_1, x_1, t_2, x_2) = 0 \tag{1.95}$$

then density g for the diffusion process is obtained:

$$g(t_1, x_1, t_2, x_2) = \frac{1}{\sqrt{2\pi(t_2 - t_1)a_2}} \exp\left[-\frac{x_2 - x_1}{2(t_2 - t_1)a_2}\right] \tag{1.96}$$

for $a_1 = 0$ and $a_2 = $ const.

Diffusion processes (Markov's processes) are widely used in physics (for studying diffusion and heat conduction), biology, and economics.

- The relationships between random input signals X_t (setpoints W_t or interferences Z_t) and output (utility) signals Y_t signals — Figure 1.4 — are examined using the static characteristics of the process. They are determined, for example, for Y_t. These are:

  1. the density of the stochastic process — $f_y(t_i, y_i)$;
  2. the expected value of the stochastic process — $m_y(t) = E(Y_t)$;
  3. the variance of the stochastic process, $var[Y(y_i, t_i)] = \sigma_y^2(t_i)$;
  4. the self-correlation functions, $K_{xx}(\tau)$, $K_{yy}(\tau)$;
  5. the cross-correlation functions, $K_{xy}(\tau)$.

It is likewise with W_t and Z_t.

In addition, the following is determined for Y_t, W_t, Z_t:

1. The self-covariance function — $C_{YY}(\tau) = K_{YY}(\tau) - m_Y^2(t)$
2. The cross-covariance function — $C_{XY}(\tau) = K_{XY}(\tau) - m_X(t)m_Y(t)$

The value of what is called the correlation coefficient, W is then calculated:

$$W_{XY} = \frac{C_{XY}(\tau)}{\sqrt{C_{XX}(0)C_{YY}(0)}} \tag{1.97}$$

The coefficient satisfies the condition:

$$-1 \le W_{XY} \le 1 \tag{1.98}$$

if:

$W_{XY} = |1|$— signals X_t and Y_t are very well correlated;
$W_{XY} = 0$— signals X_t and Y_t are independent (uncorrelated);
$W_{XY} \geq 0.7$— signals X_t and Y_t are sufficiently correlated.

• The relationships between random input signals X_t (setpoints W_t and interferences Z_t) and output signals Y_t can be successfully studied using their spectral power density functions, S determined from the correlation functions K of the signals [14, 23–25]. Using the Fourier transform, the following is derived:

$$S_{XX} = FK_{XX} = \frac{1}{2\pi} \int_{-\infty}^{\infty} K_{XX} e^{-j\omega\tau} d\tau \qquad (1.99)$$

$$S_{YY} = FK_{YY} = \frac{1}{2\pi} \int_{-\infty}^{\infty} K_{YY} e^{-j\omega\tau} d\tau \qquad (1.100)$$

$$S_{XY} = FK_{XY} = \frac{1}{2\pi} \int_{-\infty}^{\infty} K_{XY} e^{-j\omega\tau} d\tau \qquad (1.101)$$

With the spectral power density functions, spectral transmittance $G(j\omega)$ can be determined.

$$G(j\omega) = \frac{S_{XY}(j\omega)}{S_{XX}(\omega)} = P(\omega) + jQ(\omega) \qquad (1.102)$$

with:

$P(\omega)$— the real part of the spectral transmittance
$Q(\omega)$— the imaginary part of the spectral transmittance

The following is determined from the spectral transmittance:

• amplitude gain of signal y_t relative to x_t

$$A(\omega) = \sqrt{P(\omega)^2 + Q(\omega)^2} \qquad (1.103)$$

• phase shift of signal y_t relative to x_t

$$\varphi(\omega) = arctg \frac{Q(\omega)}{P(\omega)} \qquad (1.104)$$

Additionally, the following is given:

$$A^2(\omega) = \frac{S_{YY}(\omega)}{S_{XX}(\omega)} \qquad (1.105)$$

The quantities of $A(\omega)$ and $\varphi(\omega)$ are interpreted in physical terms as random vibration parameters.

A close relationship between the spectral transmittance and the time characteristics of the system is used [4, 9, 14]. This is given:

$$G(j\omega) = P(\omega) + jQ(\omega) \tag{1.106}$$

and further,

$$h(t) = \frac{2}{\pi} \int_{-\infty}^{\infty} P(\omega) \frac{\sin \omega t}{\omega} d\omega \tag{1.107}$$

where: $h(t)$—the step response of the system of interest (i.e. x_t is theoretically reduced to a function of $1(t)$). Hence, here is a reduction of the study of probabilistic systems to deterministic systems. Here, the priority of significance of ω in the process of studying systems is emphasised.

1.2.4 SYSTEM FAILURE

- The measure of reliability is the probability of failure non-occurrence— R_i [13, 14]

$$0 \leq R_i \leq 1 \tag{1.108}$$

For a system consisting of several elements connected in series, the reliability is:

$$R = \prod_{i=1}^{n} R_i \tag{1.109}$$

if $R_1 = R_2 = \ldots R_n$, then:

$$R = R_1^n \tag{1.110}$$

An analysis of the data in Table 1.3 reveals the following: a slight decrease in the reliability of the components will significantly reduce the reliability of the entire multi-component system.

Increasing the reliability of a system by increasing the reliability of its components is costly and inefficient. An excellent workaround is to introduce redundant elements into the system. This means the parallel introduction of spare, additional elements into the system, which makes the fallibility—F—of the system:

$$F = \prod_{i=1}^{n} F_i \tag{1.111}$$

TABLE 1.3

System Reliability for _n_ Elements Connected in Series

Number of elements	Average component reliability						
1	0.9999	0.999	0.99	0.9	0.8	0.7	0.6
10	0.999	0.99	0.904	0.349	0.107	0.028	0.06
20	0.998	0.98	0.802	0.122	0.012	0.0008	0.00004
50	0.995	0.951	0.605	0.005	0.00001	0	0
100	0.990	0.905	0.366	0.00003	0	0	0
200	0.979	0.819	0.134	0	0	0	0

- A measure of system fallibility is the probability of failure—F_i [3, 18, 19, 26]

$$0 \leq F_i \leq 1 \tag{1.112}$$

Subsequently, the following is given:

$$F_i = 1 - R_i \tag{1.113}$$

For a system consisting of several elements connected in parallel, the fallibility is:

$$F = F_1 \cdot F_2 \cdot F_3 ... F_n \tag{1.114}$$

if:

$$F_1 = F_2 = F_3 = F_n \text{ to: } F = F_1^n \tag{1.115}$$

It can be expressed further like so:

$$F = F_1 \cdot F_2 \cdot F_3 ... F_n = (1 - R_1)(1 - R_2)(1 - R_3)...(1 - R_n) \tag{1.116}$$

Raising the required high reliability, R, of a system. If the following is given (Figure 1.10):

FIGURE 1.10 Serial connection of system elements.

then the reliability of the system is: $R = R_1 \cdot R_2 = 0.81$

Assuming that the whole system is to have $R = 0.9$ (as its basic components do) then it would have to consist of very expensive components: $R_1 = 0.95$ and $R_2 = 0.95$. A less expensive way to achieve the same result is to introduce a redundant component (Figure 1.11).

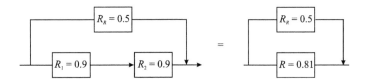

FIGURE 1.11 System with redundant element $R_R = 0.5$.

For the system shown in Figure 1.11 the following is given: $R_{12} = R_1 \cdot R_2 = 0.81$ and further, $F = (1 - R_{12}) \cdot (1 - R_R) = 0.19 \cdot 0.5 \cong 0.1$; hence: $R = 1 - 0.1 = 0.9$ Such an arrangement is less expensive and easy to operate.

- In practical terms, the description of the vulnerability of objects to failure can be reduced to the determination of the reliability characteristics of the object. Typical reliability characteristics (or fallibility characteristics) of an object are described in Polish Standards using determinate reliability indicators, defining the location of an object in an unambiguously determined state of fitness or unfitness [24, 26–32]. These are:

Reliability function:

$$R(t) = P(T \geq t) \qquad (1.117)$$

with:

$P(T \geq t)$ – the probability that the object does not fail until the instant of random variable T, where T is the random variable of fitness/durability of the object.

Fallibility function:

$$F(t) = P(T \leq t) \qquad (1.118)$$

with:

$P(T \leq t)$– the probability that the object fails after the instant of random variable T.

It follows from the definitions of the reliability function $R(t)$ and fallibility $F(t)$ that

$$R(t) = 1 - F(t) \qquad (1.119)$$
$$F(t) = 1 - R(t) \qquad (1.120)$$

Density function of the probability of failure:

$$f(t) = \frac{dF(t)}{dt} = \frac{dR(t)}{dt} \qquad (1.121)$$

Failure severity function (risk function):

$$\lambda = -\frac{d \ln R(t)}{dt} = -\frac{1}{R(t)}\frac{dR(t)}{dt} = \frac{f(t)}{R(t)} \qquad (1.122)$$

Leading function:

$$\Lambda(t) = -\ln R(t) = \int_0^t \lambda(\tau)d\tau \qquad (1.123)$$

Expected value of the time to failure of an object (to its first failure):

$$\theta = E(T) = \int_0^\infty tf(t)dt = \int_0^\infty R(t)dt \qquad (1.124)$$

Raw instant the second order of time to failure:

$$E(T^2) = \int_0^\infty t^2 f(t)dt = 2\int_0^\infty tR(t)dt \qquad (1.125)$$

Variance of time to failure:

$$VT = E(T^2) - [E(T)^2] \qquad (1.126)$$

Standard deviation of time to failure:

$$\sigma_{E(T)} = \sqrt{VT} \qquad (1.127)$$

Quantile of order p of time to failure:

$$F(t_p) = p \qquad (1.128)$$

The quantile of order $p = 0.5$ is called the median, and of order 0.25 and 0.75 are the quartiles (lower and upper, respectively). Relationship (1.128) provides information that in a certain percentage of the population (e.g. $p = 25\%$), a failure will occur already after time $tp < E(T)$ hours (years) (where T is the random variable of any selected time with respect to which the probability of failure of an object is considered).

- From the listed reliability characteristics, the machine manufacturer always provides the failure severity characteristic $\lambda(t)$ (the mean value and the upper and lower deviation) as well as the expected lifetime of the machine, $E(T)$. Selected values $\lambda(t)$ for typical machines and components of typical machines are shown in Table 1.4 [12, 18, 33].

- According to PN-77/N-04005, point estimators are determined in the process of operation, which are the basis for determining the reliability characteristics (indicators). These are:

$$R^*(t) = \frac{n(t)}{n} \tag{1.129}$$

$$F^*(t) = \frac{m(t)}{n} \tag{1.130}$$

$$f^*(t) = \frac{\Delta m(t)}{n \Delta t} \tag{1.131}$$

$$\lambda^*(t) = \frac{n(t) - n(t + \Delta t)}{\Delta t n(t)} \tag{1.132}$$

$$\theta^*(t) = \frac{1}{n}\sum_{t=1}^{n} t_i \tag{1.133}$$

with:

$n(t)$— the number of objects which did not fail in time interval <0;t>;
$m(t)$— the number of objects which did fail in time interval <0;t>;
n— the number of objects;
$n(t + \Delta t)$— the number of objects which did not fail in time interval <$t, t + \Delta t$>;
Δt— the time interval;
t— the time in which there was a failure of the ith object.

- The failure stream is ergodic. This means that the set (number) of all objects n in which failure may occur can be replaced by a sufficiently long observation time, T of the selected single object (Figure 1.12) [34].

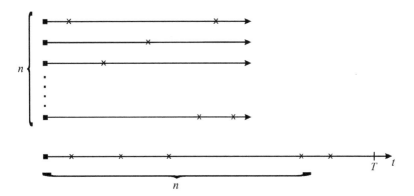

FIGURE 1.12 Illustration of the ergodicity of a failure stream.

Based on Formula 1.132, this can be expressed:

$$\lambda^*(t) = \frac{n(t) - n(t + \Delta t)}{\Delta t n(t)} = \frac{\Delta m(t)}{\Delta t n(t)} \qquad (1.134)$$

followed by:

$$n = \frac{\Delta m(t)}{\lambda^*(t)\Delta t} \cong \frac{\Delta m(t)}{\lambda(t)_{\acute{s}r} \Delta t} \qquad (1.135)$$

where, in this case: $\Delta m(t)$—the increment of failures in time Δt; $\lambda(t)_{\acute{s}r}$—failure severity (specified by the manufacturer, ref. Table 1.4).

Based on Formula 1.133, this can be expressed:

$$\theta^*(t) = \frac{1}{n}\sum_{t=1}^{n} t_i \cong \frac{\theta_{obs}}{n} \qquad (1.136)$$

followed by:

$$n = \frac{\theta_{obs}}{\Delta \theta_{\acute{s}r}} \qquad (1.137)$$

with:

θ_{obs}— the object observation time resulting from the maintenance organisation procedures'

$\Delta\,\theta_{\acute{s}r}$— the mean lifetime between failures.

- For the estimators (points) determined (without difficulty), it is necessary to determine (select) the appropriate form of reliability function $R(t)$, $F(t)$, $f(t)$, $\lambda(t)$, $E(T)$ according to the recommendations specified in the PN-79/N-04031 standard (Table 1.5).

Hence, the problem of reliability assessment is reduced to the selection of such a basic failure probability distribution function, a reliability index (which can be exponential, Weibull, normal and log-normal) which trends the closest to their estimators.

In the reliability theory, functions $f(t)$ and $F(t)$ and parameters $E(T)$, and standard deviations $\sigma_{E(T)}$ are of particular importance.

The analytical forms of the failure probability distribution functions allow a broad qualitative and quantitative analysis of reliability processes in machine maintenance [29, 30, 32, 35].

TABLE 1.4
Failure Severity of Machine Elements (The Average Value According to Experimental Tests, with the Upper and Lower Limit Values Derived by Calculation) [18]

Name of elements		Failure severity λ [10^{-6} h^{-1}]		
Manufacturer: Martin (USA)—M Manufacturer: General Electric (USA)—G		Limit Upper	Value Average	Limit Lower
Batteries	M	19.3	7.2	0.40
Starter motors	G	13.7	5.1	0.35
Alternating current generators	G	2.94	0.7	0.033
Adjustable suppressors	G	1.3	0.6	0.15
Rechargeable batteries	G	14.29	1.4	0.5
Bushing insulators	G	0.08	0.05	0.02
Fixed capacitors up to 600 V	G	0.018	0.01	0.001
Ceramic capacitors up to 600 V	G	0.133	0.0625	0.040
Oil capacitors	G	0.48	0.30	0.12
Switches	G	0.40	0.1375	0.045
Diodes, surge arresting	G	0.437	0.2	0.08
Connectors, electrical	G	0.47/k	0.2/k	0.3/k
Windings (generic)	G	0.088	0.05	0.038
Radiators	G	6.21	4.0	1.112
Electric heating element	M	0.04	0.02	0.01
Electric heating element	G	–	7.67	–
Electric heating element (overloaded)	M	18.6	15.0	2.21
Motors	M	7.5	0.625	0.15
Motors	G	0.58	0.3	0.11
Fan motors	M	5.5	0.2	0.05
Electric motors	M	0.58	0.3	0.11
AC electric motors	G	9.36	5.24	1.12
DC electric motors	G	–	9.36	–
Servomotors	M	0.35	0.23	0.11
Servomotors	G	5.61	1.51	0.101
Stepper motors	G	0.71	0.37	0.228
Gate valves	G	44.8	5.1	0.112
Ball valves	G	7.7	4.6	1.11
Pressure gauges	G	15.0	1.3	0.135
Hydraulic motors	G	2.25	4.3	1.45
Compressors	G	3.57	2.4	0.342
Pumps	G	4.90	13.5	1.12
Piping (pipeline)	G	4.85	1.1	0.25
Cylinders	G	0.81	0.007	0.005
Cylinders	M	0.12	0.008	0.005
Detachable couplings	G	1.1	0.06	0.04
Slip clutches	G	0.94	0.03	0.07
Bearings	G	5.5	0.5	0.02

(Continued)

TABLE 1.4 (*Continued*)
Failure Severity of Machine Elements (The Average Value According to Experimental Tests, with the Upper and Lower Limit Values Derived by Calculation) [18]

Name of elements		Failure severity λ [$10^{-6}\ h^{-1}$]		
Manufacturer: Martin (USA)—M Manufacturer: General Electric (USA)—G		Limit Upper	Value Average	Limit Lower
Ball bearings (medium size)	G	2.22	0.65	0.02
Roller bearings	G	1.0	0.5	0.02
Ball bearings (large size)	G	3.53	1.80	0.072
Ball bearings (small size)	G	1.72	0.875	0.35
Springs	G	–	0.112	–

Notes to distribution:

- Exponential: $t \geq 0$;
- Weibull: Euler gamma function $\Gamma(p) = \int_0^\infty x^{p-1} e^{-x} dx$;

- Normal: Laplace integral $\phi(u) = \dfrac{1}{2\sqrt{\pi}} \int_{-\infty}^0 e^{-u^2} du$;

- Log-normal: $t > 0$ if $Y = lg\ T$, then $M = lg\ e = 0.4343$; if $Y = ln\ T$, then $M = 1$.
- Exponential distribution (Table 1.5) is widely used in reliability analysis and mass maintenance theory [17, 18, 32, 33].
- Weibull distribution (Table 1.5) is widely used in the assessment of the reliability and service life of mechanical and electromechanical components and components of electronic devices [8]. Note that the Weibull distribution (Table 1.5) originated as an empirical distribution, while the theoretical basis of this distribution was developed later by B. W. Gniedenko. Therefore, it would be appropriate to call this distribution the Weibull–Gniedenko distribution [18].
- Normal distribution (Gaussian distribution) (Table 1.5) is found when differences in the value of a random variable are the result of a large number of factors homogeneous in their effect, none of which is predominant. This occurs in measurement errors, in scatter during target shooting, in scatter of dimensions of products made with automatic machine tools, etc. [17, 18, 32, 33].
- Log-normal distribution (Table 1.5) is a good mathematical model for experimental data on fatigue life of materials, determination of long-term durability of parts, correct operation time of products, etc.

With a small variation coefficient, that is, when the condition $\dfrac{\sigma}{\mu} \ll 1$ is satisfied, the log-normal distribution can be approximated with a normal distribution. This property is often used in engineering calculations by changing the actual log-normal distribution with a suitable normal distribution.

TABLE 1.5

Basic Failure Probability Distribution Functions and Reliability Indicators [32]

Distribution name/ distribution parameter	Probability distribution density function $f(t)$	Probability distribution function $F(t)$	Reliability function $R(t)$	Failure severity function $\lambda(t)$	Expected value $E(T)$
Exponential θ	$\dfrac{1}{\theta} e^{-\frac{t}{\theta}}$	$1 - e^{-\frac{t}{\theta}}$	$e^{-\frac{t}{\theta}}$	$\dfrac{1}{\theta}$	θ
Weibull a, b	$b/a(t/a)^{(b-1)} e^{(?-(t/a)^b)}$	$1 - e^{-\left(\frac{t}{a}\right)^b}$	$e^{-\left(\frac{t}{a}\right)^b}$	$\dfrac{b}{a}\left(\dfrac{t}{a}\right)^{b-1}$	$a\Gamma\left(\dfrac{1}{b}+1\right)$
Normal m, σ	$\dfrac{1}{\sigma\sqrt{2\pi}} e^{-\frac{(t-m)^2}{2\sigma^2}} = \dfrac{1}{\sigma}\varphi\left(\dfrac{t-m}{\sigma}\right)$	$\dfrac{1}{\sigma\sqrt{2\pi}}\displaystyle\int_{-\infty}^{t} e^{-\frac{(x-m)^2}{2\sigma^2}} dx = \phi\left(\dfrac{t-m}{\sigma}\right)$	$1-\phi\left(\dfrac{t-m}{\sigma}\right)$	$\dfrac{\dfrac{1}{\sigma}\varphi\left(\dfrac{t-m}{\sigma}\right)}{1-\phi\left(\dfrac{t-m}{\sigma}\right)}$	m
Log-normal m, σ	$\dfrac{M}{t\sigma\sqrt{2\pi}} e^{-\frac{(lgt-m)^2}{2\sigma^2}} = \dfrac{M}{\sigma t}\varphi\left(\dfrac{lgt-m}{\sigma}\right)$	$\dfrac{M}{\sigma\sqrt{2\pi}}\displaystyle\int_0^t \dfrac{1}{x} e^{-\frac{(lgx-m)^2}{2\sigma^2}} dx = \phi\left(\dfrac{lgt-m}{\sigma}\right)$	$1-\phi\left(\dfrac{lgt-m}{\sigma}\right)$	$\dfrac{\dfrac{M}{\sigma t}\varphi\left(\dfrac{lgt-m}{\sigma}\right)}{1-\phi\left(\dfrac{lgt-m}{\sigma}\right)}$	$e^{\left(\frac{m}{M}+\frac{\sigma^2}{2M^2}\right)}$

- Reliability indicators are determined at different stages of an object's life. These stages are:
  - Preliminary design
  - Engineering design
  - Prototype
  - Trial batch
  - Series production
  - Operation.
- The starting point for the determination of reliability characteristics is the designation of the machine type with the appropriate standardised code (PN-77/N-04010), for example, 1111.

In the process of determining the machine object code, individual questions must be answered according to the following algorithm based on Table 1.6:

- Is the machine repairable? If yes, the first digit of code is 2.
- Are there are restrictions on the operation time of the machine? This is signified with the appropriate second digit of code. The digit is 1 when operation continues until the first failure; it is 2 when operation continues until the limit state is reached; it is 3 when operation continues until the specified task is completed; it is 4 when operation continues until nth failure occurs; it is 5 when operation continues until the limit state is reached under the conditions of standby for operation.
- The type of operating duty is signified with the third digit of code. The digit is 1 when the duty is continuous; it is 2 when the duty has regular breaks; it is 3 when the duty has with random breaks.
- Is it possible for the task to be continued after a failure, depending on the time of repair? This is signified with the third digit of code. The digit is 1 when, irrespective of the repair time length, the object can continue the task which has begun; it is 2 when, irrespective of the repair time length, the object cannot continue the task which has begun; it is 3 when the feasibility to continue the task depends on the repair time length; it is 4 when, irrespective of the repair time length, the object cannot continue the task if the failure has occurred in the operating conditions.

According to the specified code, for example 1222, 2222, the baseline reliability index $R(t)$, $F(t)$, $f(t)$, $\lambda(t)$, $E(T)$ should be chosen according to the guidelines in Table 1.7 [32].

TABLE 1.6
Determination of the Technical Object Failure Code

Basis of classification	Code digit location	Class name	Code digit	Basis of subclassification	Code digit location	Subclass feature	Code digit
Repairability	I	Unrepairable	1	Lifetime restrictions	II	To failure	1
						To the limit state	2
						To complete the specific tasks	3
				Operating duty	III	Continuous operation	1
						Operation with regular breaks	2
						Operation with random breaks	3
				Task continuation feasibility after a failure	IV	The task can be continued when the failed object is replaced with a new one	1
						The task cannot be continued when the failed object is replaced with a new one	2
		Repairable	2	Operating time restrictions	II	To the first failure	1
						To the limit state	2
						To complete the specific tasks	3
						To the nth failure	4
						To the limit state in the standby for operation	5
				Operating duty	III	Continuous operation	1
						Operation with regular breaks	2
						Operation with random breaks	3
				The task can be continued after a failure, depending on the repair time length	IV	Irrespective of the repair time length, the object may continue the tasks in progress	1
						Irrespective of the repair time length, the object cannot continue the tasks in progress	2
						The task could be continued depending on the repair time length	3
						Irrespective of the repair time length, the object cannot continue the task if the failure occurs under operating conditions	4

TABLE 1.7

Selection of Basic Reliability Indicators

Code	Indicator designation and name
1	2
1111	Θ— mean time of correct operation to failure
1121	$\lambda(t)$— failure severity[1]
1131	Θ— mean time of correct operation to failure
2111	
2121	Θ— mean time of correct operation to failure
2131	
1211	
1221	
1231	Θ— mean time of correct operation to failure
2211	Θ_S— mean operating asset
2221	
2231	
1222	
1232	$R(t)$— the probability of object's correct operation in interval $(0, t >$
2222	$P(t)$— the probability of object's failure in interval $(0, t >$
2232	Θ_S— mean operating asset
2422	Θ_K— mean operating time between failures[2]
2432	
1312	$R(t)$— the probability of object's correct operation in interval $(0, t >$
2312	$P(t)$— the probability of object's failure in interval $(0, t >$
2411	$\omega(t)$— failure stream parameter
2421	Θ_S— mean operating asset
2431	
2413	K_ω— technical duty factor Θ_S— mean operating asset $\omega(t)$— failure stream parameter
2423	$\omega(t)$— failure stream parameter K_g— readiness factor
2433	Θ_S— mean operating asset Θ_n— average repair time length
2414	
2424	
2434	K_{go}— operating readiness factor
2514	Θ_S— mean operating asset
2524	
2534	

1. Apply for an exponential distribution of correct operating time.

2. Apply to repairable objects.

1.2.5   STRUCTURE OF SYSTEMS AND SYSTEM COUPLING

- A system (as explained in Section 1.1.1) is understood to mean the set of elements (arrangements) of a system and the set of specific relations between these elements (arrangements). The very set of these relations and their isomorphic transformations constitute the structure of the system. When the responses (output signals) of one system are drivers (input signals) for another system, these two systems are coupled (Figure 1.13) [3, 36].

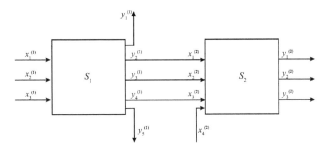

FIGURE 1.13 Coupling of systems (arrangements/components) S_1 and S_2.

Signals $x_1^{(1)}$, $x_2^{(1)}$, $x_3^{(1)}$, $y_1^{(1)}$, $y_5^{(1)}$, $x_4^{(2)}$, $y_1^{(2)}$, $y_2^{(2)}$, $y_3^{(2)}$ are non-coupling signals. Signals $y_2^{(1)}$, $y_3^{(1)}$, $y_4^{(1)}$, $x_1^{(2)}$, $x_2^{(2)}$, $x_3^{(2)}$ are coupling signals. Thus, the coupling of system S_1 to system S_2 is the transition of signals $y_{1\,to\,5}^{(1)}$ into signals $x_{1\,to\,4}^{(2)}$ (when there is no transition it is "0", when there is transition it is "1"). This coupling is described by matrix C_{21}.

$$
C_{21} =
\overbrace{
\begin{array}{ccccc}
y_1^{(1)} & y_2^{(1)} & y_3^{(1)} & y_4^{(1)} & y_5^{(1)}
\end{array}
}^{\text{output}(1)(y_{1-r})}
\begin{vmatrix}
0 & 1 & 0 & 0 & 0 \\
0 & 0 & 1 & 0 & 0 \\
0 & 0 & 0 & 1 & 0 \\
0 & 0 & 0 & 0 & 0
\end{vmatrix}
\begin{array}{l}
x_1^{(2)} \\
x_2^{(2)} \\
x_3^{(2)} \\
x_4^{(2)}
\end{array}
\Big\} \text{input}(2)(x_{1-4})
\tag{1.138}
$$

Matrix C_{21} is the structure matrix of the arrangement in Figure 1.13. Matrix C_{21} is a zero-one (binary) matrix. This matrix should contain at least one element that is a one. There should be at most a single one in each column or row.

In a generic case there is this matrix:

$$C_{sr} = \begin{array}{c} \overset{\textstyle y_1^{(r)},\ y_2^{(r)},}{} \overset{\textstyle y_n^{(r)}}{} \\ \begin{vmatrix} C_{11} & C_{12} & C_{13} & \cdots & C_{1n,} \\ C_{21} & C_{22} & C_{23} & \cdots & C_{2n,} \\ C_{31} & C_{32} & C_{33} & \cdots & C_{3n,} \\ \vdots & & & & \\ C_{m,1} & C_{m,2} & C_{m,3} & \cdots & C_{m,n,} \end{vmatrix} \begin{array}{l} x_1^{(s)} \\ x_2^{(s)} \\ \\ \\ x_m^{(s)} \end{array} \end{array}$$

r-th element previous

next / previous

s-th element next

Hence:

$$x^{(s)} = C_{sr} y^{(r)} \qquad (1.139)$$

which means that with $s = 2$, $r = 1$, this applies:

$$x^{(2)} = C_{21} y^{(1)} \qquad (1.140)$$

An example of the description of the coupling of elements S_1, S_2, S_3, S_4 shown in Figure 1.14:

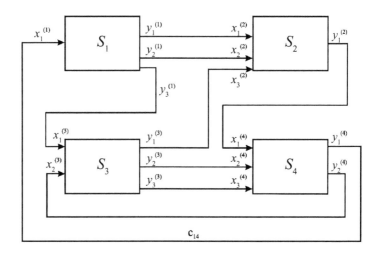

FIGURE 1.14 Arrangement of the coupling of four elements.

When determining the structure matrix, the question is whether the output of interest has an effect on a specific input for all elements. The result is $4(4 - 1) = 12$ structure matrices:

$$C_{11} = \begin{array}{c} \overset{\textstyle y_1^{(1)}\ y_2^{(1)}\ y_3^{(1)}}{} \\ \begin{bmatrix} 0 & 0 & 0 \end{bmatrix} x_1^{(1)} \end{array} \qquad C_{12} = \begin{array}{c} \overset{\textstyle y_1^{(2)}}{} \\ \begin{bmatrix} 0 \end{bmatrix} x_1^{(1)} \end{array}$$

$$
\begin{array}{cc}
\overset{\overset{(3)}{y_1}\ \overset{(3)}{y_2}\ \overset{(3)}{y_3}}{C_{13}=\begin{bmatrix}0 & 0 & 0\end{bmatrix}\overset{(1)}{x_1}} &
\overset{\overset{(4)}{y_1}\ \overset{(4)}{y_2}}{C_{14}=\begin{bmatrix}1 & 0\end{bmatrix}\overset{(4)}{x_1}}
\end{array}
$$

$$
C_{21}=\begin{matrix}\overset{(1)}{y_1}\ \overset{(1)}{y_2}\ \overset{(1)}{y_3}\\ \begin{bmatrix}1 & 0 & 0\\ 0 & 1 & 0\\ 0 & 0 & 0\end{bmatrix}\end{matrix}\begin{matrix}\overset{(2)}{x_1}\\ \overset{(2)}{x_2}\\ \overset{(2)}{x_3}\end{matrix}
\qquad
C_{22}=\begin{matrix}\overset{(2)}{y_1}\\ \begin{bmatrix}0\\ 0\\ 0\end{bmatrix}\end{matrix}\begin{matrix}\overset{(2)}{x_1}\\ \overset{(2)}{x_2}\\ \overset{(2)}{x_3}\end{matrix}
$$

$$
C_{23}=\begin{matrix}\overset{(3)}{y_1}\ \overset{(3)}{y_2}\ \overset{(3)}{y_3}\\ \begin{bmatrix}0 & 0 & 0\\ 0 & 0 & 0\\ 1 & 0 & 0\end{bmatrix}\end{matrix}\begin{matrix}\overset{(2)}{x_1}\\ \overset{(2)}{x_2}\\ \overset{(2)}{x_3}\end{matrix}
\qquad
C_{24}=\begin{matrix}\overset{(4)}{y_1}\ \overset{(4)}{y_2}\\ \begin{bmatrix}0 & 0\\ 0 & 0\\ 1 & 0\end{bmatrix}\end{matrix}\begin{matrix}\overset{(2)}{x_1}\\ \overset{(2)}{x_2}\\ \overset{(2)}{x_3}\end{matrix}
$$

$$
C_{31}=\begin{matrix}\overset{(1)}{y_1}\ \overset{(1)}{y_2}\ \overset{(1)}{y_3}\\ \begin{bmatrix}0 & 0 & 1\\ 0 & 0 & 0\end{bmatrix}\end{matrix}\begin{matrix}\overset{(3)}{x_1}\\ \overset{(3)}{x_2}\end{matrix}
\qquad
C_{32}=\begin{matrix}\overset{(2)}{y_1}\\ \begin{bmatrix}0\\ 0\end{bmatrix}\end{matrix}\begin{matrix}\overset{(3)}{x_1}\\ \overset{(3)}{x_2}\end{matrix}
$$

$$
C_{33}=\begin{matrix}\overset{(3)}{y_1}\ \overset{(3)}{y_2}\ \overset{(3)}{y_3}\\ \begin{bmatrix}0 & 0 & 0\\ 0 & 0 & 0\end{bmatrix}\end{matrix}\begin{matrix}\overset{(3)}{x_1}\\ \overset{(3)}{x_2}\end{matrix}
\qquad
C_{34}=\begin{matrix}\overset{(4)}{y_1}\ \overset{(4)}{y_2}\\ \begin{bmatrix}0 & 0\\ 0 & 1\end{bmatrix}\end{matrix}\begin{matrix}\overset{(3)}{x_1}\\ \overset{(3)}{x_2}\end{matrix}
$$

$$
C_{41}=\begin{matrix}\overset{(1)}{y_1}\ \overset{(1)}{y_2}\ \overset{(1)}{y_3}\\ \begin{bmatrix}0 & 0 & 0\\ 0 & 0 & 0\\ 0 & 0 & 0\end{bmatrix}\end{matrix}\begin{matrix}\overset{(4)}{x_1}\\ \overset{(4)}{x_2}\\ \overset{(4)}{x_3}\end{matrix}
\qquad
C_{42}=\begin{matrix}\overset{(2)}{y_1}\\ \begin{bmatrix}1\\ 0\\ 0\end{bmatrix}\end{matrix}\begin{matrix}\overset{(4)}{x_1}\\ \overset{(4)}{x_2}\\ \overset{(4)}{x_3}\end{matrix}
$$

$$
C_{43}=\begin{matrix}\overset{(3)}{y_1}\ \overset{(3)}{y_2}\ \overset{(3)}{y_3}\\ \begin{bmatrix}0 & 0 & 0\\ 0 & 1 & 0\\ 0 & 0 & 1\end{bmatrix}\end{matrix}\begin{matrix}\overset{(4)}{x_1}\\ \overset{(4)}{x_2}\\ \overset{(4)}{x_3}\end{matrix}
\qquad
C_{44}=\begin{matrix}\overset{(4)}{y_1}\ \overset{(4)}{y_2}\\ \begin{bmatrix}0 & 0\\ 0 & 0\\ 0 & 0\end{bmatrix}\end{matrix}\begin{matrix}\overset{(4)}{x_1}\\ \overset{(4)}{x_2}\\ \overset{(4)}{x_3}\end{matrix}
$$

These matrices can be expressed using a single condensed matrix, R:

$$
R=\begin{bmatrix}
0 & C_{12} & C_{13} & C_{14}\\
C_{21} & 0 & C_{23} & C_{24}\\
C_{31} & C_{32} & 0 & C_{34}\\
C_{41} & C_{42} & C_{43} & 0
\end{bmatrix}
$$

The coupling matrix can be expressed as follows:

$$
\begin{bmatrix} x_1^{(1)} \\ x_1^{(2)} \\ x_2^{(2)} \\ x_3^{(2)} \\ x_1^{(3)} \\ x_2^{(3)} \\ x_1^{(4)} \\ x_2^{(4)} \\ x_3^{(4)} \end{bmatrix} =
\begin{bmatrix}
0 & 0 & 0 & 0 & 0 & 0 & 0 & 1 & 0 \\
1 & 0 & 0 & 0 & 0 & 0 & 0 & 0 & 0 \\
0 & 1 & 0 & 0 & 0 & 0 & 0 & 0 & 0 \\
0 & 0 & 0 & 0 & 1 & 0 & 0 & 0 & 0 \\
0 & 0 & 1 & 0 & 0 & 0 & 0 & 0 & 0 \\
0 & 0 & 0 & 0 & 0 & 0 & 0 & 0 & 1 \\
0 & 0 & 0 & 1 & 0 & 0 & 0 & 0 & 0 \\
0 & 0 & 0 & 0 & 0 & 1 & 0 & 0 & 0 \\
0 & 0 & 0 & 0 & 0 & 0 & 1 & 0 & 0
\end{bmatrix} =
\begin{bmatrix} y_1^{(1)} \\ y_2^{(1)} \\ y_3^{(1)} \\ y_1^{(2)} \\ y_1^{(3)} \\ y_2^{(3)} \\ y_3^{(3)} \\ y_1^{(4)} \\ y_2^{(4)} \end{bmatrix}
$$

or in its condensed form:

$$
R = \begin{array}{c} \begin{matrix} y_1^{(1)} & y_2^{(1)} & y_1^{(2)} & y_2^{(2)} \end{matrix} \\ \begin{bmatrix} 0 & 0 & 1 & 0 \\ 1 & 0 & 0 & 0 \\ 0 & 1 & 0 & 0 \\ 0 & 0 & 0 & 1 \end{bmatrix} \begin{matrix} x_1^{(1)} \\ x_2^{(1)} \\ x_1^{(2)} \\ x_2^{(2)} \end{matrix} \end{array}
$$

Matrix R is called the structure matrix of the arrangement (system).

1. Matrix R is a zero-one (binary) matrix.
2. Minimum number of couplings $= N - 1$ (N is the number of elements).
3. An element that is not coupled to another element is called a boundary element.
4. The submatrices C_{12}, C_{13}, ..., C_{23}, ... located above the diagonal of the matrix represent the feedback of the arrangement.
5. The arrangement structure matrix can be extended with an additional row and an additional column, which will mean that the arrangement is linked to its environment. Then, matrix R^* will take this form:

$$
R^* = \begin{bmatrix}
0 & C_{U1} & C_{U2} & \cdots & C_{UN} \\
C_{1U} & 0 & C_{12} & \cdots & C_{1N} \\
C_{2U} & C_{21} & 0 & \cdots & C_{2N} \\
C_{NU} & C_{N1} & C_{N2} & \cdots & 0
\end{bmatrix}
$$

The structure matrix can be developed into an arrangement (system), for example when it is experimentally determined that the structure matrix takes this form:

$$R = \begin{bmatrix} 0 & 0 & 1 & 0 \\ 1 & 0 & 0 & 0 \\ 0 & 1 & 0 & 0 \\ 0 & 0 & 0 & 1 \end{bmatrix} \begin{matrix} x_1^{(1)} \\ x_2^{(1)} \\ x_1^{(2)} \\ x_2^{(2)} \end{matrix} \qquad (1.141)$$

with column headers $y_1^{(1)}\ y_2^{(1)}\ y_1^{(2)}\ y_2^{(2)}$

then its equivalent two-element arrangement can be determined (Figure 1.15):

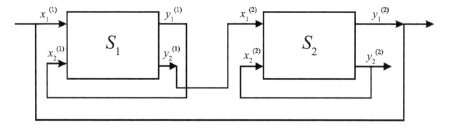

FIGURE 1.15 Arrangement composed of elements S_1 and S_2 equivalent to structure matrix R (Formula 1.141).

1.2.6 THE ESSENCE OF REGULATION AND CONTROL

The essence (gist) of regulation is to bring the output state of arrangement (system) y to a state defined by a constant standard, $y^* = const.$ according to the law of regulation:

$$\Delta y = y - y^* \leq E \qquad (1.142)$$

where E is the permissible deviation from the standard.

The very way of bringing y to y^* is called regulation.

- The typical regulation methods include:

    1. interference elimination—Figure 1.16;
    2. interference compensation—Figure 1.17;
    3. deviation offset—Figure 1.18.

Examples:

The systems in Figures 1.16 and 1.17 require detection of interferences (disturbances). The interference signal $\hat{x}$ is measured. The system in Figure 1.18 does not require interference detection $\hat{x}$. The measured signal is $\tilde{y}$, that is, the effect of the $\hat{x}$ signal after its compensation with signal Δx produced by the controller.

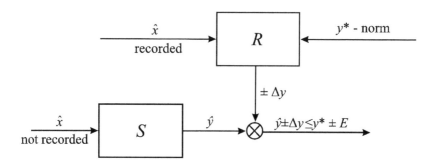

FIGURE 1.16 Regulation system with interference elimination $\hat{x}$—the disturbed input signal $\hat{y}$—the disturbed output signal, Δy—the signal produced by the controller eliminating the interference from signal $\hat{y}$.

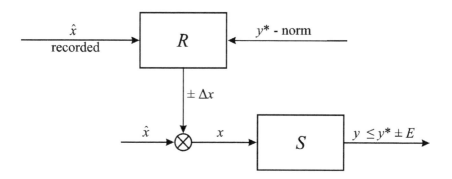

FIGURE 1.17 Regulation system with interference compensation Δx—the signal produced by the controller compensating for the interference in signal $\hat{x}$.

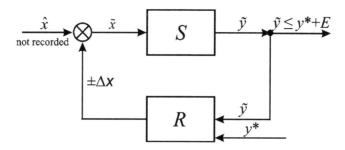

FIGURE 1.18 Regulation system with deviation offset $\tilde{x}$—the input signal with compensation of the deviation in signal $\hat{x}$; $\tilde{y}$—detected disturbed output signal; Δx—the signal produced by the controller on the basis of $\tilde{y}$ and y^*.

- The essence of control is to bring the output state of arrangement (system) y to the state defined by the changing norm $y^* = f(t)$ according to the control law:

$$\Delta y = y - y^* = y - f(t) \leq E \tag{1.143}$$

The typical control methods include:

1. programming (of flight trajectories, production plans, consumption development, etc.);
2. adaptive control;
3. follow-up control;
4. feedforward (anticipating) control.

In programming control, the deviations of output states y are observed at particular time periods from norm y^* which varies according to the time function $f(t)$ and it is checked whether the deviations are within acceptable tolerances defined by probability conditions:

$$P\{|y - f(t)| < 2\sigma\} > 1 - \alpha \tag{1.144}$$

with:

σ— standard deviation;
2σ— standard deviation for significance level $\alpha = 5\%$;
$u = 1-\alpha$— confidence level, here: $u = 95\%$.

This means that if individual differences $y - f(t)$ are larger in absolute value than the 2σ values calculated from these differences and occur more frequently than implied by the significance level, α, then it can be assumed that some significant change is taking place in the system.

Adaptive control involves maintaining the initial state of the system at a level dependent on the levels achieved in previous periods. Here, the norm is a function depending on the $yt - p$ states reached in previous time periods:

$$y^*_t = f(y_{t-1}, y_{t-2}, \ldots, y_{t-p}) \tag{1.145}$$

Here, time is the fundamental variable for leading, developing, or achieving goals. Examples of adaptive (step) control are processes of adaptation of living organisms to new environmental conditions, learning processes, planning of production or purchase orders, etc.

In follow-up control, the reference basis is the states of external elements x_k, especially those that cannot be changed arbitrarily. Here, the norm takes this form:

$$y^*_t = f(x_1, x_2, \ldots, x_k) \tag{1.146}$$

Examples of follow-up control are the movement of a ship along a coastline, purchasing decisions based on prices, income, or supply (which are external factors), production decisions based on customer orders, opportunities for procurement of materials, etc.

Feedforward control is the feasibility of forecasting (predicting) the achieved output states by applying in advance appropriate activities and regulatory measures intended to achieve compliance of these states with the desired norm. Examples of this control are ambient temperature control based on changes in external temperature, aircraft piloting characterised by the fact that the pilot predicts future states of the aircraft based on the state the aircraft is currently in, predictive regulation, whose characteristic is that the output signal from a predictive controller appears earlier than the output signal from a non-predictive controller.

1.2.7   Basic Regulation Pattern: Balance and Stability of Systems, Signal Dating, Proprietary and Feed Components in Systems

Based on Figures 1.3 and 1.4, a regulating system can be represented on a block diagram; see Figure 1.19.

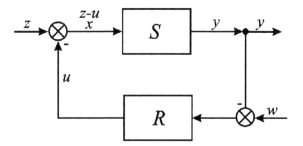

FIGURE 1.19 Block diagram of a regulating (control) system.

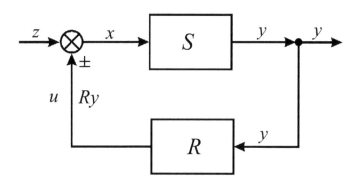

FIGURE 1.20 Block diagram of a basic regulating (control) system.

This system, or arrangement, is described by the transmittances:

$$H_z = \frac{Y}{Z} = \frac{S}{1+RS} \text{ —interference transmittance} \qquad (1.147)$$

$$H_w = \frac{Y}{Z} = \frac{RS}{1+RS} \text{ —follow-up transmittance} \qquad (1.148)$$

The basic regulation pattern is transmittance H_z. It is because of the ambiguity of transmittance H_w, because $R_1 = 3$, $S_1 = 2$, $H_{w1} = 6/7$ and for $R_2 = 2$, $S_2 = 3$ also gives $H_{w2} = 6/7$. Although the arrangements are different, the H_w transmittances remain identical. By analysing transmittance H_z, different transmittances of the arrangement are obtained: $H_{z1} = 2/7$ and $H_{z2} = 3/7$, which is consistent with the reality described. Hence, H_z is the basic regulation pattern used to study an arrangement (a system).

- Stability of an arrangement is understood as the ability of the arrange-ment to automatically reduce the effects of interference until they are completely eliminated (extinguished) during a time approaching infinity. This means that a stable arrangement will, over time, move towards an equilibrium state which is not necessarily the same as it was at the begin-ning. A diagram of the basic regulating arrangement with positive and negative feedback is shown in Figure 1.20 [3].

If input signal $x = x_1$ appears in an object (a phenomenon, an organ, or an organism) designated S, then output signal $y = y_1$ appears in the object. Hence:

$$y_1 = Sx_1 \qquad (1.149)$$

As a result of triggering feedback, there is a change in the signal at the object input. Hence, for positive feedback, there will be x_2 instead of x_1 previously:

$$x_2 = x_1 + Ry_1 = x_1 + RSx_1 = (1 + RS)x_1 \qquad (1.150)$$

this new signal, x_2, triggers a new signal, y_2:

$$y_2 = Sx_2 = S(1+RS)x_1 = (1+RS)Sx_1 \qquad (1.151)$$

Then again, from the effect of feedback, signal x_2 changes change to a new signal, x_3:

$$x_3 = x_1 + Ry_2 = x_1 + R(1+RS)Sx_1$$
$$x_3 = \left[1 + RS + (RS)^2\right]x_1 \qquad (1.152)$$

Further from this new signal, x_3, a new output signal y_3 is generated:

$$y_3 = Sx_3 = \left[1 + RS + (RS)^2\right]Sx_1 \qquad (1.153)$$

And again, the feedback effect will change the input of object S from x_3 to x_4:

$$x_4 = x_1 + Ry_3$$
$$x_4 = \left[1 + RS + (RS)^2 + (RS)^3\right]x_1 \qquad (1.154)$$

This signal changes signal x_4 to y_4:

$$y_4 = Sx_4 = \left[1 + RS + (RS)^2 + (RS)^3\right]Sx_1 \qquad (1.155)$$

The new input, x_5, will be:

$$x_5 = x_1 + Ry_4$$
$$x_5 = \left[1 + RS + (RS)^2 + (RS)^3 + (RS)^4\right]x_1 \qquad (1.156)$$

resulting—again—in the following:

$$y_5 = Sx_5 = \left[1 + RS + (RS)^2 + (RS)^3 + (RS)^4\right]Sx_1 \qquad (1.157)$$

Finally, it can be expressed like so:

$$y_n = \left[1 + RS + (RS)^2 + \ \ldots \ + (RS)^{n-1}\right]Sx_1 \qquad (1.158)$$
$$y_{n+1} = \left[1 + RS + (RS)^2 + \ \ldots \ + (RS)^{n-1} + (RS)^n\right]Sx_1 \qquad (1.159)$$

The square brackets of Formula (1.159) hold this:

$$\frac{(RS)^n}{(RS)^{n-1}} = \frac{(RS)^3}{(RS)^2} = \frac{(RS)^2}{RS} = RS = q \qquad (1.160)$$

This is the expansion of the sum of geometric progression.
    It is why it can be expressed like so:

$$y_n = \frac{(RS)^n - 1}{RS - 1} Sx_1 \qquad (1.161)$$

Since
$$1 + RS + (RS)^2 + \ldots (RS)^{n-1} = \frac{(RS)^n - 1}{RS - 1}$$

Formula 1.161 can be expressed as follows:

$$y_n = \frac{1 - (RS)^n}{1 - RS} Sx_1 \qquad (1.162)$$

An analysis of Formula 1.162 shows the following:

1. If $RS > 1$, then $y_n \rightarrow \infty$

Such an arrangement cannot stabilise itself. It does not seek equilibrium.

2. If $RS < 1$, then

$$y_n = \frac{1}{1-RS} Sx_1 \tag{1.163}$$

Such an arrangement stabilises itself. It seeks equilibrium.
For negative feedback (Figure 1.20), this is obtained:

$$y_n = \frac{1-(-RS)^n}{1+RS} Sx_1 \tag{1.164}$$

An analysis of Formula 1.164 shows the following:

1. If $RS > 1$, then $y_n \rightarrow -\infty$

2. If $RS < 1$, then

$$y_n \rightarrow \frac{1}{1+RS} Sx_1 \tag{1.165}$$

Such an arrangement stabilises itself. It seeks equilibrium.
Finally, with positive and negative feedback, the condition of stability, of seeking equilibrium, can be written as follows:

$$|RS| < 1 \tag{1.166}$$

which is

$$|S| < \frac{1}{|R|} \tag{1.167}$$

with:

$|R|$ — regulator power
$|S|$ — power of the object (an arrangement or a phenomenon)

where:

$|S| < \dfrac{1}{|R|}$ — compensating feedback

$$|S| > \frac{1}{|R|} \quad \text{— cumulative feedback}$$

$$|S| = \frac{1}{|R|} \quad \text{— the arrangement is at borderline stability}$$

Expression $\frac{1}{|R|}$ refers to the critical graph $K(A) = \frac{1}{I(A)}$ [1, 4, 5, 7, 9]

- In a more detailed analysis of the process of stabilising output signal y, it is necessary to consider the obvious fact that the simple and complex operations taking place in the arrangement require a certain amount of time to be completed. Hence, the need to date the signals. When signal x_t passes through object S, signal y_{t-1} is output. By the action of this output signal, signal x_t changes to signal $x_t + Ry_{t-1}$ (Figure 1.20) (whereby signal y_{t-1}, to be considered with signal x_t, must be a signal from an earlier instant of the arrangement's operation) [3].

Knowing that $y = S_x$ always applies, the following is obtained:

$$y_t = S(x_t + Ry_{t-1})$$
$$y_t = SRy_{t-1} + Sx_t \tag{1.168}$$

and for any $x_t = x$:

$$y_t = SRy_{t-1} + Sx \tag{1.169}$$

Formula 1.169 shows that the output signal of the arrangement at a given instant t depends on the signal at the previous instant, $t - 1$, for each x. Previous instants can reach the initial state, y_0, for each x.
Hence:

$$y_0 = SRy_0 + Sx$$
$$y_0 = \frac{S}{1 - SR} x \tag{1.170}$$

The further behaviour of the arrangement can be analysed from the difference $\hat{y}_t$ of signals $y_t - y_0$ at any instant t relative to the initial state t_0:

$$\hat{y}_t = y_t - y_0 = y_t - \frac{S}{1 - SR} x \tag{1.171}$$
$$\hat{y}_t = SRy_{t-1} + Sx - \frac{S}{1 - SR} x \tag{1.172}$$
$$\hat{y}_t = SRy_{t-1} + Sx(1 - \frac{1}{1 - SR}) \tag{1.173}$$

$$\hat{y}_t = SRy_{t-1} - \frac{S^2 R}{1 - SR} x = SR(y_{t-1} - \frac{S}{1 - SR} x) \qquad (1.174)$$

If it was previously like so:

$$\hat{y}_t = y_t - \frac{S}{1 - SR} x \text{ (Formula 1.171)}$$

whereas Formula 1.174 holds this:

$$y_{t-1} - \frac{S}{1 - SR} x = \hat{y}_{t-1} \qquad (1.175)$$

the ultimate result is:

$$\hat{y}_t = SR\hat{y}_{t-1} \text{ — for positive feedback} \qquad (1.176)$$

$$\hat{y}_t = -SR\hat{y}_{t-1} \text{ — for negative feedback} \qquad (1.177)$$

It follows from these formulas that the deviation in the next instant $\hat{y}_t$ depends on the deviation in the previous instant, and on the product of SR.

A graphical interpretation of Formulas 1.176 and 1.177 is shown in Figures 1.21–1.25:

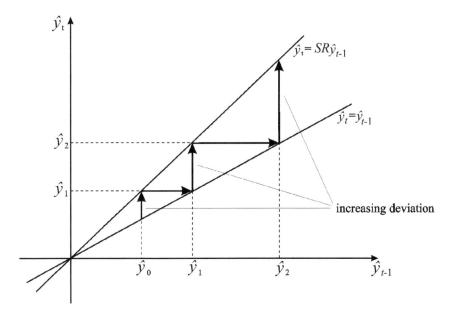

FIGURE 1.21 Graphical interpretation of Formula $\hat{y}_t = SR\hat{y}_{t-1}$ with $SR > 1$.

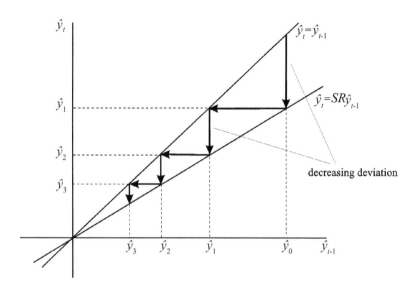

FIGURE 1.22 Graphical interpretation of Formula $\hat{y}_t = SR\hat{y}_{t-1}$ with $SR < 1$.

It is known that SR can be negative (this is the case when there is negative feedback). This is the result:

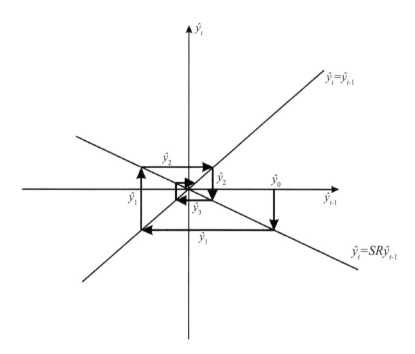

FIGURE 1.23 Damped oscillations for arrangement $SR < 1$.

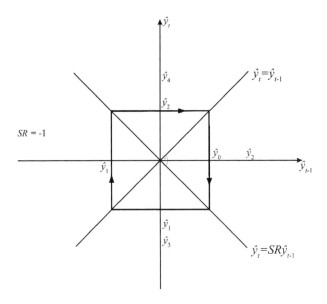

FIGURE 1.24 Periodic oscillations for arrangement $SR = 1$.

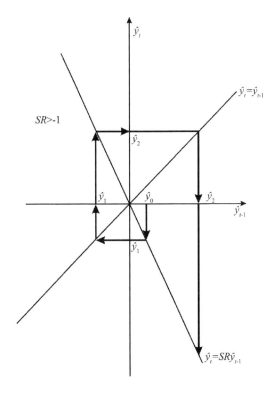

FIGURE 1.25 Oscillations rising—explosive oscillations—arrangement unstable.

Finally, it can be stated that the function (relation)

$$\hat{y}_t = SR\hat{y}_{t-1} \tag{1.178}$$

allows the study of arrangements at time t on the basis of their behaviour at time $t - 1$, where the arrangements whose (and especially these arrangements) R and S are proportional members.

- Additional information about the arrangement (system) can be obtained from the analysis of its proprietary component and feed component. Based on the equation of deviation from equilibrium, this can be expressed:

$$\hat{y}_t = (SR)\hat{y}_{t-1} \tag{1.179}$$

and further:

$$\hat{y}_t = (SR)\hat{y}_{t-1} = (SR)^2\,\hat{y}_{t-2} = (SR)^3\,\hat{y}_{t-3} = \ldots = (SR)^n\,\hat{y}_{t-n} \tag{1.180}$$

If it is assumed that there is time Δt between deviations of, for example, 2 and 3, then: $n\Delta t = t$ and $t - n\Delta t = 0$, the result is:

$$\hat{y}_t = (SR)^t\,\hat{y}_0 \tag{1.181}$$

Thus, the deviation at any time t depends on time t and the product of the power of the object and of the regulator, and the initial deviation $\hat{y}_0$ at time $t = 0$.

Knowing that the definition provides this:

$$\hat{y}_t = y_t - y_0 \text{ (Formula 1.170)}$$

it is possible to determine the following:

$$y_t = \hat{y}_t + y_0 \tag{1.182}$$

After substitutions (Formulas 1.181 and 1.170), the result is:

$$y_t = (SR)^t\,\hat{y}_0 + \frac{S}{1 - SR}\,x \tag{1.183}$$

Formula 1.183 shows that the initial state y_t depends on two components: (1) the proprietary component (which does not depend on input signal x), and (2) the feed component (which depends on x). Only the feed component is examined in the regulation process. If $SR<1$, then the proprietary component has no meaning (for $t\rightarrow\infty$).

1.2.8 A CYBERNETIC APPROACH TO ECONOMIC SYSTEMS: KEYNES MULTIPLIER AND ITS IMPORTANCE IN SYSTEM ANALYSIS

In economic systems the relationships between domestic product, Y, investment expenditures, a, and consumption, C, are studied. An expression can be formulated as follows:

$$Y = A + C \tag{1.184}$$

It can further be assumed that consumption is a linear function of domestic product:

$$C = cY \tag{1.185}$$

Formula 1.184 provides the following:

$$Y = A + cY \tag{1.186}$$

$$Y = \frac{1}{1-c}A \tag{1.187}$$

Thus, the system can be represented as a block diagram (Figure 1.26).

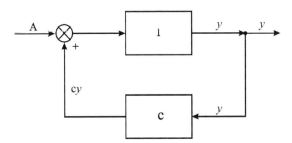

FIGURE 1.26 Block diagram of an economic system built on the Keynesian multiplier.

Figure 1.26 shows there is a basic regulating system (Figure 1.19) where $S = 1$ and $R = c$. Hence, all the conclusions of the previous considerations in Section 1.1.7 can be used to study the operation of this system.

With Formula 1.142 and assuming $S = 1$ and $R = c$, this follows:

$$Y_n = \frac{1-(RS)^n}{1-RS}SX_1 = \frac{1-c^n}{1-c}A \tag{1.188}$$

So the system will be stable (in equilibrium) if:

$$0 < c < 1 \tag{1.189}$$

because for $n \to \infty$ a constant value is obtained

$$Y_n = \frac{1}{1-c}A \tag{1.190}$$

This only applies to positive feedback (because negative consumption c does not exist).

Formula 1.179, considering the dating of signals, provides the relations between deviations $\hat{y}$ at time t and $t - 1$:

$$\hat{y}_t = SR\hat{y}_{t-1} = c\hat{y}_{t-1} \tag{1.191}$$

The analysis of deviations from equilibrium should be carried out according to Figures 1.21 to 1.25. It is possible to observe fluctuations of $\hat{y}_t$, their amplitude and frequency over time.

From Formula 1.183 describing the relations between the proprietary component and the feed component of the system, the following is provided:

$$y_t = (SR)^t \hat{y}_0 + \frac{S}{1-SR}x = c^t \hat{y}_0 + \frac{1}{1-c}A \tag{1.192}$$

Formula 1.192 shows that for any $c < 1$ and $t = 0$, the proprietary component of the system is $\hat{y}_0$ and with $t = \infty$, the proprietary component is 0. Between these points, the trend of y_t strongly depends on c. Based on Formula 1.192, the dependence of the domestic product on the value of the consumption coefficient c can be studied. If $c > 1$, the entire economic system becomes deregulated and goes into self-destruction.

1.2.9 OPERATION OF SYSTEMS UNDER MUTUAL CONFLICT CONDITIONS: GAME WITH NATURE—THE MINIMAX AND MAXMINI STRATEGIES

Conflict situations between systems are the focus of a branch of mathematics called the "game theory" [9, 37].

Models of conflict situations occur in the decision-making processes of various fields of human activity (and in this section, humans are construed to be "players" of games). The object of focus in game theory is to find the optimal strategy for a given player in the set of all possible strategies for a given game. A player's strategy is an instruction that unambiguously defines each of the player's moves in any situation, if the move is possible within the framework of the accepted rules of the game. In games (like chess), the number of possible moves is very large, so it is very difficult or outright impossible to determine the strategy of players.

If the number of possible moves is finite (although it can be very large and the number of players is also finite), then the game is called a finite game. This type of game is encountered in the theory of economic planning, the theory of tactical operations, and the theory of competitive activities. The operation of systems under conditions of mutual conflict is shown in Figure 1.27.

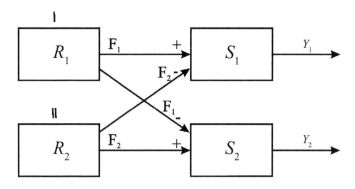

FIGURE 1.27 The oblique effect of two control systems, R_1 and R_2 on control objects S_1 and S_2: "+" is a positive impact and "–" is a negative impact.

It can be seen in the figure above that the control unit, R_1 (player I), generates a positive signal, F_1, for the "improvement" of its object S_1, which is at the same time a signal harmful for the foreign object, S_2, resulting in the deterioration of the latter object's functioning. Control unit R_2 (player II) works in a similar way.

A two-player game involves the development of a set of action strategies F_1 by player I and F_2 by player II. For finite games, any set of strategies F_1 or F_2 is finite. Each element from these sets can be numbered and represented as a game matrix; see Table 1.8:

TABLE 1.8
Two-Player Game Matrix

F_2 \ F_1	f_{11}	f_{21}	$\ldots$	f_{n1}
f_{1II}	a_{11}	a_{12}	$\ldots$	a_{1n}
f_{2II}	a_{21}	a_{22}	$\ldots$	a_{2n}
$\ldots$	$\ldots$	$\ldots$	$\ldots$	$\ldots$
f_{nII}	a_{n1}	a_{n2}	$\ldots$	a_{nn}

To solve a given game described by an $n \times m$ matrix means to find for each player such a strategy of moves that the average gain in a large number of games is maximum. Game theory allows each player F_1 to choose the move that will give him the maximum possible gain, designated "Z", in the case of the worst-case move of his opponent, F_2, who has to suffer a loss, designated "S". For a game with two players:

$$Z(f_1, f_2) + S(f_1, f_2) = 0 \tag{1.193}$$

and that the function of convenience (goodness) is like so:

$$M(f_1, f_2) = Z(f_1, f_2) = -S(f_1, f_2) \tag{1.194}$$

The matrix elements:

$$a_{mn} = M(f_1, f_2)$$ (1.195)

They are equal to the values of the gain function $Z(f_1, f_2)$.

The strategies of player F_1 and player F_2 consist in choosing the appropriate element of the game matrix.

For player F_1, the best-case strategy will be to choose the largest element of the smallest ones in each row. This strategy is called the "maxmini" strategy. For player F_2, the best-case strategy will be to choose the smallest element of the largest ones in each row. This strategy is called the "minimax" strategy. These strategies are expressed as follows:

$$
\begin{aligned}
a_{kp} &= \underset{i}{maks} \ \underset{j}{min} \ aij \\
a_{ql} &= \underset{j}{min} \ \underset{i}{maks} \ aij
\end{aligned}
$$ (1.196)

The following conflict situations are encountered:

- in nature, during the struggle for existence (a field of wheat verus a meadow);
- in economic systems (employer versus employee);
- in management systems (competition between businesses);
- in political systems (capitalism versus socialism).

The examples of conflict situations presented here can be reduced to the following games:

- game against nature;
- game against a rational opponent;
- game of complete contradiction of interests.

In a game against nature, the rule is that gain and loss shall be equal. Hence:

$$Z + S \neq 0$$ (1.197)

The farmer mows the meadow and harvests hay (Z), whereas the nature, meaning the meadow in this instance, does not lose the grass (S) forever, as the grass quickly grows back stronger. On the other hand, there is the example of a forester who cuts forest trees to source timber (Z), whereas the nature loses trees which do not grow back quickly (S).

In a game against a rational opponent, the rule by which gain plus loss equals zero does not apply either. In this case the following applies, too:

$$Z + S \neq 0$$ (1.198)

Opponents (competitors) want to act rationally. It is not about ruthless destruction of the competition. Military conflicts (e.g. Japan versus USA) are an example of this game. This game guarantees moderate gain which the "good loser" can receive from the "good winner".

In a game of complete contradiction of interests, the absolute rule is that what one player loses another player gains. Hence:

$$Z + S = 0 \qquad (1.199)$$

The interests of the players in the game are opposed.

- Decision-making in conflict situations requires a large number of logical and arithmetic operations. These operations consist in calculating the elements of the game matrix and calculating the probabilities of the game strategy [9, 37, 38].

1.2.10 RISKS IN DECISION-MAKING PROCESSES

Risk refers to decision-making processes in management, games, and other areas. Risk is not an inevitable destiny; it can be high or low, depending on the probability of adverse events caused by one's decision and on the potential consequences (meaning the price) of the occurrence of adverse events.

The following definition of risk is adopted:

"Risk is the product of the value (price) of the consequence of a hazard and the probability of occurrence of the hazard".

$$R = P \cdot S \qquad (1.200)$$

with:

R— risk;
P— probability of hazards;
S— relative value of the consequence of the hazard

Risks are determined in the following areas of human activity:

- design— R_p
- production (manufacturing)— R_w
- purchase— R_z

The risk value for an entire execution process is a set of risks.

$$R = \{R_p, R_w, R_z\} \qquad (1.201)$$

The requirement follows:

$$R = \leq R(a) \qquad (1.202)$$

where $R(a)$ is the acceptable risk.

TABLE 1.9

Risk Assessment Criterion Matrix

P.S. S.Z.	0	0.25	0.5	0.75	1
1	0	0.25	0.5	0.75	1
0.75	0	0.187	0.375	0.562	0.75
0.5	0	0.125	0.25	0.375	0.5
0.25	0	0.062	0.125	0.187	0.25
0	0	0	0	0	0

There are opportunities to reduce the assessed unacceptable risk value $R(n)$ to the acceptable risk value $R(a)$ by performing appropriate corrective and preventive measures (O).

$$R(n) \xrightarrow{(O)} R(a) \qquad (1.203)$$

If $R(n)$ cannot be reduced to $R(a)$, then the execution of the decision process in question is unreasonable.

Determining the value of risk requires estimation of the following:

- the value of the hazard consequence (e.g. % of the product price)
- the likelihood of the hazard

It is therefore possible to determine a risk assessment criterion matrix (Table 1.9).

with:

P.S.— likelihood (probability) of loss
S.Z.— consequence (price) of hazards:

It is assumed that low risk is between 0 and 0.25, medium risk is between 0.25 and 0.75, and high risk is between 0.75 and 1.

The selection of a team of experts is of great importance in the risk assessment. The experts the price of actual hazard, $S.Z.$, and the likelihood of the hazard, $P.S.$

Risk of road traffic collisions (Great Britain)
Risk D— number of casualties

$$D = AN^\alpha P^\beta \qquad (1.204)$$

with:

N— number of vehicles;
P— population;
A, α, β— experimental output data

Ultimately:

Risk D as the number of casualties (hazards to life):

$$D = 0.0003(NP^2)^{1/3} \qquad (1.205)$$

Risk of loss (USA)

$$r(R) = S \cdot E \cdot P \tag{1.206}$$

where:

$r(R)$— risk
S— possible consequences of the event (losses)
E— frequency of hazard
P— probability of the event

with

$r < 20$— negligible
$1.5 < r < 48$— acceptable
$48 < r < 270$— medium
$270 < r < 1440$— high
$r > 1440$— unacceptable

1.2.11 LARGE SYSTEMS: CONTROL TASKS IN A LARGE SYSTEM—MONTE CARLO METHOD

- A large system is a collection of subsystems linked by a common objective (goal) or action. It is characterised by its high complexity and the fact that the actions of the system and its elements are highly indeterminate. The characteristic properties of a large system are the presence of various complex parts in it, varying in physical nature, like people, machines, natural environment, material and energy resources, as well as various information channels between these parts and between other large systems (voice, telephone, or mobile network). Such systems exist in technology, biology, economics, and nature [16, 37, 38].
- The control tasks carried out in a large system are conventionally divided into the following:
  - operational tasks—related to the choice of structure and interaction of system components and to the analysis of system behaviour and assessment of its performance.
  - functional tasks—related to the performance of tasks.

For example, the following operational tasks occur in a business management system:

- stock control—accumulation and maintenance of reserves (which can be human, material, or financial)
- execution of complicated complex facilities—construction or recon-struction of enterprises; launching and mastering production of new products

- maintaining the system in working order (in a state of fitness) for equipment and people. Repairs to machinery; provision of rest and health care for the staff.
- use of resources—controlling the disposal of human, material and financial resources necessary for the functioning of the system
- selection of energy (material) and information paths—control of material stream movement, distribution of energy streams, control of flow (circulation of information)
- maintaining a sufficiently high level of business—approaching increasingly effective methods, broader scope and higher efficiency of operation; upgrading and improving manufacturing methods
- choice of undertakings under conditions of competitive struggle (contradiction of interests); game against nature; game against a rational opponent; game of complete contradiction of interests. Protection of own interests against those of competitors
- control of the sale of production—investigating demand, choosing the production portfolio, organisation of advertising, pricing
- organisation of work—training of personnel, system improvement, work pay, improvement of working conditions and safety

The following functional tasks occur in a business management system:

- ensuring the required manufacturing process
- performing manufacturing operations in the correct order
- coordination of activities of different elements at the same time.

The functional tasks of control in large systems are solved with a whole host of means and methods of operation, namely:

- regulation
- adaptation
- development and execution of action plans
- learning
- games

Thus, in conclusion, it can be said that an example of a large system is a multidimensional dynamic arrangement whose structure and parameters change in a random (chance) manner.

- Control quality indicators of large systems are used to assess the control quality of any system (including large systems). Control quality indicators determine the compliance of the system's operation with the control tasks. In automatic control systems, these indicators are preset. It is required that the static error e_{st}, the overshoot χ, the regulation time $_{tr}$, the modulus reserve ΔL and the phase reserve $\Delta\phi$ are appropriate and set in advance (preset) for all *UARs* [1, 4, 5].

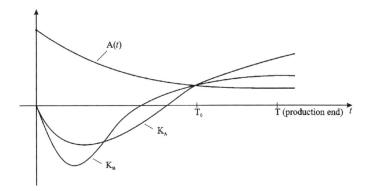

FIGURE 1.28 Basic characteristics for system quality assessment. $A(t)$—attractiveness characteristics of the product; K_A, K_B—gain from production for process A and process B; T_0—time constant of product ageing; Θ—production time.

In the case of large systems, the quality indicators, "J", the numerical value of which will characterises the performance of a given control [38], must be individually determined for each specific system.

The indicator J can be determined from the expected values of gains Z and losses S and their weight $A(t)$ at the time of production (Figure 1.28).

The system quality indicators are calculated from this formula:

$$J = \int_0^T (Z-S)A(t)\,dt \qquad (1.207)$$

whereby:

$$Z - S = K \qquad (1.208)$$

- One of the important and difficult tasks in developing a large system is to establish its structure. The following systems exist:
  - centralised
  - hierarchical

1.2.11.1 Centralised systems

All information about the state of each control system component and about the external effects on the system is fed to a centralised control centre. Hence, the centralised control centre accumulates a great number of diverse pieces of information. Their processing often becomes impossible. The disadvantages of a centralised system are particularly evident when people are its elements. A human being, like any cybernetic system, can only efficiently process a finite and relatively small quantity of information. Decisions properly developed by humans in the ordinary practice of life can lead to adverse consequences if the decisions apply to a large number of elements. A human being can effectively direct a few elements (e.g. soldiers) and fails when the number of elements is 200 000 for example. An example of such a system was an Inca army of 200 000 each warrior of which was directed by the chieftain; the army was defeated (and dispersed) by 168 men of Pizarro the conquistador [38].

The high unreliability of this system and its low efficiency are obvious.

1.2.11.2   Hierarchical systems

A characteristic feature of a hierarchical system is its subdivision into subsystems between which there are relations of subordination, see Figure 1.29.

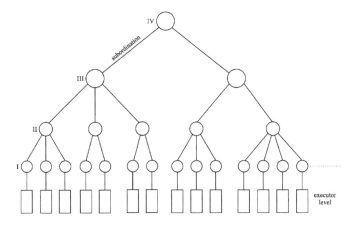

FIGURE 1.29 Hierarchical structure of a system.

Level I—solves basic control tasks (detailed information)
Level II—coordinates the actions of Level I elements (less detailed information)
Level III—coordinates the actions of Level II elements (general information)
Level IV—guidelines for the actions of Level III elements (general guidelines, assumptions, and quality indicators).

The quantity of information on each level is reduced accordingly and thus adapted to the information throughput of the decision-makers on these levels.

- A large system such as a factory, a company, a university, for example, is difficult to describe mathematically. However, there are specific requirements to ensure optimal control of this type of system (which is difficult to achieve without a model). Hence the idea to build a "machine simulating" the action of a human being (an analogue of humans), a manager (being a decision-maker) in the process of system optimisation, considering that a human manager often makes decisions based on intuitive premises. Action methods based on intuitive premises are called heuristic. An example of a heuristic method for system performance optimisation is shown in Figure 1.30 [38].

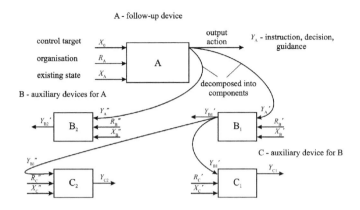

FIGURE 1.30 Hierarchical control diagram of a large system.

As shown in Figure 1.30, the result of the action of element A is an output Y_A, which can be an instruction, guidance, decision, etc. If signal Y_A does not provide optimal control of the system, then the control element can decompose the signal into signals $Y_{A'}$ and $Y_{A''}$ and relay them it to auxiliary devices, B_1 and B_2, respectively, which will generate refining signals Y_{B1} and Y_{B2}. Further on, assume that signal Y_{B1} can be decomposed by B_1 into signals $Y_{B1'}$ and $Y_{B1''}$ and passed to lower-level auxiliaries C_1 and C_2 which will generate further refining signals Y_{C1} and Y_{C2}. This way of building a hierarchical system is continued until the approximation of actual state X_A to control objective X_0 (Figure 1.30) is optimal. It is also clear from Figure 1.30 that the final control system Y consists of the "coarse" signal Y_A and the corrections from iterative approximations, Y_{B1} and Y_{C1}. The result is:

$$Y = Y_A + Y_{B1} + Y_{C1} \qquad (1.209)$$

To analyse the performance of a specific system, in addition to theoretical studies (based on mathematical models), heuristic studies (based on beliefs, intuition), and a manager (expert), experimental methods are applied and based on:

- a passive experiment (observation of the behaviour of the system during normal operation (observation of an engine in operation));
- an active experiment (observation of the behaviour of the system when actuated by specifically selected input function signals (observation of an engine during ground tests)).

Active and passive experimental research is very expensive. It is generally limited to normal working conditions. These methods cannot be used to assess the behaviour of a system under emergency conditions. The most important disadvantage of these methods is that they cannot be applied to systems in their design stage, meaning: before systems are executed and implemented for use.

Their mathematical, heuristic, and experimental studies are further complicated when they are used for probabilistic phenomena. Hence, a dedicated method based on a special substitute experiment has been developed to solve this type of phenomenon. It is called the Monte Carlo method [13, 38, 39].

Example (Figure 1.31): The system under test consists of elements A, B, and C.

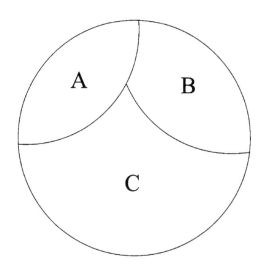

FIGURE 1.31 New system composed of three known systems.

These elements are known. From these elements, new complex systems need to be built: ABC, AB, AC, and BC (Figure 1.31). These systems have a property that when one of the components of the unit (A or B or C) stops operating properly, then the whole system is unfit. The question arises: what will be the correct operation of the new units ABC, AB, AC, and BC when the data on the probability of failure of each part A, B, and C after $X(t)$ weeks of operation are known? (Table 1.10).

The average operating time of elements A, B, and C is:

$$\bar{X}_A = \sum p_i x_i = 0.05 \cdot 5 + 0.10 \cdot 10 + 0.15 \cdot 15 + 0.20 \cdot 20 + 0.20 \cdot 25 +$$
$$+ 0.15 \cdot 30 \cdot 0.10 \cdot 35 + 0.05 \cdot 40 = 22.5 \, week$$
$$\bar{X}_B = \sum p_i x_i = 13.6 \, week$$
$$\bar{X}_C = \sum p_i x_i = 21.8 \, week$$

TABLE 1.10
Data on the Probability of Correct Operation of System Components

Part A $X_A(t)$	Failure probability P	Part B $X_B(t)$	Failure probability P	Part C $X_C(t)$	Failure probability P
0	00	00	00	00	00
5	0.05	5	15	5	30
10	0.10	10	35	10	10
15	0.15	15	30	15	10
20	20	20	10	20	05
25	20	25	05	25	04
30	15	30	03	30	06
35	10	35	02	35	15
40	05	40	00	40	10
45	00	45	00	45	05
50	00	50	00	50	05
55	00	55	00	55	00

TABLE 1.11
Characteristics of the Component A Model

Weeks, X_A	Number of balls, $P_A(x)$	Colour
5	5	Red
10	10	Blue
15	15	Yellow
20	20	White
25	20	Black
30	15	Green
35	10	Orange
40	5	Violet
	100 balls	

The probability of failure of systems ABC, AB, AC, and BC can be determined using the Monte Carlo method, which consists in performing a substitute experiment. The substitute experiment is as follows:

100 coloured balls are placed in a jar, according to the probability of failure (unfitness) of component A (Table 1.11).

Derived from Table 1.11 are:

$$P_A = 0.05$$
$$P_A' = 0.10 \text{ etc.}$$

In this way, a surrogate model of the failure characteristics of component A is obtained.

The colours can be converted into Monte Carlo numbers for component A (Table 1.12).

TABLE 1.12
Characteristic Data of Component A with a Monte Carlo Number Description

X_A	$P_A(x)$	Colour	Monte Carlo number
5	5	Red	00 to 04
10	10	Blue	05 to 14
15	15	Yellow	05 to 29
20	20	White	30 to 49
25	20	Black	50 to 69
30	15	Green	70 to 84
35	10	Orange	85 to 94
40	5	Violet	95 to 99

TABLE 1.13
Characteristic Data of Components B and C with a Monte Carlo Number Description

Part B (jar no. 2)			Part C (jar no. 3)		
Operating weeks, X_B	Failure probability $P_B(x)$	Monte Carlo number	Operating weeks, X_C	Failure probability $P_C(x)$	Monte Carlo number
5	0.15	00 to 14	5	0.30	00 to 29
10	0.35	15 to 49	10	0.10	30 to 39
15	0.30	50 to 79	15	0.10	40 to 49
20	0.10	80 to 89	20	0.05	50 to 54
25	0.05	90 to 94	25	0.04	55 to 58
30	0.03	95 to 97	30	0.06	59 to 64
35	0.02	98 to 99	35	0.15	65 to 79
40	–	–	40	0.10	80 to 89
45	–	–	45	0.05	90 to 94
50	–	–	50	0.05	95 to 99

The same procedure is done for components B and C. Thus jars B and C are each filled with 100 balls, marked with Monte Carlo numbers (Table 1.13).

Having the probability models of the correct operation time for components A, B, and C, the correct operation time can be determined for ABC, for example. The balls are drawn from jar A, B, and C in turn. For each ball drawn, the number MC is read, followed by X_A, X_B, and X_C (the number of correct operation weeks) (Table 1.14).

$$X_{\min ABC} = 5,10,5,15,5,10,5,10,10,5$$
$$X_{\min AB} = 15,10,5,15,5,10,15,10,20,20$$
$$X_{\min AC} = 5,15,5,15,5,20,5,10,10,5$$
$$X_{\min CB} = 5,10,15,20,5,10,5,25,10,5$$

TABLE 1.14

Example of Drawing the Correct Operation Times from Jars A, B, and C

Sequential drawing no.	Part A Number MC	X_A	Part B Number MC	X_B	Part C Number MC	X_C	Unit ABC $X_{min\,ABC}$
1	87	35	50	15	10	5	5
2	98	40	42	10	44	15	10
3	03	5	60	15	65	35	5
4	27	15	88	20	83	40	15
5	84	30	10	5	12	5	5
6	44	20	41	10	51	20	10
7	55	25	62	15	29	5	5
8	10	10	92	25	74	35	10
9	68	25	81	20	34	10	10
10	70	30	86	20	18	5	5

TABLE 1.15

Probability of the System ABC Operation

X_{min}	Times of X_{min}	$P(X_{min\,ABC})$
5	5	0.50
10	4	0.40
15	1	0.10

X_{min}— number of weeks after which failure of system ABC, AB, AC, or CB occurs, respectively

The result X_{minABC} is converted into probabilities $P(X_{minABC})$, $P(X_{minAB})$, etc. Table 1.15 shows that after only 5 weeks, only 50% of system ABC will be operating correctly.

The Monte Carlo method can be used to solve a variety of problems. Example: Three parts are needed to assemble a device. Half of the parts are larger than the nominal size, and the other half are smaller than the nominal size. The device will not work if all three parts are larger than nominal. Find the probability that the device will not work. This problem can be solved using:

- the 3 coin toss (with 100 or more tosses)
- draw lots per the Monte Carlo algorithm (3 jars, in each there is 50% (no. 1 to 49) and 50% (no. 50 to 99)).

1.2.12 LARGE SYSTEMS: OPERATIONAL RESEARCH

Effective management of operations always requires solving the following problems:

1. Develop an optimal plan for the execution of operations, including a break-down of activities and the execution of individual activities.
2. Ensure that operations are carried out in sufficient compliance with the optimum plan under conditions of inevitable disturbances.

Solution to these problems is possible when a mathematical model exists that sufficiently faithfully reflects the relationships between the elements of the system (people or machines) and its environment (material, human, and financial resources) with methods of the system's solution, verification, and inspection of performance.

The whole activity concerning the description of the assessment of the quality of performance, verification, and inspection of a large system, which can be an enterprise, a construction office, or a sales network, is called operational research [37, 38, 40].

- In large system operational research, the network model is commonly used [38]. The network model—or simply, a "network"—is a particular form of graph without a feedback loop (Figure 1.33), as a substitute for system graph with loop (Figure 1.32).

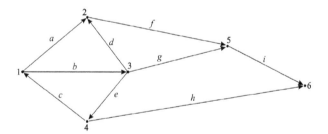

FIGURE 1.32 System graph (includes loop 1-3-4-1).

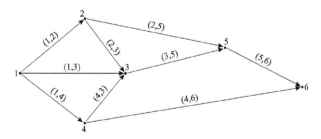

FIGURE 1.33 System network (does not include loops).

In network models:

- the nodes •1, •2, etc. indicate the start and end events of activities (1,2) and of the whole operation (1,6)
- edges 1• → •2, indicate the individual operation activities (1,2), (2,5) Activities in network models should be understood as follows:
- the work requiring a certain amount of material resources and time
- an expectation that does not require material resources but adequate time only, for example, curing of concrete
- an abstract activity requiring neither material resources nor time, but requiring the occurrence of a specific expected event, which is making a decision.

An example of a network model of an operation involving the positioning of a motor on a specially made baseplate: this operation includes the following activities [38]:

1. Sending an order for a baseplate
2. Production of the baseplate
3. Transporting the baseplate to the motor installation site
4. Preparing the substrate for the foundation structure
5. Form placement
6. Casting the foundation structure concrete
7. Concrete curing
8. Installation of the baseplate
9. Ordering and picking the motor from the warehouse
10. Transporting the motor to is installation site
11. Installing the motor

The following network (Figure 1.34), which is the network model, can be developed from the sequence of activities resulting from the performance method of the given operation.

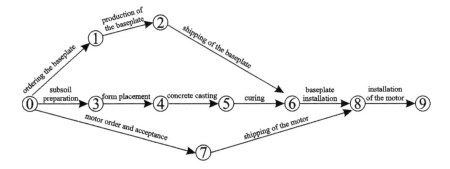

FIGURE 1.34 Network model for installation of a motor on a baseplate.

The network shown illustrates the conditions under which it is acceptable to start each next activity when all activities ending at the node under consideration have been completed.

For example, there are the following events at specific nodes:

0— make a decision
1— the baseplate was ordered (sending the order was completed)
6— the baseplate was delivered and concrete curing was completed
8— installation of the baseplate was completed and the motor was delivered.

Naturally, the activities included in the operation require a certain amount of time and resources. Resources are mostly unlimited in engineering and human terms (within common sense, of course).

It is assumed that to solve the problem presented here, one should limit oneself only to temporal characteristics which include the durations, for example, $t(i,j)$ of the individual work activities (ij) between events i and j.

Activity durations can be assessed (predicted), estimated, or adopted from reference standards (Figure 1.35).

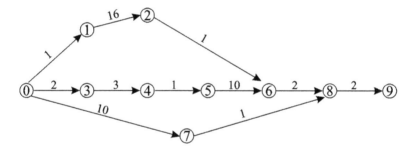

FIGURE 1.35 Network model of an operation with estimated durations of activities.

Transition times between characteristic events can be used to assess the quality of network performance. These events are 6, 8, 9. These times are:

$T(0, 1, 2, 6) = 1 + 16 + 1 = 18$ days
$T(0, 3, 4, 5, 6) = 2 + 3 + 1 + 10 = 16$ days
$T(0, 1, 2, 6, 8) = 20$ days
$T(0, 3, 4, 5, 6, 8) = 18$ days
$T(0, 7, 8) = 11$ days
$T(0, 1, 2, 6, 8, 9) = 22$ days
$T(0, 3, 4, 5, 6, 8, 9) = 20$ days
$T(0, 7, 8, 9) = 13$ days

The longest transition time from event 0 to event 9 is called the critical path, T_K. In this case, $T_K = 22$ days. The critical path includes only the longest path of events

and activities of the process. Therefore, other activities may take place with some delay. It means there is a time reserve when performing some activities, T_{Sj}.
For event 7, the following latest event time T_{S7}:

$$T_{S7} = T_k - T(7, 8, 9) = 22 - (1+2) = 19 \text{ days}$$

This means that instead of 10 days (Figure 1.35) it could be 19 days without any consequences for the execution of the whole operation.
The time reserve before event 7 occurs is:

$$R_7 = T_{S7} - T(0, 7) = 19 - 10 = 9 \text{ days}$$

Determining the critical path and time reserves before events are among the main tasks of network analysis.
A network with the critical path and the time of the earliest and latest instances of events is shown in Figure 1.36.

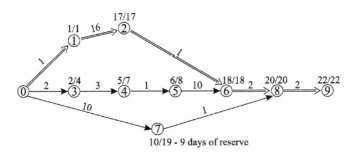

10/19 - 9 days of reserve

FIGURE 1.36 Critical path of the network with earliest and latest acceptable times of events.

The duration of the whole operation, as well as the durations of the individual activities, can be reduced by increasing the number of contractors, the power of the machines, etc. It is therefore possible to arrive at a situation where all paths from the beginning to the end of an operation are critical. A state is sought to ensure that all paths of the network of operations are critical and, in addition, the path is the shortest possible, which requires an appropriate plan of operation.

- The condition of criticality of the working time demand (work intensity) of all paths is a necessary but not sufficient condition in the process of optimising an operation schedule. In addition, the critical path should be the shortest. Example: A network satisfying the criticality conditions is given (Figure 1.37):

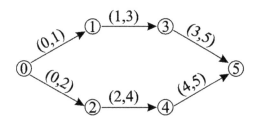

FIGURE 1.37 Network model of an operation with equal critical paths.

TABLE 1.16
Work Intensity and Acceptable Number of Personnel for a Specific Activity

Activity No.	Activity work intensity (man-hours)	Acceptable number of personnel to carry out the activity
0 to 1	12	4
0 to 2	12	4
1 to 3	4	1
2 to 4	4	1
3 to 5	12	4
4 to 5	12	4

The maximum number of contractors and the work intensity of each activity are given in Table 1.16.

It is assumed that 4 workers were employed to execute out the operation. There are many decisions to perform this operation, from which the decision of optimality must be chosen:

Decision option I

1. For work 0–1 and 0–2, 2 workers are assigned; these activities will then be completed after 6 hours.
2. After completing activities 0–1 and 0–2, one worker is assigned to each of activities 1–3 and 2–4, which will be completed after 4 hours (unfortunately 2 workers are idle at the moment).
3. Once activities 1–3 and 2–4 have been completed, two workers each are assigned to activities 3–5 and 4–5. The required activities will then be performed after 6 h. In this case, the operation duration is 16 hours.

$$T(0, 1, 3, 5) = 6+4 + 6 = 16 \text{ hours}$$
$$T(0, 2, 4, 5) = 6+4 + 6 = 16 \text{ hours}$$

The condition of criticality of the duration of all paths of operation was met. 2 employees do not work for 4 hours.

Decision option II

1. For the following work:

   - 0–1, 3 workers are assigned and the work takes 4 hours
   - 0–2, 1 worker is assigned who works 4 hours out of 12 (all employees are under equal workload)

2. 4 workers are appointed to complete work 0–2. This work will take 12–4 = 8:4 = 2 h. Naturally, work 0–1 lasted 4 hours and work 0–2 lasted longer, meaning 6 hours.
3. After completing work 0–1 and 0–2, 1 worker each is assigned to complete work 1–3 and 2–4. Unfortunately, 2 employees are idle at this time. This work takes 4 h.
4. After work 2–4 is completed, 3 workers are assigned to work 4–5 and one worker is assigned to work 3–5. This work will take 4 h and 6 h, respectively.

In this case, the network takes the following form (Figure 1.38):

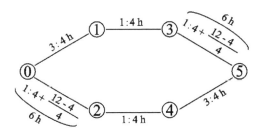

FIGURE 1.38 Illustration for option II of the operation plan.

Eventually it is concluded that the operation duration is:

$$T(0, 1, 3, 5) = 4 + 4 + 6 = 14 \text{ hours}$$
$$T(0, 2, 4, 5) = 6 + 4 + 4 = 14 \text{ hours}$$

Here, too, 2 workers are idle for 4 hours, but work duration on the site is reduced to 14 hours. This is the result of increasing the number of workers from 2 to 3 to do work 0–1.

Decision option III: the optimum

1. 4 employees are assigned to work 0–1. The work takes 3 h.
2. After completing work 0–1, one worker remains to complete work 1–3. This work takes 4 h. The other 3 workers carry out work 0–2, which will take 4 h.
3. After work 1–3 and 0–2 (which are finished equally), one worker is assigned to work 2–4 and completes it after 4 h, while three workers are assigned to work 3–5, which is finished after 4 h.
4. The final step is to assign 4 workers to complete work 4–5 (3 h).

In this case, the network takes the following form (Figure 1.39):

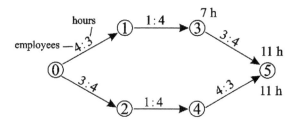

FIGURE 1.39 Illustration for option III of the operation plan.

Eventually it is concluded that the operation duration on site is:

$T(0, 1, 3, 5) = 3 + 4 + 4 = 11$ hours
$T(0, 2, 4, 5) = 4 + 4 + 3 = 11$ hours

From the comparison of the decision options presented here for the organisation of work on the site, option III is the best. All work was completed in 11 h.

However, the duration of an operation is not always a measure of the plan's effectiveness. Other criteria are often adopted when planning, like the cost of operation performance and the maximum number of workers needed to perform the operation.

1.3   SELECTED ELEMENTS OF INFORMATION THEORY

1.3.1   System Interactions

There is interaction between different systems and between different elements of a system. The interaction is:

- exchange of energy and/or matter according to the law of conservation of energy and mass;
- exchange of information on energy conservation in accordance with the principles of information theory.

Energy and matter are fundamental concepts and therefore do not need to be redefined. There are many definitions of the term "information". One of them states that "information is any message about processes and states of any matter that can be perceived by systems (humans, nature, economy)". To rephrase it in brief, "information is everything which exists and is neither mass or energy".

It was recognised that there is an relationship between energy and information [3, 38, 40, 41]:

- in the absence of information, energy consumption is higher;
- energy can be replaced by information up to certain limits;
- information helps to conserve energy.

The sources of information include:

- own experience;
- examples of the experience of other researchers.

The price of information should be less than the price of the energy conserved:

- price of information ≤ price of conserved energy;

Optimal systems are fed by energy and information. It is possible to distinguish their energy and information parts

1.3.2   TYPES OF INFORMATION

Different types of information exist. The information can be [3, 42]:

- optical
- acoustic
- sensual
- abstract
- cybernetic

1.3.2.1   Optical Information

It is the richest in terms of its content. It expresses itself in a large scale of colours, shapes, and sizes of images. Related to this information is visual memory, which is a memory type with the most capacity.

1.3.2.2   Acoustic Information

The content of acoustic information is sound. The sound parameters are:

- pitch (vibration frequency of 20 to 20000 Hz);
- volume (wave frequency N/m^2, or sound frequency);
- timbre or tone quality (defined by "tones": fundamental tone f, and the tones called harmonics, $2f$, $3f$, $4f$).

1.3.2.3   Sensory Information
- Vision (optical information)
- Hearing (acoustic information)
- Touch
- Taste
- Smell
- Balance
- Extra-sensory (prediction of future states "by intuition" or "by feeling")

This type of information is primarily associated with humans and other living organisms.

1.3.2.4   Abstract Information

The following typical forms of abstract information can be distinguished:

- print or writing
- drawings, photographs, sketches
- sound recordings
- musical notes
- formulas and scientific symbols
- diplomatic and military ciphers
- road signs
- algorithms and programs

1.3.2.5   Cybernetic Information

This is information related to the control processes of systems (arrangements). The control actuators are the receptor and the effector, which are interconnected by an information channel (path). The receptor detects stimuli. The effector is used to produce a reaction, that is, to perform work. The effector therefore requires "information" and "energy". The disposer of "information" and "energy" is called an "organiser".

1.3.3   Information/Energy Relations in Systems

An organised arrangement is the simplest system that uses information, I, and energy, E, taken from the surroundings, and then processes both for a specific purpose, see Figure 1.40 [3].

An example is the "hammer, a knife, or a scythe in the hands of the user" who is the "organiser" of the performance of a certain activity.

A controlled system additionally features an energy reservoir (a battery). Such systems implement the mechanisation of processes, see Figure 1.41.

$E = E_0 + E_d$;

E_0—idle energy; E_d—available energy

An example is any appliance fitted with an energy storage, for example, a motor car, a machine tool, and a washing machine.

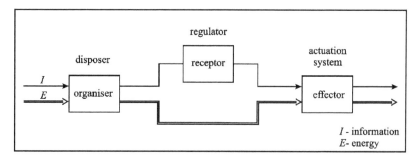

FIGURE 1.40 Organised arrangement.

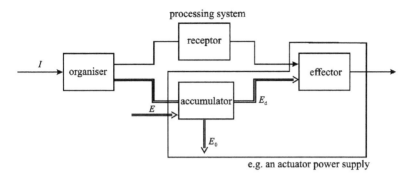

FIGURE 1.41 Controlled system.

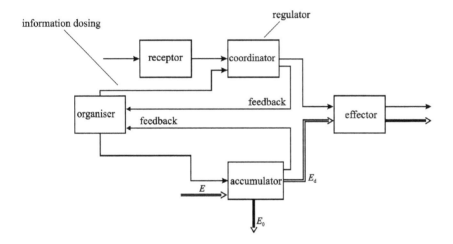

FIGURE 1.42 Self-controlled system.

A self-controlled system features an additional information processing element, which is the "coordinator". Such systems implement the automation of processes, see Figure 1.42.

Automatic control systems for various processes are an example of this system.

A system like this can operate with reduced performance of the "organiser" (e.g. an aircraft pilot), for example, during the flight of an air plane controlled by its autopilot.

Standalone (autonomous) system features an additional element for internal control of a system called the structure change system. Such systems implement adaptation processes, see Figure 1.43.

This is the highest level of organisation in a control system. Examples of standalone systems include all living organisms. They eliminate all interference. They adapt to different conditions.

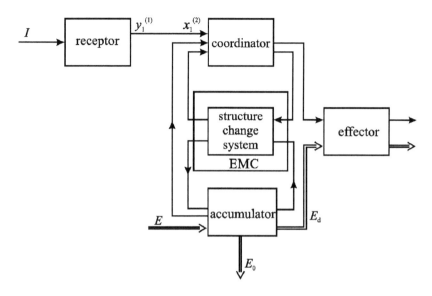

FIGURE 1.43 Autonomous system.

In the systems under consideration, there is feedback occurring through their environment.

1.3.4 TRANSMISSION OF INFORMATION: MAXWELL'S DEMON

The transfer of information between system elements is shown in Figure 1.44 [3, 38, 42, 43]. A signal can carry information about an event or a process.

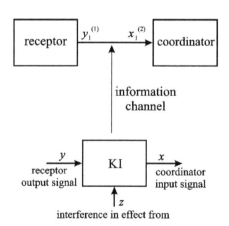

FIGURE 1.44 Information transmissions—information channel *KI*.

The disturbances (interferences) z are random in nature and originate from the variable environment acting on the information channel and from random failures of channel components. There are two problems with the transfer of information:

- evaluation of the quantity of information carried by a signal;
- evaluation of the capacity (throughput) of channels carrying a signal with a given quantity of information.

The quantity of information h_i is a measure of information. Each message contains some data about a specific event S; this data can be, for example, the value of x_i in instance t_i. The quantity of information depends on the probability of occurrence of the message:

$$h_i = \log_2 \frac{1}{P_i} = -\log_2 P_i \qquad (1.210)$$

$$P_i = \frac{n_i}{N} \qquad (1.211)$$

n_i — number of specific events x_i
N — number of all events/experiences

If each of x_i is equally likely, then one information occurs with this probability:

$$P_i = \frac{1}{N} \qquad (1.212)$$

The maximum information quantity is obtained, naturally.

$$h_{i\,max} = -\log_2 \frac{1}{N} = \log_2 N \qquad (1.213)$$

$$h_{i\,max}(N) = \log_2 N \qquad (1.214)$$

Example: Message $a\,(n_i)$ is one of N_1 possible messages and message $b(n_i)$ is one of N_2 possible messages, which are independent of message a. It means that the number of all the different possibilities of these messages is $N_1 \cdot N_2$. The information quantity in this example is:

$$h_{max}(N_1, N_2) = \log_2 N_1 \cdot N_2 = \log_2 N_1 + \log_2 N_2 = h_{max}(N_1) + h_{max}(N_2) \quad (1.215)$$

Thus, the quantity of information contained in two independent messages is equal to the sum of the quantity of information in each message, which is consistent with human intuition.

The average information quantity (information entropy) H is a measure of the indeterminacy of a system.

Thus, similarly for the energy channel, for the information channel this is produced:

$$H = \sum_{i=1}^{k} P_i h_i = \sum P_i \log_2 \frac{1}{P_i} = -\sum_{i=1}^{k} P_i \log_2 P_i \qquad (1.216)$$

where H is the average information quantity (in other words, the information quantity per message); h_i is the information quantity in a message; P_i is the probability of a message.

The unit of information quantity is such a simple message which carries a logically closed, obvious content, for example in the sentence "yes or no", the statement "yes" or "no" is unambiguously understood.

Hence in a sentence, "yes" or "no" $P_{tak} = \frac{1}{2}$ and $P_{nie} = \frac{1}{2}$;

In sentence, "1" or "0" $P_1 = \frac{1}{2}$ and $P_0 = \frac{1}{2}$

therefore, in a "yes" or "no" statement in the sentence "yes, no", this is given:

$$h_i = \log_2 \frac{1}{\dfrac{1}{2}} = \log_2{}^2 = 1 \text{ [bit]} \qquad (1.217)$$

Therefore, this unit content is 1 bit.

It is also possible to determine the average quantity of information per the "yes" or "no" message of the sentence "yes, no":

$$H = \sum_{i=1}^{2} P_i h_i = \sum (\frac{1}{2} \cdot 1 + \frac{1}{2} \cdot 1) = 1 \text{ [bit]} \qquad (1.218)$$

Intuitively, one will also confirm that the average quantity of information in the "yes" or "no" statements of this sentence is 1[bit].

- Information entropy is used to calculate the ordered state of a system [38, 40, 41]. A measure of a system order (ordered state) is accepted to be:

$$R = 1 - \frac{H}{H_m} \qquad (1.219)$$

with:

R— system redundancy (degree of deviation from equilibrium). Redundancy varies from 0 (chaos) to 1 (complete system order).

H— average information quantity (the amount of missing information) or information entropy

H_m— maximum value of information entropy.

If the following is give in time θ_0:

$$R_0 = 1 - \frac{H_0}{H_m}$$

After some time, in θ_1, this exists:

$$R_1 = 1 - \frac{H_1}{H_m}$$

The system order will increase when $R_1 > R_0$, hence:

$$1 - \frac{H_1}{H_m} > 1 - \frac{H_0}{H_m}$$

hence:

$$H_1 < H_0 \quad \Rightarrow \quad -p_1 \log_2 p_1 < -p_0 \log_2 p_0 \Rightarrow p_1 > p_0$$

Thus, for a system order to grow, the system must take negative entropy of information in order to increase the probability of the system working. Increasing the probability of working requires an additional energy feed. This energy feed can be realised with an appropriate information feed.

- The way to increase the system order based on the retrieved information can be illustrated as follows in Figure 1.45 (Maxwell's demon).

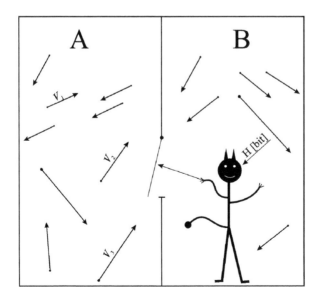

FIGURE 1.45 Maxwell's demon.

At the beginning, there is complete chaos in vessel $A + B$ ($R = 0$), $H = H_m = 1$. A partition with a window is placed in the vessel, which divides the vessel into parts A and B. The "demon" opens the window according to the information it has about the velocity of a given gas molecule, so that it lets high-velocity molecules into part B and low-velocity molecules into part A. In this way, the temperature in B is raised and that in A is lowered without loss of total energy. There is an ordering of molecules into fast and slow molecules in parts A and B thanks to the information $H(bit)$ available to the "demon". The relationship between entropy ΔS and information ΔH given by Maxwell [3, 12, 38, 40] is as follows:

$$\Delta S = -10^{16} \Delta H \; [\text{erg/K}] \tag{1.220}$$

It follows from Formula 1.220 that information has a significant effect on entropy (hence on energy) only when the information quantity reaches an enormous value, of the order of 1016 bits. In artificial systems (with 1000 elements), a much smaller entropy of information, equal to 105 [bits] accumulated in 1 s is used. For a human, this value is 1010 [bits]. However, when the information gathering time will be long (as measured in light years) and the number of elements is immensely huge (like the number of stars in the sky), then Formula 1.220 becomes very important for theoretical considerations.

- The practical quantities related to the information quantity are:
  - information throughput, $C =$ information quantity/time [bit/s] or [baud] ([baud] stems from the surname "Baudot");
  - information density, $G =$ information quantity/surface area [bit/m^2].

Throughput and density are of particular importance when calculating the information capacity of transmission channels and the value of accumulated information in the information source.

The throughput [bauds] is directly related to the information capacity [bit] of the channel, because:

- information capacity $C_t =$ throughput × dwelling time of the information in the channel.

Information in human sensory organs can be estimated by assuming that humans are information channels (Figure 1.46) [42].

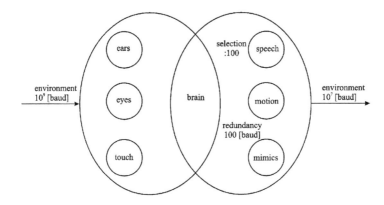

FIGURE 1.46 Human information throughput.

For example, sensory organ receptors (Figure 1.46) are assumed to have:

C_{eye} = 1010 [bauds]
C_{ear} = 5 × 104 [bauds]
$C_{pressure}$ = 105 [bauds]
C_{temp} = 103 [bauds]
C_{smell} = 102 [bauds]
C_{taste} = 101 [bauds]

Knowing that information can be retained in the brain for about 10 s, an indicative information capacity of a human being can be calculated.

$C_t = C \cdot t \equiv 1015$ [bits]

A capacity of 106 [bits] is necessary to use speech.
C_t— is the amount of information that can be registered in the brain, a computer, etc.

• Information transfer is an important and complex phenomenon of communication between systems.

It is very common to witness scenarios in which an information transmitter generates continuous signals. Using appropriate sampling, the continuous signal can be converted into a discrete signal that is easily transferable.

The fundamental period is taken to be the duration T of the signal, and the fundamental frequency is taken to be $f_d = 1/T$, and $T = 1/f_d$.

The frequency response is determined when all multiples of frequency f_d are known.

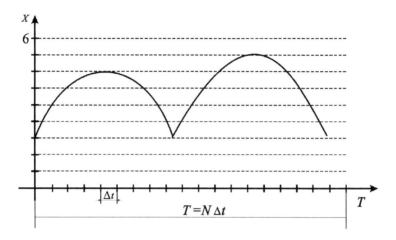

FIGURE 1.47 Example of digitisation of an entire signal X.

The frequency response is:

$$\Delta f = (f_g - f_d) \text{ where } f_g \text{ is a multiple of } f_d \qquad (1.221)$$

A bandwidth-limited process is fully determined if the signal values at successively small enough time intervals Δt are known, that is, if $N \cdot \Delta t$ can be given for the entire interval T (Figure 1.47).

The problem then is to determine a sufficiently small interval Δt, called the Nyquist interval:

$$\Delta t = \frac{1}{2\Delta f} = \frac{1}{2(f_g - f_d)} \qquad (1.222)$$

The number of necessary signal samples with duration T will be [42, 43]:

$$N = \frac{T}{\Delta t} = 2T\Delta f = 2T(f_g - f_d) \qquad (1.223)$$

If $f_g \gg f_d$, then:

$$N = 2Tf_g$$

$$N > 2Tf_g \text{ (Kotielnikov's theorem)} \qquad (1.224)$$

or

$$\frac{N}{T} > 2f_g$$

$$\frac{1}{\Delta t} \geq 2f_g \; \rightarrow \; \Delta t < \frac{1}{2f_g}$$

Knowing the effect of the useful signal P_u and the interference signal P_z, it is possible to calculate the capacity of the information channel

$$C = \Delta f \log_2 (1 + \frac{P_u}{P_z}) \; [baud] \; (Shannon's \; formula) \qquad (1.225)$$

with: P_u—power of the useful signal; P_z—power of the interference signal

1.4   SUMMARY

Making an optimal decision requires a comprehensive, multi-criteria analysis of the phenomenon, process, system, or object under consideration. Without a correct description of the item under consideration, it is impossible to arrive at the solution (decision) sought. Hence, mathematical models are created which are specialised for the problems under analysis. The models are based on the principles of cybernetics, which are oriented towards the study of the quality of functioning of systems that are in constant motion and development in a changing environment. Different models are therefore built to reproduce the current operation of the system in Newtonian time t and its development in Bergsonian time θ.

The following system models are presented in a condensed way:

- deterministic models, which can be differential equations, operator equations, operator transmittances, spectral transmittances, and equations of state. Time and frequency characteristics can also be deterministic models;
- probabilistic models for the development of which "probability calculus", "mathematical statistics", and "stochastic processes" are used.

Basic problems of system fallibility (unreliability) and the ways leading to improved system reliability are also presented. Methods for studying system structures are specified. The essence of regulation and control is described. The problem of identifying a basic regulation pattern is addressed. With a novel approach, the following topics are outlined:

- the study of the equilibrium of systems;
- signal dating;
- testing the proprietary component and feed components of systems;
- the role of the Keynesian multiplier in economic systems.

Issues relating to the operation of systems in mutual conflict are also addressed. Conflict situations reduced to games are presented. The Monte Carlo method and its importance in the study of large (hierarchical) systems are presented. An example of a network model in operational research is given. The relations between information entropy and energy are described. Their analysis was carried out using the "Maxwell's demon" model.

REFERENCES

1. Antoniewicz J.: Automatyka. WNT, Warszawa 1973.
2. Cempel C.: Teoria i inżynieria systemów. Wyd. Naukowe Instytutu Technologii Eksploatacyjnej, PIB, Radom 2006.
3. Mynarski S.: Elementy teorii systemów i cybernetyki. PWN, Warszawa 1974.
4. Pełczewski W.: Teoria sterowania. WNT, Warszawa 1980.
5. Bisztyga K.: Poradnik inżyniera automatyka pod red. Findeisen W. WNT, Warszawa 1969.
6. Lindstedt P.: Praktyczna regulacja maszyn i jej teoretyczne podstawy. Wyd. ITWL, Warszawa 2010.
7. Brzózka J.: Regulatory i układy automatyki. MIKOM, Warszawa 2004.
8. Manerowski J.: Identyfikacja modeli dynamiki ruchu sterowanych obiektów latających. Wyd. Nauk. ASKON, Warszawa 1999.
9. Krasowski A.A., Pospiełow G.S.: Podstawy automatyki i cybernetyki technicznej. WNT, Warszawa 1965.
10. Osiowski J.: Zarys rachunku operatorowego. WNT, Warszawa 1981.
11. Staniszewski R.: Cybernetyczna teoria projektowania. Ossolineum, Wrocław 1986.
12. Lindstedt P., Sudakowski T., Grądzki R.: Eksploatacyjna niezawodność maszyn i jej teoretyczne podstawy. Wyd. ITWL, Warszawa 2016.
13. Lindstedt P., Sudakowski T., Grądzki R.: Prediction of estimates of technical object's reliability on the basis of damage determined from Linderg Levy's claim and multiplicity of the set specified from ergodicity stream damage. Journal of KONES, vol. 20, no. 1, pp. 179–184, 2013.
14. Grądzki R., Golak K., Lindstedt P.: Parametric and nonparametric diagnostic models for blades in the rotating machinery with environment elimination. Journal of KONES, vol. 23, no. 2, pp. 137–145, 2016.
15. Grądzki R., Lindstedt P.: Method of assessment of technical object aptitude in environment of exploitation and service conditions. Eksploatacja i Niezawodnosc— Maintenance and Reliability, vol. 17, no. 1, pp. 54–63, 2015.
16. Bubnicki Z.: Podstawy informatycznych systemów zarządzania. Wyd. Politech. Wrocławskiej, Wrocław 1993.
17. Plucińska A., Pluciński E.: Probabilistyka. PWN, Warszawa 2017.
18. Sotskow B.S.: Niezawodność elementów i urządzeń automatyki. WNT, Warszawa 1973.
19. Sztarski M.: Niezawodność i eksploatacja urządzeń elektronicznych. WKiŁ, Warszawa 1972.
20. Mańczak K.: Metody identyfikacji wielowymiarowych obiektów sterowania. WNT, Warszawa 1971.
21. Miller J.: Statystyka i chemometria w chemii analitycznej. PWN, Warszawa 2016.

22. Sołodnikow W.W.: Dynamika statystyczna liniowych układów sterowania automatycznego. WNT, Warszawa 1964.
23. Bendat J.S., Piersol A.G.: Metody analizy i pomiaru sygnałów losowych. PWN, Warszawa 1976.
24. Bracewell R.: Przekształcenie Fouriera i jego zastosowania. WNT, Warszawa 1968.
25. Szabatin J.: Podstawy teorii sygnałów. WKŁ, Warszawa 2016.
26. Jaźwiński J., Ważyńska-Fiok K., Żurek J.: Wybrane rozkłady prawdopodobieństwa wykorzystywane w symulacyjnych badaniach bezpieczeństwa systemów transportowych. Zagadnienia Eksploatacji Maszyn, vol. 30, no. 2 (102), 1995.
27. Bobrowski D.: Modele i metody matematyczne teorii niezawodności w przykładach i zadaniach. WNT, Warszawa 1985.
28. Bojarski W.W.: Wprowadzenie do oceny niezawodności działania układów technicznych. PWN, Warszawa 1967.
29. Borowczyk H., Lindstedt P., Manerowski J.: Premises for a practical computer-aided parametric method of evaluation of the technical object reliability. Journal of KONES, vol. 16, no. 2, pp. 29–37, 2009.
30. Lewitowicz J., Borgoń J., Zabkowicz W.: Podstawy badań i eksploatacji techniki lotniczej, t. i II. Wyd. ITWL, Warszawa 1993.
31. Lindstedt P., Sudakowski T.: Prediction the bearing reliability on basis diagnostics information. Journal of Konbin, vol. 1, no. 3, pp. 27–49, 2007.
32. Niezawodność w technice. Zestaw norm Wyd. Normalizacyjne ALFA-WERO, Warszawa 1997.
33. Praca zbiorowa pod red. Migalski J.: Inżynieria niezawodności. Poradnik ZETOM, Warszawa 1992.
34. Hebda M., Mazur T.: Podstawy eksploatacji pojazdów samochodowych. WKiŁ, Warszawa 1980.
35. Praca zbiorowa pod redakcją M. Woropaya: Podstawy racjonalnej eksploatacji maszyn. ITE-ATR, Radom-Bydgoszcz 1996.
36. Smalko Z.: Podstawy eksploatacji technicznej pojazdów. Oficyna Wyd. Polit. Warszawskiej, Warszawa 1998.
37. Sadowski W.: Teoria podejmowania decyzji. PWE, Warszawa 1976.
38. Lerner A.J.: Zarys cybernetyki. WNT, Warszawa 1971.
39. Jędrzejowicz P.: Wybrane modele decyzyjne w produkcji i eksploatacji. WKiŁ, Warszawa 1981.
40. Wiener N.: Cybernetyka czyli sterowanie i komunikacja w zwierzęciu i maszynie. PWN, Warszawa 1971.
41. Ashby R.W.: Wstęp do cybernetyki. PWN, Warszawa 1963.
42. Drischel H.: Podstawy biocybernetyki. PWN, Warszawa 1976.
43. Hagel R., Zakrzewski J.: Miernictwo dynamiczne. WNT, Warszawa 1984.

2 Cybernetic Operating System

2.1 INTRODUCTION

Complex—and often costly—technical objects consist of many different components which must meet stringent requirements in terms of material and technology, as well as durability and reliability. These objects operate in a variable and arduous environment due to the difficult and complex, often excessive, requirements of their operating programs. Technical objects (especially those with a service life of several tens of thousands of hours or more) require special care in maintenance, adjustment, and diagnostics to ensure their reliability and safety characteristics. Maintenance should be characterised by a high degree of diligence and accuracy in performance of prescribed actions and by the fact that a significant share of the components is to be operated in accordance with the principles of technical status (condition)-based diagnostics. Maintenance is therefore faced with enormous and complex problems of maintaining and predicting the fitness of technical objects, which cannot be solved effectively when deprived of adequate scientific interdisciplinary support in the areas of regulation, diagnostics, and reliability [1–6].

2.2 ELEMENTS OF A CYBERNETIC OPERATING SYSTEM OF A TECHNICAL OBJECT

Machines (technical objects) are subject to the same destructive processes as living organisms (biological objects) and nature as a whole. A new machine ages and thus transforms into an old machine (machine wreck), just as a child transforms into an adult and finally becomes old (human wreck), or a young plant grows and ages into a centuries-old tree [7, 8].

This process is inevitable and irreversible, and technical, biological, and natural objects have no influence on its course. This is because the process progresses in the space of irreversible time, or evolutionary time, or Bergsonian time—θ. Bergsonian time can take different values $0<\theta<\infty$, with the additional rule by which the following always applies: $\theta_0<\theta_1<\theta_2$. Therefore, in the path of the passage of time θ, there is present time (e.g. θ_1), past time (θ_0), and future time (e.g. θ_2). Thus, Bergsonian time can be used to describe the relations between the past, the present, and the future of the state of energy, material, and information status in large technical, economic, and natural systems [8–11].

DOI: 10.1201/9781032638447-2

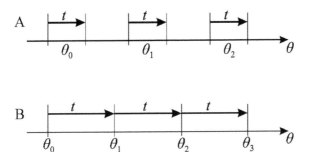

FIGURE 2.1 Bergsonian time θ and Newtonian time t. A—sequential method of testing an technical object; B—continuous method of testing an technical object.

It was discovered that there are sufficiently short instances, $\Delta\theta$, in which Bergsonian time practically "freezes". Nevertheless, in these instances (which have no relevance to the course of Bergsonian time θ), important work can be done to establish the current status of operation and the current technical status. These instances form a space of reversible time, called Newtonian time t. During this time, various tests are performed, leading to the identification of the object. Ultimately, it is concluded that the process of testing an object or a system in the time space t (i.e. the reversible Newtonian time of testing and identification) can be programmed or planned as required. This time can be expanded or reduced. It can be reversed from the final value (end of testing) to the initial value (which beans back to the start of testing). By examining the relations between t and θ, it is possible to state the obvious fact: Newtonian time overlaps with Bergsonian time (Figure 2.1).

When studying case A (Figure 2.1) of the relation between time t and θ, it is found that, for example, θ_0, θ_1, and θ_2 the short time t of an experiment is autonomous time, especially in terms of tests that can be repeated many times, and thus time t is reversible. An example of such tests is testing the wear of products in lubricating oil in tribological systems (the oil can be repeatedly sampled and tested).

When studying case B (Figure 2.1) of the relations between t and θ, it is found that time t in periods θ_0 to θ_1, θ_1 to θ_2, and so on, fully coincides with time θ. Since time t fills time θ by 100%, one could erroneously conclude that time t and θ are identical. Extending time t to the whole time period, for example, θ_0 to θ_1, does not mean that it has the characteristics of time θ. The conclusion is completely unreasonable, for the past, the present, and the future cannot be considered in time t. In addition, what happens in time t can be reversed, corrected, or cancelled (e.g. results from observations of an object in time θ_0 to θ_1 can be disregarded, meaning as non-existent), even though time θ has irreversibly progressed from time θ_0 to time θ_1. An example of research contemplated here could be the continuous testing of a vibroacoustic signal (e.g. the signal in time θ_0 to θ_1 can be studied in different ways or outright cancelled). Bergsonian time θ and Newtonian time t are used to describe processes occurring in operating systems [5–8].

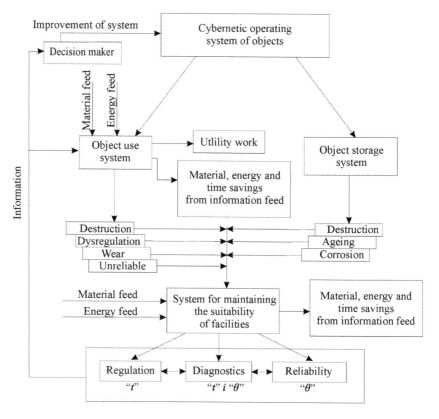

FIGURE 2.2 Main elements of a cybernetic operating system of objects: t—dynamic (Newtonian) time, θ—operating (Bergsonian) time [6].

A schematic diagram of the model of a cybernetic operating system for a technical object is shown in Figure 2.2, which indicates that during the use and storage of the object there is its continuous and inevitable destruction (changes in regulation, wear, increasing unreliability), and that adequate operation of the object is possible with an adequate feed of energy, material, and information. It is also recognised that the existing destruction phenomenon determines the shape of the system for maintaining the fitness (operation) of the object, where the system ensures the required relation between the material, energy, and information portions of the object.

The maintenance system should consist of regulation, diagnostics, and reliability systems.

The aim of regulation is to maintain optimum operating quality of the technical object in accordance with the information resulting from the principles of automation. It is always conducted in Newtonian (dynamic) time, t. The measure of regulation status is the relation between signals, expressed by regulation quality indicators.

The purpose of diagnostics is to acquire information on changes in the technical status that occur during the operation of an object; the information should be acquired with indirect methods, without the need to disassemble the object, using the measured diagnostic signals of the object and the signals of the environment. In diagnostic systems, a distinction is made between the maintenance activity which is carried out in dynamic time t (object identification) and the maintenance activity which is carried out in operating time θ. Knowledge (information) about changes in technical status provides the foundation for optimum (safe and cost-effective) operation of objects based on their technical status.

The objective of reliability is to continuously refine the reliability characteristics based on knowledge of the failures that have occurred (including catastrophic, parametric, and transient failures) during the operation of an object. Today, methods are increasingly used for the determination of reliability characteristics based on parametric and transient failures prior to the always hazardous, catastrophic failures which lead to disastrous consequences. The reliability characteristics are described in operating time θ.

A special role in the system for maintenance of object fitness is played by diagnostics through its direct link with the regulation and reliability systems.

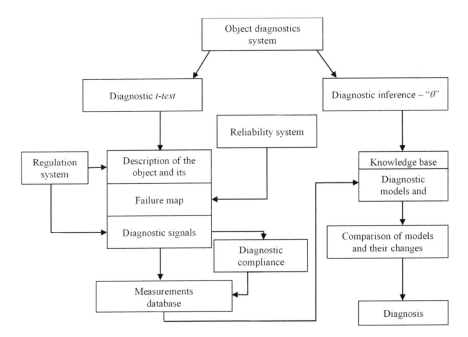

FIGURE 2.3 Schematic diagram of a diagnostic system and its relations with regulation and reliability systems [6].

2.3 DIAGNOSTICS IN CYBERNETIC OPERATING SYSTEMS OF OBJECTS AND ITS RELATIONS WITH RELIABILITY AND REGULATION

A schematic diagram of a technical object diagnostic system and its links with the regulation and reliability systems is shown in Figure 2.3 [4–6, 12].

An analysis of Figure 2.3 shows that diagnostics equally applies both to the object being diagnosed and its environment, and that diagnostics is performed at two different times—Newtonian t and Bergsonian θ—yet these times are closely related by the diagnostic activity, which always includes: diagnostic testing (carried out in time t) and diagnostic inference (carried out in time θ).

- Diagnostic testing (Figure 2.3) is a fundamental element of diagnostics and largely determines its effectiveness. It is divided into several stages, among which are as follows:

Object Identification

In this stage of diagnostic testing, a broad knowledge of the object and its environment should be acquired and it should include:

- a formal description of the object, a description of its construction and operation in the environment (including equations of motion and static and dynamic characteristics), the manufacturing technology of the object, the reliability and safety characteristics, including a set of typical failures and the diagnostic signals they generate;
- a description of diagnostic signals with their physical nature and degree of interference (disturbance).

Measurement of Diagnostic Signals

Here is where the necessary measuring equipment is selected and precise instructions for measurement performance are developed. The instructions should prevail in an unchanging form throughout the lifetime of the object. Of particular importance here is the required assurance of appropriately constant accuracy (class) of measurements and repeatability (identity) of the settings of the measuring equipment in relation to the object during subsequent diagnostic tests.

Interference Suppression in Diagnostic Signals

This process is performed by applying appropriate filters (which can be: low pass, high pass, band pass, comb, Wiener, etc. filters) or (what is more effective and universal) correlators in the measuring systems for transformation of the measured signal trends (in dynamic time t) into correlation function trends (at shift time τ), followed by transformation of the latter into the spectral power density function of the signal (which is dependent on frequency ω). Note that time τ and frequency are just another form of expression of time space t. In addition, it is known that the two measured signals $x(t)$ and $y(t)$ can be transformed into three correlation signals, $R_{xx}(\tau)$, $R_{xy}(\tau)$, and $R_{yy}(\tau)$, and into three spectral power density signals, $S_{xx}(\omega)$, $S_{xy}(\omega)$, and $S_{yy}(\omega)$, and into the square of amplitude gain $\left|A^2\right| = \dfrac{S_{yy}}{S_{xx}}$ and the phase shift $\varphi = Arg\,\dfrac{S_{xy}}{S_{xx}}$ [6, 13, 14].

Forming of Diagnostic Signals

This activity is intended to reduce all measured signals into a dimensionless form. The reference value of the measured diagnostic signal is its design value resulting from the object design, the value determined during factory tests, or the value determined during the transfer of the object from the production system to the operating system. This way, the "past" θ_0 resulting from the object design is introduced to the "present" θ_1 (e.g. a pump design provides for a discharge pressure of 210 [atm] at a flow rate of 10 [l/s], and the manufacturer has produced a pump with 200 [atm] and 9 [l/s], respectively, so the relative values referenced to the design are 0.95 and 0.9, which should be considered a poor result). It is significant that the object assessment is produced already at the onset of diagnostic testing [5, 12, 15].

Development of the Database

The database is the tables of the trend quality indicators for the formed signals, of the correlation function of the signals, and of the spectral power density function of the signals. The quality indicators adopted should relate, by their physical nature, to the "regulation time" and the "overshoot value" used in assessment of automatic regulation system quality. The database can also be the parameter matrices of mathematical models determined with static and dynamic identification methods. The development of the database is the final stage of diagnostic testing, the object identification [5, 12].

- Diagnostic inference (Figure 2.3) is another element of diagnostics as important as diagnostic testing. It involves processing the results of diagnostic testing (the database) and other information about the object and its environment (the knowledge base) into diagnosis, genesis, and prognosis. In diagnostic inference, several different stages are distinguished [5, 8]:

Development of the Diagnostic Model

It consists of linking (by following the available knowledge) the diagnostic signals to the changes in the technical status (failures) of the object. Formal linking of the diagnostic signals, the signal trend quality indicators, and the diagnostic parameters to failures is absolutely essential in the diagnostic process. The diagnostic model allows "memorising" the (constantly changing) technical status of the object at the current diagnostic instance θ_0 and storing it until the next diagnostic instance—θ_1, θ_2, etc. Thus, without a diagnostic model, it is not possible to realise the principles of diagnostics based on comparing the current (present) states of the object with its previous (past) and projected (future) states.

Development of Algorithms for Comparison Between Diagnostic Models

It includes the principles of comparison between the models from current diagnostics and the previous models from the history of the object's life (time θ). The resulting changes in the form and parameters of the model are processed into changes in the technical status of the object.

Computer-Aided Diagnostic Inference

It addresses the issue of effectively eliminating the subjective action of the diagnostician from the diagnostic inference process and replacing it with an objective expert system (always acting identically, now and after many years). It turns out (as proved by practice) that the identity of diagnostic inference, which is ensured by computer technology, is much more effective than the intelligence of a diagnostician who is in the present time and of the completely different diagnosticians who follow.

- To implement diagnostic activities, the following terms and definitions are used (always for a specific given object):
  1. Diagnostic object—an aircraft, an airframe, an engine, a powerplant, an equipment unit, an assembly and functional arrangement of an airframe or an engine; a structural component which is being diagnosed and its environment.
  2. Diagnostic system of an aircraft, an airframe, or an engine—a set of elements which execute the diagnostic methods, including the diagnostic object in its environment, the methods, models, and means of diagnostics, the activities of diagnosticians, users, maintenance services, and decision-makers, and the information on the relevant relations between these elements.
  3. Object technical status assessment—verification of conformity of measurement results against their requirements, driving and followed by determination of the properties which define the technical status of the object in question. An analysis of the current and past verifications done by a diagnostician or a diagnostic device (which is automatic) leads to the formulation of diagnosis. The diagnosis defines the technical status of the object with the required accuracy, at the time of diagnostic testing, and the ability of the object to perform its task.
  4. Supervision—routine observation of the technical status of the diagnostic object, performed continuously or sequentially. Supervision is used in the process of inspecting the wear of the diagnostic object.
  5. Reliability status genesis—the effect of diagnostic activity, determining the time, location, and causes of the resulting unfitness status. Diagnostics—which is current and from previous diagnostic testing—of certain reliability characteristics, severity, and the duration of action of component wear and failure factors is required to develop the genesis. The genesis

is essential for the determination of the causes of particularly hazardous conditions that threaten flight safety; it is also used in flight accident investigations. The results of the genesis are used to plan preventive measures.

6. Failure location—the search for the location of the failure origin of the diagnostic object being tested.

7. Technical status forecasting—a diagnostic activity intended to determine the future fitness status of the diagnostic object. Forecasting is driven by a technical status assessment of the time of diagnostic testing and the knowledge of past statuses, as well as the knowledge of the severity and duration of the wear and failure factors. The fitness status forecast of an object is determined with a certain probability, considering a certain time that no shorter than the latest departure or the next diagnostic.

8. Monitoring—continuously collecting information and informing the object's user about the operating status of the diagnostic object (also by means of special systems which serve to alert the object's user) and instructing and advising the user to optimise the object's performance during emergencies.

9. Diagnostic procedure—a structured diagnostic activity intended to diagnose the technical status of the diagnostic object. Diagnostic procedures are a component of maintenance procedures and usually precondition the maintenance work accordingly. If, as a result of diagnostic work, it is found that the diagnostic object is fit, then preventive maintenance work is undertaken (which means the activities are carried out on a scheduled basis). Otherwise, repair work is necessary (regulation, repair, or replacement) to restore the lost technical fitness of the diagnostic object.

10. Diagnostic model—the expressed relation between changes in the technical status of the diagnostic object and the diagnostic parameters and signals of the object generated by the changes. Application of a diagnostic object facilitates the following:
    - analysis of complex objects to determine their diagnostic compliance and the sensitivity of individual diagnostic signals to changes in the technical status of the object;
    - selection of the diagnostic parameters and signals for the object and the development of diagnostic procedures;
    - selection of the diagnostic methods and synthesis of diagnostic systems.

11. Diagnostic compliance—a property of the diagnostic object (system) that defines its fitness for performing the diagnostic process. Diagnostic compliance is shaped by the design and production process of, for example, an aircraft. It includes knowledge of the object to be diagnosed and the properties of the object to facilitate diagnostic testing.

12. Diagnostic requirements—a quantitative or qualitative description of the features that the aircraft diagnostic system should have (i.e. the diagnostic object, the diagnostic methods and measures, and the diagnostic activity). Diagnostic requirements are taken into account in the concept and design engineering stages of aircraft and their operating

systems. Diagnostic requirements concern increasing the diagnostic compliance of aircraft, adapting them better to the needs of diagnostics, and are linked to the problems resulting from the growing number of instruments in the diagnostic process.

13. Diagnostic station—a diagnostic kit at a diagnostic activity station. Diagnostic stations can be stationary or mobile.

14. Operating potential—the resource of the possible durability and resistance of the diagnostic object to the predicted loads resulting from the anticipated process of use.

2.4 REGULATION IN OPERATING SYSTEMS OF OBJECTS AND ITS RELATIONS WITH RELIABILITY AND DIAGNOSTICS

According to the principles of automation, it is required that a technical object is immune to interference signals originating in its environment and that the object is capable of following the control signals set by the object's user [6, 14, 15].

In the process of operation, it has been observed that during their operation, objects wear out and this causes, among other things, maladjustment (loss of regulation). In the process of its operation, an object is brought to its correct operating status by changing the settings of the regulating devices of the object. Thus, any change in the required regulator settings resulting from ensuring the required quality of operation of the object (regulation of the object) stems from the change in structural parameters of the object, meaning its technical status (diagnostics of the object).

However, the degree of dependence between the regulation status of an object and its technical status varies. In extreme cases, a functionally unfit object may be technically fit (like a poorly regulated engine), while an object that is technically unfit can be functionally fit (like a broken blade or vane) [2, 16].

- The severity of effects of the object elements and parameters and the object's surrounding on the quality of functioning can be assessed by analysing the function of structural, parametric, and interference sensitivity [5, 6, 13, 14].

A technical object with its control unit in an open system is illustrated in Figure 2.4.

An technical object with its control unit in a closed system is illustrated in Figure 2.5.

As shown in Figures 2.4 and 2.5, the setting w of the utility signal y is input to the control unit, US. Since the object (the system) is always affected by undefined interference z, the required value of the utility signal can be unsatisfactory (it can deviate significantly from the setting w) [6, 16]. In such an adverse situation, the settings n of the control unit US must be adjusted accordingly (and the adjustment shall be continuous for Figure 2.4 and periodic for Figure 2.5), so that the system fulfils its utility tasks with appropriate quality. In short, the control unit US must be regulated accordingly.

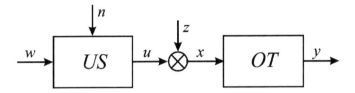

FIGURE 2.4 Technical object with its open-system control unit *OT*—technical object; *US*—control unit; *w*—utility signal setting value; *n*—control unit settings; *u*—the signal of *US* effect on *OT*; *z*—interference; *y*—utility signal; *x*—object's driving signal [based on 6].

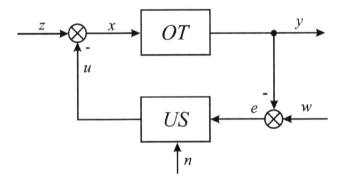

FIGURE 2.5 Technical object with its closed-system control unit *OT*—technical object; *US*—control unit; *w*—utility signal setting value; *n*—control unit settings; *u*—the signal of *OT* effect on *US*; *z*—interference; *y*—utility signal; *x*—object's driving signal; *e*—offset signal [based on 6].

The problem of control unit (regulator) regulation is complex. It can be solved by following the widely construed principles of automation. It is required that each system, after the completion of the regulation process, be stable, follow up, and have adequate static and dynamic quality.

It can be concluded that a significant change in the technical status (the change of status signals or parameters) of an object will cause a change in its regulation state (the performance quality indicators change) and—at the same time—cause a change in its reliability characteristics. Since it is required that operation and reliability are always correct and constant, it is necessary to regulate the settings of the control unit (*n*, see Figure 2.5) to the functional needs of the object, and the use should be regulated to the current reliability characteristics. Thus, any required change in the control unit settings (made during the maintenance of the object) also indicates a change in the technical and reliability status of the object. It should be presumed that a situation may occur in the operation of a technical object where the selection of control unit settings for an excessively worn (failed) object will not be possible. This fact, if predicted, becomes the foundation for predicting the reliability characteristics of the object.

It can be concluded that any significant change in the technical status (diagnostics) performed in time t and θ will result in a change of the regulation settings according to the principles of automation (time t) and hence the need to re-determine the reliability characteristics (time θ) [16].

- The following definitions (always for the specific object of interest) are given for the implementation of regulation activities:
  1. Regulated object—an aircraft engine—a machine that converts the fuel and air supplied to it into mechanical energy, that is controlled torque, controlled thrust, or controlled power. In this standard, an aircraft engine is considered a regulated object.
  2. Aircraft engine fuel supply system—equipment which facilitates the delivery of the required quantity of fuel with the correct parameters to the combustor of the aircraft engine.
  3. Aircraft engine control system—an aircraft engine with the fuel supply system and the equipment which facilitates control of the correct air and fuel ratios delivered to the engine combustor.
  4. Aircraft engine control system structural diagram—a technical drawing—made at an appropriate degree of simplification—of an aircraft engine control system, detailing and specifying all components of the aircraft engine control system.
  5. Aircraft engine control system functional diagram—a technical drawing—made at an appropriate degree of simplification—of an aircraft engine control system, detailing and specifying the component assemblies and their input and output signals and the designations and values of the signals at steady states (e.g. low engine speed, cruise range, maximum range).
  6. Aircraft engine control system block diagram—an indicative drawing which shows the units of the aircraft engine control system in the form of identical blocks (rectangles) and the summing and information blocks, respectively, interconnected by signals in the form of vectors of different lengths (resulting from the layout of the drawing), which have no relation to signal values.
  7. Aircraft engine regulator—the basic unit of an aircraft engine control system, into which the set value is input and which, in accordance with the structurally established control algorithm, generates an appropriate control signal output that affects the change of the flow rates of air fuel delivery to the engine combustor.
  8. Aircraft engine control system correction—technical elements introduced into the main path and feedback of an aircraft engine control system to improve the static and dynamic quality of the system. In the case of aircraft engines, these elements are most often implemented as additional feedback from the regulator; the feedback can be fixed (proportional), flexible (differential), or adaptive (isodromic).

9. Aircraft engine identification—determination of transmittance and its parameters by means of a computer program explicitly specified by the manufacturer.

10. Aircraft engine control system sensitivity—sensitivity of operation (functioning) of the aircraft engine control system to changes in the parameters of the object and regulation settings, as well as of the corrector.

11. Aircraft engine control system monitoring—the continuous acquisition, storage, and processing of information about the relations between automatic control signals, with reporting to the user on the actual operating status of the aircraft engine control system, by means of specific systems designed to alert the user and to instruct and advise the user to ensure proper operation during an emergency status of the aircraft engine control system.

12. Aircraft engine regulation requirements—a quantitative and qualitative specification of the features that the aircraft engine control system should have, the means of regulation, and the basic duties and requirements for aircraft engine maintenance personnel.

13. Regulation procedure—structured activities intended to identify the operating status of an aircraft engine control system and bring it to the required status. The regulation procedure is a component of maintenance procedures.

2.5   RELIABILITY IN OPERATING SYSTEMS OF OBJECTS AND ITS RELATIONS WITH DIAGNOSTICS AND REGULATION

The properties of an object that determine the fitness of the object for a given application can be described with measurable functions of the essential characteristics of the object. Changes in the essential characteristics of a technical object result in changes to their reliability status. Total or partial loss of fitness, a change in the essential characteristics of a technical object, is a phenomenon which, according to the reference Polish Standard, is defined by the term "failure" [10, 17–20].

All failures are random events. A failure may be characterised by abrupt (sudden) changes in the basic parameters due to various random causes related to internal component defects, inappropriate changes in the operating conditions, or operator errors. In the case of a slow, gradual failure, a gradual, smooth, and slow change of parameters is observed, which is the result of age-related wear and tear of individual components as well as of the entire system. Other common failures are characterised by that they can spontaneously disappear on their own without any intervention by the operator once the root cause of the failure has disappeared. The often causes of this type of failure are non-nominal operating conditions [11, 21, 22].

The number of failures and their occurrence in time are the absolute basis for determining the reliability indicators of an object. Note, however, that failure can already be such an undesirable status in which the essential characteristic of the object's properties, U, permanently exceeds its limit values, u_g or u_d, and the object will permanently transition from its fitness status to its unfitness status [5, 23, 24].

Therefore, there is a need to predict this type of failure, which in turn requires continuous observation of changes in an often inaccessible, measurable essential property of an object.

The prediction is facilitated by the application of the following diagnostic principles:

1. Any change in a technical condition (status) characteristic generates measurable and accessible diagnostic signals.
2. Diagnostic signals facilitate indirect observation of inaccessible essential characteristics of technical status.
3. Diagnostic signals facilitate predictions about whether an essential characteristic of technical status will reach the limit values u_g or u_d.

The potential failures predicted in accordance with the principles of diagnostics facilitate verification of the required reliability characteristics in the operating process before actual failure occurs [6, 25].

- Relevant Polish Standards, which are synthesised in Section 1.1.4, are applied to complete the activities in the reliability determination process.

2.6 SUMMARY

It can be concluded that a change in the technical status (its parameters) of an object (Figures 2.4 and 2.5) causes a change in its operating status (the performance quality indicators change). Since it is required that the performance quality is always correct and constant, it is necessary to regulate (tune) the settings of the control unit to the present changes of the object (Figures 2.4 and 2.5). Thus, any required change in the control unit settings (made during the maintenance of the object) also indicates a change in the technical status of the object. It is prudent to assume that in the course of operating a technical object, a situation may arise where the selection of control unit settings for an excessively worn and failed technical object is difficult. This fact (preferably when predicted) becomes the foundation for predicting the reliability characteristics of the object.

Hence the basic conclusion that regulation, diagnostics, and reliability of a technical object are in a close relationship, which can be optimally implemented in the cybernetic operation system of the object.

Information about the regulation status, technical status, and reliability status (Figure 2.2) is transmitted to the maintenance staff of the object (to improve the quality of maintenance activities), to the object's user (to adapt the conditions of use to the technical capacities of the object), and to the decision-maker (to continuously improve the system order), and finally converted (according to Maxwell's formula: $\Delta E = 10^{-16} \Delta I \left[\dfrac{erg}{K} \right]$, which links the increase of energy, ΔE, to the increase of information, ΔI) into the savings of time, material, and energy [6–8, 26].

According to the principles of cybernetics in the process of maintenance of technical objects, observed and documented changes occurring in the regulation, diagnostics, and reliability of the objects drive the planning of maintenance of the objects (which include machines and equipment).

Examples of the self-transformation of information or knowledge (attainments) into material and energy savings are widely perceptible. The increase in information about the technical status of an object reduces the energy required to operate the object. Example:

1. Compressor blade—and the knowledge of 2 mm of its material loss facilitates blending of the blade and its continued, safe operation. The economic (material) saving is obvious. There is no need to replace the blade. However, a 3 mm loss of material requires a different treatment. The blade must be removed. A material loss this large is a risk of the blade breaking away, destroying the entire engine and the aircraft, resulting in a large economic and material loss.
2. Railway track rail—the knowledge of the flaking of the rails provides the opportunity to continue operation of the rail, provided that train speed is reduced. Failure to reduce the speed can lead to an accident and severe property damage.
3. Aircraft pilot—during a pre-flight medical examination, knowledge is gained about the pilot's health (well-being). A pilot completely unfit to fly is a presumption of a possible aircraft accident, leading to considerable material and social losses.
4. Bus driver—sobriety test and rest time. This knowledge helps reduce the likelihood of an accident.
5. Wear (abrasion) of car tyres—the knowledge of the condition of the tyre allows matching the speed of the vehicle to the condition of the tyre (instead of driving at 140 km/h, the speed is reduced to 80 km/h, for example).
6. Sea—Beaufort wind force scale from 0 to 9—at Force 9, ships and ferries do not leave port as there is a high risk of sinking.

These examples clearly prove that the acquired and applied information (knowledge) allows to avoid material, energy, and social losses.

REFERENCES

1. Boliński B., Stelmaszczyk Z.: Eksploatacja silników turbinowych. WKŁ, Warszawa 1981.
2. Borowczyk H., Lindstedt P. + zespół: Model zintegrowanego systemu diagnostycznego płatowca i zespołu napędowego statków powietrznych, Opracowanie ITWL Nr 12020/I. ITWL, Warszawa 1997.
3. Lewitowicz J., Kustroń K.: Podstawy eksploatacji statków powietrznych, t. 2. Wyd. ITWL, Warszawa 2003.

4. Lindstedt P., Błachnio J.: Automatyka i diagnostyka podstawą systemu obsługiwania maszyn, Materiały V Krajowej Konferencji Naukowo-Technicznej DPP'01. Wyd. Politechniki Zielonogórskiej, Zielona Góra 2001.
5. Lindstedt P.: Praktyczna diagnostyka maszyn i jej teoretyczne podstawy. Wydawnictwo Naukowe ASKON, Warszawa 2002.
6. Lindstedt P.: Praktyczna regulacja maszyn i jej teoretyczne podstawy. Wydawnictwo Naukowe ITWL, Warszawa 2010.
7. Lerner A.J.: Zarys cybernetyki. WNT, Warszawa 1971.
8. Wiener N.: Cybernetyka czyli sterowanie i komunikacja w zwierzęciu i maszynie. PWN, Warszawa 1971.
9. Ashby R.W.: Wstęp do cybernetyki. PWN, Warszawa 1963.
10. Borowczyk H., Lindstedt P., Manerowski J.: Premises for a practical computer aide parametric method of evaluation of the technical object reliability. Journal of KONES, vol. 16, no. 12, 2009.
11. Żółtowski B., Ćwik Z.: Leksykon diagnostyki technicznej. Wyd. ATR, Bydgoszcz 1996.
12. Szczepanik R., Lindstedt P., Borowczyk H.: Diagnostyka techniczna w systemie obsługiwania silników lotniczych, Problemy Badań i Eksploatacji Techniki Lotniczej, tom V rozdział 4. Wyd. ITWL, Warszawa 2004, pp. 85–100.
13. Pełczewski W.: Teoria sterowania. WNT, Warszawa 1980.
14. Staniszewski R.: Sterowanie zespołów napędowych. WKŁ, Warszawa 1980.
15. Lindstedt P., Sabak R.: Nowe techniki w diagnostyce lotniczych silników turbinowych, Materiały Seminarium Wydz. M.E.L. PW. Wyd. Politechniki Warszawskiej, Warszawa 2005.
16. Lindstedt P., Szczepanik R.: Regulacja i diagnostyka w obsłudze technicznej silników lotniczych, VII Międzynarodowa Konferencja AIRDIAG'01. Wyd. ITWL, Warszawa 2001.
17. Bobrowski D.: Modele i metody matematyczne teorii niezawodności. WNT, Warszawa 1985.
18. Niezawodność w technice. Zestaw Norm. Wyd. Normalizacyjne ALFA-WERO, Warszawa 1997.
19. Praca zbiorowa pod red. Migalski J.: Inżynieria niezawodności. Poradnik ZETOM, Warszawa 1992.
20. Praca zbiorowa pod redakcją M. Woropaya: Podstawy racjonalnej eksploatacji maszyn. ITE-ATR, Radom-Bydgoszcz 1996.
21. Woropay M.: Diagnostyka a niezawodność systemów technicznych. Postępy Cybernetyki, Ossolineum, no. 2, 1983.
22. Zboiński M., Lindstedt P., Kotlarz I.: Stałe i aktualizowane statystyczne tribologiczne progi diagnostyczne i ich znaczenie w procesie bieżącej oceny stanu technicznego układu łożyskowania silnika lotniczego. Journal of Konbin, vol. 1, no. 17, 2011.
23. Sztarski M.: Niezawodność i eksploatacja urządzeń elektronicznych. WKiŁ, Warszawa 1972.
24. Żurek J., Krutkow A., Stawiński Ł.: Symulacyjne badania algorytmu doboru modelu matematycznego rozkładu. Materiały Szkoły Zimowej Niezawodności, Szczyrk 1991.
25. Sotskow B.S.: Niezawodność elementów i urządzeń automatyki. WNT, Warszawa 1973.
26. Mynarski S.: Elementy teorii systemów i cybernetyki. PWN, Warszawa 1974.

3 Decision Support in Turbine Jet Engine Control

3.1 INTRODUCTION

Regulation is one of the more difficult forms of human interaction with a technical object. It is because the testing and regulating of an object is almost always done from the setting (w) and used in a complex environment, where the testing and regulating are also done from random interferences (z). It appears it is not always true that an object well-regulated from setting w will perform well in a random, hardly predictable predict environment, that is, from the interference z (see Section 1.1.7, Figure 1.19, Formulas 1.147 and 1.148). This problem applies in particular to turbine jet engines. There are often conflicting cases where a jet engine that has been regulated correctly (according to the maintenance engineer's judgement) from setting w during the ground test (with the regulation done on the ground) will perform incorrectly (according to the pilot's judgement) in the engine's environment when an undefined interference (disturbance) z acts on the engine (in flight). This phenomenon is particularly true of regulations made on turbine jet engines after their production, overhaul, or maintenance. What follows is that during ground tests, the engine is regulated only from setting w, after which—during the flight of the aircraft—the resistance of the engine to disturbance z is tested. This two-stage (convoluted) solution to the engine regulation process is dictated by the fact that during ground tests:

- The w signal can be input to the engine regulator by operating the *DSS* (engine control lever).
- The z signal shall not be input to the engine (partial obstruction of the engine intake/exhaust is not permitted).

Therefore, the regulation activities done on the ground are incomplete, which makes them uncertain. This situation is further complicated by that when one improves the regulation state to the value w, there is an undesirable deterioration of the regulation status by disturbance z. As it turns out, the signals w and z are in conflict, and the whole regulation process becomes a "game" (see Section 1.1.9, Figure 1.26) of the turbine jet engine and its environment.

DOI: 10.1201/9781032638447-3

3.2   DESCRIPTION OF THE TURBINE JET ENGINE AND ITS ENVIRONMENT

- The turbine jet engine whose structural diagram is shown in Figure 3.1 is a technical object of complex structure [1, 2]. Due to the applied technologies of production and overhaul and the operating methods of this engine, its maintenance is complex and complicated. For these reasons, the process of in-service testing of the engine, followed by the required regulation process, is difficult to perform (there are many different regulation points) and can only be done strictly in accordance with a regulation method manual developed by the engine manufacturer, using specialised engine instruments (the measures to perform all maintenance operations: maintenance tools, measuring/test instruments, measuring/ test apparatus, data recorders, and software) [3–8].
- Regardless of the type of jet engine, the principles of its operation are the same. The engine draws air through the intake; the air is compressed by the compressor and delivered to the combustor. The air is mixed with fuel (e.g. kerosene) in the combustor, and the air/fuel mix is combusted (the air/fuel mix ignition during starting is achieved with the use of a spark plug; once the engine is in operation, combustion is sustained by the combustor internal temperature), generating large amounts of heat with rapid decompression of air. The resulting exhaust gas, which is a mixture of air and combustion products, is directed to the blades of the high-pressure turbine, which drives the compressor (by which the engine

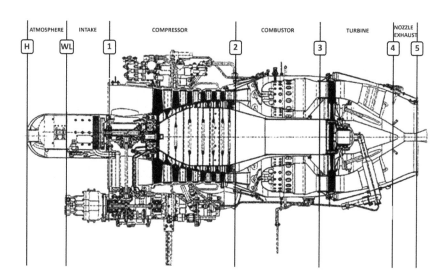

FIGURE 3.1 Structural diagram of a single-rotor turbine jet engine: *H*, *WL*, *1*, *2*, *3*, *4*, *5*—engine cross-sectional views [5].

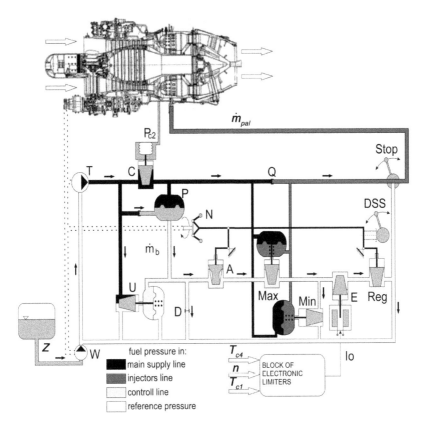

FIGURE 3.2 Functional diagram showing the operating principle of the EUP-150S fuel delivery and control system of the K-15 engine: A—starting and acceleration governor valve; C—starting and acceleration unit needle; D—deceleration control nozzle; DSS—engine control lever; E—electrohydraulic control valve (electronic limiter unit actuator); Max—maximum fuel flow rate restrictor valve; Min—minimum fuel flow rate restrictor valve; N—centrifugal engine speed sender; P—comparator valve (couples the mainline to the control line); Q—fuel flow rate volumetric orifice; Reg—engine speed hydromechanical regulator; $Stop$—fuel injector stop valve; T—main plunger pump; U—fuel bleed valve; W—auxiliary impeller pump; z—fuel tank; p_{c2} (p_2)—compressor downstream total air pressure; $\dot{m}_{pal}$ (m_p)—fuel delivery mainline mass flow rate; $\dot{m}_b$—control line fuel mass flow rate; I_0—electrohydraulic valve driver input; p_4—compressor downstream air pressure; n—engine (rotational) speed [based on. 5, 13].

keeps running). The exhaust gas is discharged at high velocity from the HP turbine, around the exhaust nozzle, and into the atmosphere. Through the interaction of the flow passage walls with the exhaust gas washing the walls, thrust is generated [1, 9–12]. A functional diagram of a turbine jet engine with its fuel delivery and control system is shown in Figure 3.2.

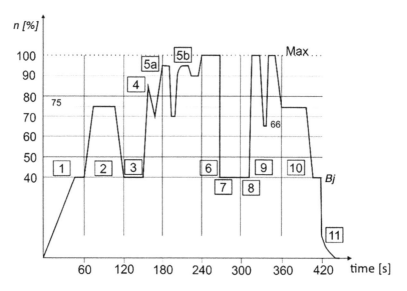

FIGURE 3.3 Basic proof test chart for the K-15 engine [15].

- The automatic control system (*UAR*) of the K-15 engine (Figure 3.2) is a hydro-mechanical follow-up system whose main objective is to maintain the engine rotor speed (*n*) set with the *DSS*, regardless of the effects of the environment on the ground and in flight. It also includes electronic limiters for maximum rotor speed (*n*) and maximum turbine downstream temperature (t_4). Other tasks performed by the *UAR* include limiting the maximum fuel delivery flow to the injectors (which is designed to limit the maximum power output of the turbine), protecting against engine stalling (by ensuring a continuous minimum fuel delivery flow to the engine), and controlling the acceleration, deceleration, and engine starting [5, 14]. The engine speed sender output is represented by displacement and its change of rate. The engine regulator implements a *PI* algorithm [5].
- Ground testing of turbine jet engines to check their regulation status follows a strict program. The program specified both the value of engine speed setting, the time for which the engine speed is maintained, and the rate of engine speed change input with the engine control lever (*DSS*). A chart of the proof test for the K-15 engine is shown in Figure 3.3.

A detailed description of the activities carried out during the standard proof test of the K-15 engine is shown in Table 3.1.

During the tests, the trends of automatic control (regulation) of the engine are recorded: the inputs, the outputs, and the auxiliary signals. A set of automatic control signals for an aircraft jet engine (K-15) recorded during a standard ground test is shown in Table 3.2 [7, 16].

TABLE 3.1
Specification of the K-15 Engine Proof Test Activities [15]

No. of step	Activity
1	Start the engine.
2	Preheat the engine, duration 60 s at n=75% of max. engine speed.
3	Check the idling Bj parameters.
	Set the DSS to idle and wait 15 s.
	Once the engine speed has been established, record the instrument readings.
4	Check the fuel bleed valve (failure of the bleed valves to open/close; incorrect engine speed to actuate the valves).
	Slowly increase the engine speed to $n = 85\%$ while monitoring the engine speed indicator and the fuel bleed valve trigger indicators.
	Slowly reduce the engine speed to $n = 70\%$ while monitoring the engine speed indicator and the fuel bleed valve trigger indicators.
5a	Do a functional test of the electronic engine speed limiters (verify that the engine speed is limited and to what level).
	Toggle the RPM LIMIT TEST switch ON.
	Slowly move the DSS to the setting of $n = 95\%$.
	Wait until the engine speed limited by the limiter is stable (approximately 20 s)
	Toggle the RPM LIMIT TEST switch OFF.
5b	Do a functional test of the electronic exhaust gas temperature limiters (verify that the exhaust gas temperature is limited and to what level).
	Set the engine speed to $n = 70\%$.
	Toggle the TEMP LIMIT TEST switch ON.
	Slowly move the DSS to the setting of $n = 95\%$.
	Wait until the exhaust gas temperature limited by the limiter is stable (approximately 30 s).
	Toggle the TEMP LIMIT TEST switch OFF.
6	Check the engine operating parameters with the DDS set in its maximum position (maximum limit overrun)
	Set the DSS to nMAX and wait 15 s
	Once the engine speed has been established, read the instrument readings
7	Test quick deceleration from the MAX range to Bj and the engine proneness to stalling.
	Quickly (within 0.5 s) move the DSS from MAX to Bj.
8	Test the engine speed acceleration from Bj to MAX and the engine proneness to overspeeding.
	Wait for the engine speed to become stable and wait 30 s more.
	Quickly (within 0.5 s) move the DSS from Bj to MAX.
	Start the stopwatch simultaneously with the movement of the DSS.
	Stop the stopwatch as soon as the engine speed is reached.
	Read the instantaneous values of t_z and n (the swing).
9	Test the acceleration from the engine speed $n = 66\%$ (10494 rpm) in landing approach to the MAX range (the proneness to overspeed).
	Set the engine speed to $n = 66\%$ of MAX.
	Wait for the engine speed to become stable and wait 30 s more.
	Quickly (within 0.5 s) move the DSS to MAX.
	Start the stopwatch simultaneously with the movement of the DSS.
	Stop the stopwatch as soon as the engine speed is reached.
	Read the instantaneous values of t_z and n (the swing).
10	Cool down the engine.
	Set the DSS to Bj.
11	Shut down the engine.
	Shut down the engine while measuring the coasting time.

TABLE 3.2

Signals Recorded During In-Service Testing of the K-15 Engine [16]

m_p	**Fuel delivery mainline pressure**
DSS	Position of the engine control lever
n	Engine shaft speed
p_2	Compressor downstream total air pressure
p_4	Engine exhaust gas nozzle pressure
T_4	Turbine downstream exhaust gas pressure
$WIBR$	Engine lateral vibration level
T_H	Ambient temperature
. . . with the following set of binary (on/off) signals	
$SMCO$	Minimum engine oil pressure
$SMCP$	Min. engine fuel pressure indication
$SZFP$	Fuel filter clogging indication
$UALUP$	Air bleed valve power
$UROZ$	Starting fuel valve power

The trends of the engine automatic control signals at different operating ranges (which are related to the time of observation of the signals) are fundamental to the assessment of the engine's operating status. The maximum and steady values of the engine automatic control signals are verified with their acceleration and deceleration [11].

3.3 PROBLEMS OF JET ENGINE OPERATION DURING GROUND AND FLIGHT TESTS

- Significant differences in performance are often present between individual engines of the same type. The differences are noticeable by aircraft pilots and can stem from many root causes (the manufacturing process of engine components, operating hours, overhauls, past periodic maintenance sessions, and regulations). These differences cause uncertainty of the pilots about the fact that engines of the same type will react differently to the same input functions from sources such as firing missiles, intake of jet blasts another aircraft's engine, advanced piloting manoeuvres, crosswind. (for example, some aircraft suffer from an engine stall when firing a missile, while other aircraft units are unaffected by this issue).

The difference in responses to interference (in engines of the same type identical nominal characteristics and which have been correctly regulated during ground tests) combined with the short distances between the individual aircraft units in group flight may give rise to premises that aircraft accidents can occur [11, 12, 17–23].

A method is therefore sought to provide precise information about engine behaviour as needed by the pilot in flight, preferably obtained already during ground testing of engines. This information will allow the aircraft to be better prepared for flight.

3.4   SIMULATION TESTING OF TURBINE JET ENGINES FROM SIGNAL *W* ON THE GROUND AND FROM SIGNAL *Z* IN FLIGHT

- During ground tests, maintenance personnel acts on the engine with signal *w* which is easily input to the engine regulator with the engine control lever (*DSS*). When the aircraft is in flight, the environment acts on the engine with signal *z* input to the regulated object (Figure 3.4). The primary task of aircraft maintenance is to establish the relationship between the system's follow-up (the response to *w*) and the system's resistance to disturbance (the response to *z*).

For this purpose, a simplified analogue model of the automatic control system of the rotational speed of a turbine jet engine was built to test it both from the value set with the engine control lever, *DSS* (input *w*), and from the disturbance (interference) value (input *z*) (Figure 3.4).

The simplified model of the turbine jet engine presented here facilitates studying the response of the turbine jet engine to a setting input with the *DSS* (input *w* for the ground test) and simultaneously to a disturbance (input *z* in flight).

- Jet engine performance is known to change with changes in flight parameters (e.g. altitude) [27]. The sensitivity of the engine to a change in its parameters can be described by a sensitivity function [28]. It is possible to calculate *T(H)* and *k(H)*, which are respectively the time constant and the gain of the jet engine at a certain altitude, *H*. *T(H)* and *k(H)* of the engine in flight are calculated from the following relations [9, 29]:

$$k(H) = \frac{p_H}{p_0} \cdot k \qquad (3.1)$$

$$T(H) = \frac{\sqrt{T_H/T_0}}{p_H/p_0} \cdot T \qquad (3.2)$$

where:

p_0 and p_H— respectively, the pressure on the ground and at altitude *H*
T_0 and T_H— temperature on the ground and at height *H*.

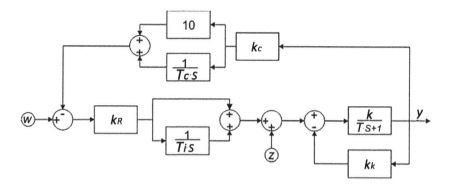

FIGURE 3.4 Simplified regulation diagram of the K-15 turbine jet engine rotational speed, with: w—setting (input with the *DSS*); z—interference (disturbance); y—engine output (rotational speed, rpm); k_R—regulator gain; T_I—regulator time constant; k_C—sender (sensor) time constant; T_C—sender (sensor) time constant; k—object gain factor; T—object time constant; k_K—object corrector time constant [based on 5, 9, 11, 24–26].

Table 3.3 shows the values of parameters $T(H)$ and $k(H)$ at altitudes $H = 0$ m, $H = 4000$ m, and $H = 8000$ m above sea level, as well as the regulator parameters k_R and T_I, the sensor constants k_C and T_C, and the corrector k_K, where the parameters are selected according to the principles of automation.

- Changes in the engine parameters that occur in flight determine the depth and extent of simulation tests (options ① to ⑤). The test program is shown in Table 3.4.

TABLE 3.3

Values of Object Parameters k and T for Altitudes $H_0 = 0$ m ASL, $H = 4000$ m ASL, and $H = 8000$ m ASL

Altitude H [m ASL = above sea level]	Temperature [K]	Pressure [Pa]	k	T	k_R	T_I	k_C	T_C	k_K
0	288.15	101327	0.45	1.7	15.6	0.68	0.1	3.5	0.075
4000	262.15	61645	0.274	2.665	25.5	1.08	0.1	3.5	0.075
8000	236.15	35606	0.158	4.380	44.3	1.76	0.1	3.5	0.075

For the adopted parameters of the object shown in Table 3.3, the step responses of the engine to the input function of setting w and disturbance z were determined according to the test program shown in Table 3.4.

TABLE 3.4

Simulation test Program

No.	H	k	T	k_R	T_i	$k_R\downarrow$	$T_i\downarrow$	$k_R\uparrow$	$T_i\uparrow$	$k_R\uparrow$	$T_i\downarrow$	$k_R\downarrow$	$T_i\uparrow$
1		0.36	1.36	15.6	0.68	12.48	0.544	18.72	0.816	18.72	0.544	12.48	0.816
2	0	0.45	1.7	15.6	0.68	12.48	0.544	18.72	0.816	18.72	0.544	12.48	0.816
3		0.54	2.04	15.6	0.68	12.48	0.544	18.72	0.816	18.72	0.544	12.48	0.816
4		0.328	2.132	25.5	1.08	20.4	0.864	30.6	1.296	30.6	0.864	20.4	1.296
5	4000	0.274	2.665	25.5	1.08	20.4	0.864	30.6	1.296	30.6	0.864	20.4	1.296
6		0.219	3.198	25.5	1.08	20.4	0.864	30.6	1.296	30.6	0.864	20.4	1.296
7		0.189	3.504	44.3	1.76	35.44	1.408	53.16	2.112	53.16	1.408	35.44	2.112
8	8000	0.158	4.38	44.3	1.76	35.44	1.408	53.16	2.112	53.16	1.408	35.44	2.112
9		0.126	5.256	44.3	1.76	35.44	1.408	53.16	2.112	53.16	1.408	35.44	2.112
				①		②		③		④		⑤	

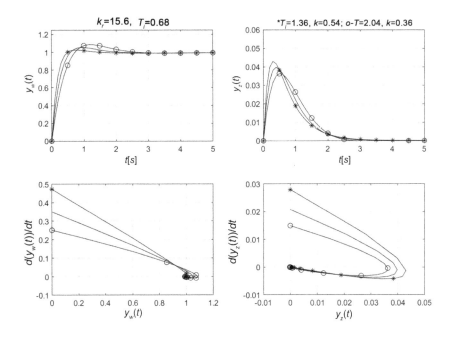

FIGURE 3.5 Step responses from w and from z with phase trajectories for the changes of parameters, with: $k_R = 15.6$, $T_i = 0.68$; $-k = 0.45$, $T = 1.7$; $\star - k = 0.54$ and $T = 1.36$; $o - k = 0.36$ and $T = 2.04$; $H = 0$, option ①, Table 3.4.

Figures 3.5–3.9 show the simulation test results for the test program listed in Table 3.4. The responses to step input functions w—$y_w(t)$, from z—$y_z(t)$, the output signals from the regulator, $u_w(t)$, $u_z(t)$, and the phase trajectories are presented.

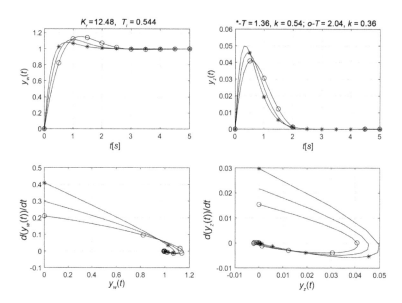

FIGURE 3.6 Step responses from w and from z with phase trajectories for the changes of parameters, with: $k_R = 12.48$, $T_i = 0.544$; $-k = 0.45$, $T = 1.7$; $\star - k = 0.54$ and $T = 1.36$; $o - k = 0.36$ and $T = 2.04$; $H = 0$, option ②, Table 3.4.

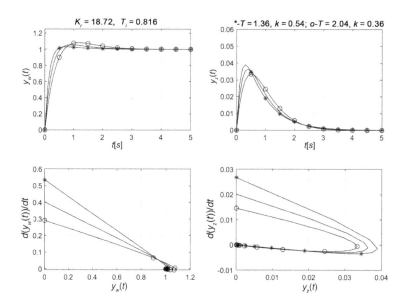

FIGURE 3.7 Step responses from w and from z with phase trajectories for the changes of parameters, with: $k_R = 18.72$, $T_i = 0.816$; $-k = 0.45$, $T = 1.7$; $\star - k = 0.54$ and $T = 1.36$; $o - k = 0.36$ and $T = 2.04$; $H = 0$, option ③, Table 3.4.

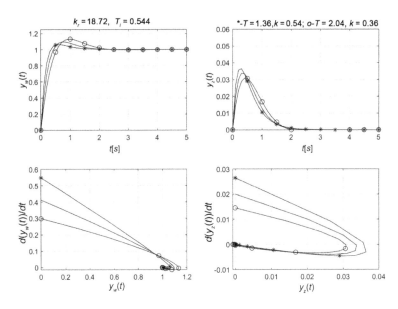

FIGURE 3.8 Step responses from w and from z with phase trajectories for the changes of parameters, with: $k_R = 18.72$, $T_i = 0.544$; $-k = 0.45$, $T = 1.7$; $\star - k = 0.54$ and $T = 1.36$; $o - k = 0.36$ and $T = 2.04$; $H = 0$, option ④, Table 3.4.

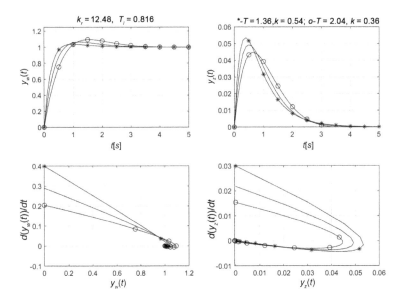

FIGURE 3.9 Step responses from w and from z with phase trajectories for the changes of parameters, with: $k_R = 18.72$, $T_i = 0.544$; $-k = 0.45$, $T = 1.7$; $\star - k = 0.54$ and $T = 1.36$; $o - k = 0.36$ and $T = 2.04$; $H = 0$, option ⑤, Table 3.4.

TABLE 3.5
Maximum Values for the Step Input Function from *w* and from *z*

No.	H	k	T	H_w					H_z				
				①	②	③	④	⑤	①	②	③	④	⑤
1		0.36	1.36	1.024	1.080	1.030	1.065	1.037	0.043	0.050	0.039	0.037	0.053
2	0	0.45	1.7	1.053	1.115	1.054	1.097	1.065	0.040	0.046	0.036	0.034	0.049
3		0.54	2.04	1.085	1.152	1.081	1.131	1.094	0.036	0.041	0.033	0.031	0.045
4		0.328	2.132	1.049	1.080	1.008	1.065	1.037	0.027	0.031	0.023	0.023	0.033
5	4000	0.274	2.665	1.079	1.115	1.031	1.096	1.065	0.025	0.028	0.022	0.021	0.030
6		0.219	3.198	1.110	1.152	1.058	1.131	1.094	0.023	0.025	0.020	0.019	0.027
7		0.189	3.504	1.031	1.081	1.031	1.067	1.039	0.015	0.018	0.014	0.013	0.019
8	8000	0.158	4.38	1.060	1.117	1.055	1.098	1.066	0.014	0.016	0.013	0.012	0.017
9		0.126	5.256	1.092	1.154	1.082	1.132	1.096	0.013	0.014	0.012	0.011	0.016

TABLE 3.6
Stabilisation Time t_p[s] for Step Input Function from *w* and from *z*

No.	H	K	T	H_w					H_z				
				①	②	③	④	⑤	①	②	③	④	⑤
1		0.495	1.53	0.94	1.62	1.17	1.29	1.64	2.93	2.08	3.42	2.16	3.45
2	0	0.45	1.7	1.59	2.02	1.85	1.65	2.36	2.73	1.94	3.33	1.98	3.25
3		0.405	1.87	2.17	2.46	2.44	2.02	3.02	2.50	3.54	3.11	2.62	3.06
4		0.246	2.399	2.34	2.57	0.69	2.05	2.60	4.44	3.30	5.71	3.44	5.48
5	4000	0.274	2.665	3.15	3.20	2.15	2.62	3.75	4.14	3.08	5.59	3.15	5.17
6		0.301	2.931	3.93	3.90	3.32	3.20	4.79	3.87	5.60	5.24	4.08	4.86
7		0.142	3.942	2.92	4.23	3.13	3.38	4.35	7.60	5.35	8.83	5.59	8.90
8	8000	0.158	4.380	4.61	5.25	4.85	4.30	6.18	7.12	5.01	8.59	5.12	8.38
9		0.174	4.818	6.10	6.38	6.36	5.25	7.86	6.52	9.16	8.02	6.79	7.89

The basic quality indicators of the speed output trend from the step change *w* and *z* are shown in Tables 3.5 and 3.6.

A study of the test results shown in Table 3.5 reveals, for example, that with *H* = 0 and a change in *k* and *T* at # 2 and # 1 of option ①, there is an improvement of the maximum value from 1.053 to 1.024 caused by the input function w and a simultaneous deterioration from 0.040 to 0.043 caused by disturbance *z*.

A study of the test results shown in Table 3.6 reveals, for example, that with *H* = 4000 and # 4 and case ① (Table 3.4), there is a stabilisation time for the signal from w equal to 2.34 s (improvement) and for the signal from z equal to 4.44 s (degradation), while for case ② (Table 3.4) the stabilisation time for the signal from *w* is 2.57 s (there is deterioration with respect to ①) and for the signal from z is 3.30 s (there is improvement with respect to ①). Therefore, it can be clearly stated that the improvement of the regulation status "on the ground" means also the deterioration of the regulation "in flight", and that the regulation "on the ground" should be carried out considering the behaviour of the engine in flight.

3.5 ASSESSMENT METHOD FOR THE TURBINE JET ENGINE PERFORMANCE IN FLIGHT BASED ON THE ENGINE'S GROUND TESTS

3.5.1 THEORETICAL FOUNDATIONS

For testing the operating quality of a turbine jet engine from z (in flight) by its tests from w (during ground tests), it is necessary to identify the transmittance of the individual components of the automatic control system of the engine. The simplified diagram of the automatic control system (UAR) of the aircraft jet engine (Figure 3.4) can be reduced to a standard diagram of an automatic control system [30, 31]. A schematic of this system is shown in Figure 3.10:

Directly from this diagram is how the components of the system and the entire system are identified.

The identification of the object from w (assuming that $z = 0$) where the input signal to the object is u and the output signal is y is to determine:

$$G_{OW} = \frac{Y}{U} \tag{3.3}$$

The identification of the regulator from w (assuming that $z = 0$) where the input signal is $w - y$, $1 - y$, or $0 - y$, and the output signal is u.

$$G_{RW} = \frac{U}{W - Y} = \frac{U}{1 - Y} = \frac{U}{-Y} \tag{3.4}$$

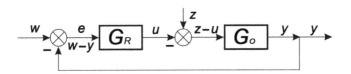

FIGURE 3.10 Structural diagram of the engine control system, with: G_R—transmittance of the regulator; G_O—transmittance of the object; w—input signal (engine control lever setting); z—input signal (disturbance/interference); y—output signal (engine speed); $e = w - y$—input signal to the regulator (regulation offset); u—output signal from the regulator (control signal) [based on 31].

The identification of the object from z (assuming that $w = 0$) where the input signal is $z - u$, 1-u or 0-y, and the output signal is y.

$$G_{OZ} = \frac{Y}{Z-U} = \frac{Y}{1-U} = \frac{Y}{-U} \qquad (3.5)$$

The identification of the regulator from z (assuming that $w = 0$) where the input signal is y, and the output signal is u.

$$G_{RZ} = \frac{U}{Y} \qquad (3.6)$$

From an analysis of Figure 3.10, the transmittances H_W (for $z = 0$) and H_Z (for $w = 0$) shown below can be obtained [9, 11, 22, 32]:

$$H_W = \frac{G_{OW}G_{RW}}{1+G_{OW}G_{RW}} \qquad (3.7)$$

$$H_Z = \frac{G_{OZ}}{1+G_{OZ}G_{RZ}} \qquad (3.8)$$

The transmittances (3.7) and (3.8) are different.

Comparing H_W to H_Z, it is found that by multiplying the transmittance H_W obtained during the ground test of the engine, by the inverse of the regulator transmittance, G_{RW} from the same ground test, it is possible to obtain transmittance H_{ZW} identical in form to transmittance H_Z, and obtained without the need for a test from z [20].

$$H_{ZW} = \frac{G_{OW}G_{RW}}{1+G_{OW}G_{RW}} \cdot \frac{1}{G_{RW}} = \frac{G_{OW}}{1+G_{OW}G_{RW}} = H_W \cdot \frac{1}{G_{RW}} = -H_Z \qquad (3.9)$$

since:

$$\frac{G_{OW}}{1+G_{OW}G_{RW}} = -\frac{G_{OZ}}{1+G_{OZ}G_{RZ}} \rightarrow G_{OW} = -G_{OZ} \rightarrow \frac{Y}{U} = -\left(-\frac{Y}{U}\right)$$

In addition, it is found that transmittances H_{ZW} and H_W are determined from the same signals, which are: y, u, and w.

Having the relations between H_{ZW} and H_W, it is feasible to find relations between transmittances H_{ZW} and H_Z, and ultimately, between transmittances H_W and H_Z.

According to the principles of automation, the transmittances of system components G_{OW}, G_{OZ}, G_{RW}, and G_{RZ} can be described by the quotient of the spectral density of the mutual power of the output and input signals, S_{yz}, S_{yw}, and S_{yu}, and the spectral density of input eigenpower S_{ww}, S_{zz}, S_{uu}, S_{yy} [20, 33]

$$G_{OW} = \frac{Y}{U} = \frac{S_{yu}}{S_{uu}} \tag{3.10}$$

$$G_{RW} = \frac{U}{W-Y} = \frac{S_{u(w-y)}}{S_{(w-y)(w-y)}} \overset{w=\delta(t)}{=} \frac{S_{u(-y)}}{S_{(-y)(-y)}} \tag{3.11}$$

$$G_{OZ} = \frac{Y}{Z-U} = \frac{S_{y(z-u)}}{S_{(z-u)(z-u)}} \overset{w=\delta(t)}{=} \frac{S_{y(-u)}}{S_{(-u)(-u)}} \tag{3.12}$$

$$G_{RZ} = \frac{U}{Y} = \frac{S_{uy}}{S_{yy}} \tag{3.13}$$

Hence, transmittances H_W, H_Z and H_{ZW} based on Formulas 3.7–3.9, assuming pulse responses y_z and y_w are sought, take this form:

$$H_W = \frac{S_{yu}S_{u(-y)}}{S_{uu}S_{yy} + S_{uy}S_{u(-y)}} \tag{3.14}$$

$$H_Z = \frac{S_{yy}S_{y(-u)}}{S_{yy}S_{uu} + S_{uy}S_{y(-u)}} = \frac{S_{yz}}{S_{zz}} \tag{3.15}$$

$$H_{ZW} = H_W \cdot \frac{1}{G_{RW}} = \frac{S_{yu}S_{yy}}{S_{uu}S_{yy} + S_{uy}S_{u(-y)}} \tag{3.16}$$

Assuming that

$$S_{u(-y)} = S_{(-y)u}$$

$$\frac{H_Z}{H_W} = \frac{S_{yy} \cdot S_{y(-u)}}{S_{yu} \cdot S_{u(-y)}} = \frac{S_{yy}}{S_{yu}} \tag{3.17}$$

Finally, a relation is obtained between transmittances H_Z and H_W and the signals measured during the ground test:

$$H_Z = H_W \cdot \frac{S_{yy}}{S_{yu}} = \frac{S_{u(-y)} \cdot S_{yy}}{S_{yy}S_{uu} + S_{uy}S_{u(-y)}} \tag{3.18}$$

Therefore, using transmittance H_{ZW}, transmittance H_Z can be determined. Ultimately, a direct relation between transmittances H_Z (the engine model in flight) and H_W (the engine model on the ground) is obtained. It is therefore possible to determine the engine characteristics from z (in flight) using the signals from w recorded during the ground test.

Transmittances H_W and H_Z describe the system in the frequency domain (ω). Based on the expressions of the real parts of the spectral transmittances $H_W(j\omega)$, $H_Z(j\omega)$, it is possible to move to the time domain (t). Response to the step input function according to the algorithm (3.19) (see Section 1.1.2, Formulas 1.27 and 1.28).

$$y_{Z_i}(t_i) = \sum_{n=1}^{n=\infty} \frac{2}{\pi} \cdot \frac{\sin(\omega_n \cdot t_i)}{\omega_n} P_{Z_i n}(\omega) \cdot \Delta\omega \qquad (3.19)$$

3.5.2   VERIFICATION OF THE OPERATING STATUS OF A TURBINE JET ENGINE ON THE GROUND FROM SIGNAL W AND IN FLIGHT FROM SIGNAL Z BASED ON THE RESPONSE FROM SIGNAL W

The operation of a turbine jet engine during ground tests (from the set signal w) and in flight (from the interference signal z) is represented by the model shown in Figure 3.4. This model can be represented as shown in Figure 3.11 for simulation [6, 9, 11, 14, 20].

An arrangement (system) that executes the multiplication of the transmittance that describes the engine during its ground test (with $z = 0$) with the inverse of the regulator transmittance $1/G_R$ (Formula 3.9) outputs signal y_{zw} (Figure 3.12) from interference z. Here, signal w mimics signal z.

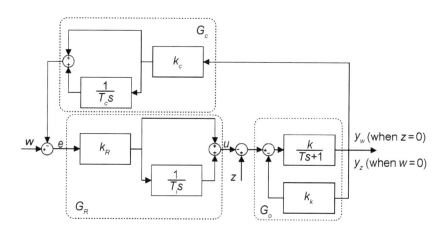

FIGURE 3.11 Simplified model of the engine speed control system, with: w—DSS setting; z—disturbance (interference) setting; y_w—response from the input function applied to the regulator; y_z—response from the input function applied directly to the object; T_p, T, and T_c—time constants of the regulator, the object and the sensor (sender), respectively; k_c, k_R, k, and k_K—gains of the engine speed control, the sensor, the regulator, the object, and the object corrector, respectively [6].

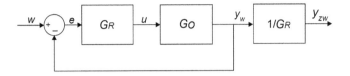

FIGURE 3.12 Simplified engine model from interference z [6].

For the adopted parameters [2, 9, 14]:

$T = 1.7$ $k = 0.45$ $k_K = 0.075$
$k_R = 15.6$ $T_I = 0.68$
$k_C = 0.1$ $T_C = 3.5$

The substitute transmittances of the system from w and from z take this form:

$$H_W(s) = \frac{y_w}{w} = \frac{16.71s^2 + 29.34s + 7.02}{4.046s^3 + 20.32s^2 + 30.52s + 7.722} \qquad (3.20)$$

$$H_Z(s) = \frac{y_z}{z} = \frac{1.071s^2 + 0.306}{4.046s^3 + 20.32s^2 + 30.52s + 7.722} \qquad (3.21)$$

In order to prove the correctness of the transformations, the operation of the system shown in Figure 3.12 was simulated for step and pulse input functions from w and from z, and the step and pulse responses were determined, see Figure 3.13.

The resulting step responses are consistent with the step responses (Figure 3.5) obtained directly from the diagram shown in Figure 3.4.

To determine the characteristics (Figure 3.13), the transmittances of the object and the regulator (Figure 3.12) need to be explicitly determined. During the ground test of the engine, signals are obtained that, when converted into their eigenpowers and reciprocal powers, facilitate the relations between them to be determined only in the form of spectral transmittances. The real parts of the transmittances determined in this way facilitate the determination of the time characteristics, like the step response. Thus, the basic problem is to determine the real part of the spectral transmittance from the power of the corresponding signals recorded during the ground test of the engine. The real parts of the spectral transmittance of the system in Figure 3.12 were determined using the corresponding signals from Figure 3.13 and signal $z(t)=1(t)$ see Figure 3.14.

(a) $P_{Z1}(\omega) = real(\dfrac{S_{y_{zw}z}(\omega)}{S_{y_{zw}y_{zw}}(\omega)})$ – real part of the transmittance from signal z obtained directly from the substitute transmittance of the system—Figure 3.12 (Formula 3.15);

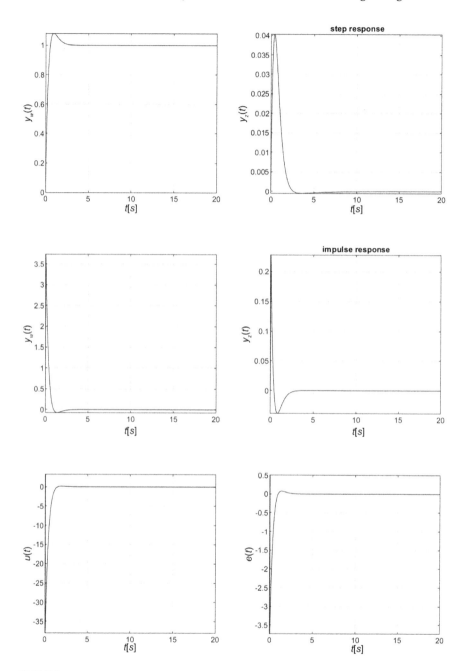

FIGURE 3.13 Response to step and pulse inputs from w and z determined from Formulas 3.20 and 3.21 and based on the block diagrams in Figures 3.12 and 3.10.

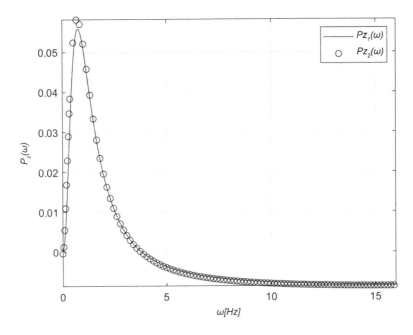

FIGURE 3.14 Comparison of the real parts of the spectral transmittances obtained from the pulse input function.

(b) $P_{Z2}(\omega) = real(\dfrac{S_{y_w w}(\omega)}{S_{ww}(\omega)}\dfrac{S_{ee}(\omega)}{S_{ue}(\omega)})$ – real part of the transmittance from signal z obtained from response signals from w using regulator signals e and u—Figure 3.12 (Formula 3.16).

$$P_{Z1}(\omega) = real(\dfrac{S_{y_{zw} z}(\omega)}{S_{y_{zw} y_{zw}}(\omega)}), \text{ and } P_{Z2}(\omega) = real(\dfrac{S_{y_w w}(\omega)}{S_{ww}(\omega)}\dfrac{S_{ee}(\omega)}{S_{ue}(\omega)})$$

A calculation was then performed to move from the frequency domain to the time domain (Figure 3.19). The results obtained were compared with $y_z(t)$ which is the response to the step input of transmittance H_Z (Formula 3.21) shown in Figure 3.15.

According to the completed simulation test, it is found that the step responses obtained directly from transmittance $H_Z(s)$, resulting from the block diagram transformation (Formula 3.21), and from spectral transmittance $H_{Z1}(j\omega)$ and spectral transmittance $H_{Z2}(j\omega)$ (Figure 3.14) using the measurable signals u and y are the same. This means that signal power S_{uy}, $S_{u(-y)}$, S_{yy}, S_{uu} linked to setting w facilitate the step responses from the unavailable signal z to be determined.

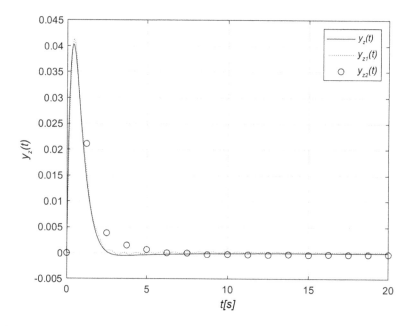

FIGURE 3.15 Comparison of the response to step input function, where $y_z(t)$ from the response of transmittance $H_z(s)$ (Formula 3.19), $y_{z1}(t)$ results from applying Formula 3.19 and the real part of transmittance $P_{Z1}(\omega)$; $y_{z2}(t)$—results from Formula 3.19 and the real part of transmittance $P_{Z2}(\omega)$.

As a result of the completed research, it can be concluded that it is feasible to assess the regulation status of the engine in flight based only on its ground tests. As a result of the completed simulation test, it was found that the transmittance of the engine determined during the ground test, H_W, and the inverse of regulator transmittance, $1/G_R$, also determined during the same ground test, allow to obtain transmittance H_Z which is the model of the engine in flight. It was also demonstrated that the necessary transmittances, H_W and H_Z, can be determined based on the power density of the signals recorded only during ground tests (Formulas 3.14 and 3.18). The correctness of the transformations was proven by the simulation (Figure 3.15).

3.6 THEORETICAL FOUNDATIONS FOR GENERATING MODIFIED SIGNALS WHICH DESCRIBE ENGINE INPUTS AND OUTPUTS

- In the process of assessing the regulation status of the engine (Figure 3.16), four basic signals are considered [5, 12, 23, 25, 34]:
  - p_2— compressor downstream air pressure (input signal)
  - m_p— injection fuel pressure differential (input signal)

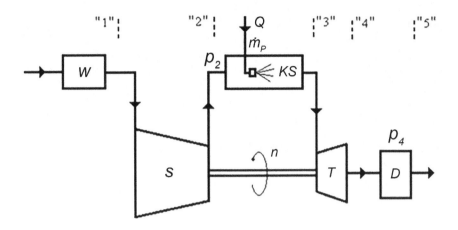

FIGURE 3.16 Engine regulation diagram (with: *w*—intake; *S*—compressor; *KS*—combustor; *T*—turbine; *D*—exhaust/nozzle; *1,2,3,4,5*—characteristic cross-sectional views) [5].

- p_4— engine exhaust gas nozzle pressure (output signal)
- *n*— engine speed (output signal)

- To assess the performance quality of the engine, all the relations between the main signals are tested, which are described by the following transmittances [5, 12, 14, 25, 35]:

$$G_{1m_p} = \frac{\Delta n}{\Delta m_p} \tag{3.22}$$

$$G_{1p_2} = \frac{\Delta n}{\Delta p_2} \tag{3.23}$$

$$G_{2m_p} = \frac{\Delta p_4}{\Delta m_p} \tag{3.24}$$

$$G_{2p_2} = \frac{\Delta p_4}{\Delta p_2} \tag{3.25}$$

It is assumed that it is possible to reduce the model in the form of four transmittances to one comprehensive model with such a preferable property that the engine performance quality determined during ground tests will also provide the required knowledge of its performance quality in flight.

Following the removal of inputs Δn and Δp_4 from Formulas 3.22 to 3.25, the following is obtained:

$$G_{1m_p p_2} = \frac{\Delta m_p}{\Delta p_2} \tag{3.26}$$

$$G_{2 p_2 m_p} = \frac{\Delta m_p}{\Delta p_2} \tag{3.27}$$

Next, input signals Δm_p and Δp_2 removed, by which Formulas 3.22 to 3.25 provide the following:

$$G_{1np_4} = \frac{\Delta n}{\Delta p_4} \tag{3.28}$$

$$G_{2np_4} = \frac{\Delta n}{\Delta p_4} \tag{3.29}$$

It follows from the above relations that it is correct to replace the input and output signals of a turbine jet engine speed control system with modified signals:

$$u = mp_2 = m_P / p_2 \tag{3.30}$$

$$y = np_4 = n / p_4 \tag{3.31}$$

These signals describe all the basic recorded input and output quantities of the turbine jet engine and significantly simplify its description with the spectral power densities of the signals (Formulas 3.14 and 3.18).

3.7 ASSESSMENT OF THE REGULATION QUALITY OF A TURBINE JET ENGINE IN FLIGHT BASED ON ITS GROUND TESTS

- The regulation quality assessment for a turbine jet engine was completed with the trends of the signals recorded during standard ground tests (Figure 3.17).

From the range of the signals recorded during the ground tests, the following will be used for further analysis: DSS (engine control lever position/setting), p_2, m_p, p_4, and n.

These signals are normalised and then modified signals are generated from them—$u = m_p/p_2$ (describing the engine input) and $y = n/p_4$ (describing the engine output) according to the relations (Formulas 3.30 and 3.31).

The next step is to calculate signal e which is input to the regulator. The signal is the difference between the signal input set with the engine control lever (DSS) and the output signal represented by modified signal $y = n/p_4$.

$$e = -y \tag{3.32}$$

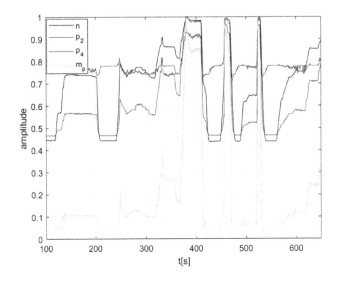

FIGURE 3.17 Real trends of normalised (relative) signals recorded during a ground test of the jet engine [11].

The signals are divided into intervals of different duration, defined according to the trend of the *DSS* input function signal, as shown in Figure 3.18.

The obtained signals are shaped with the Hanning window of a certain width; next, the necessary self-correlations are calculated with cross-correlations of the signals are calculated (Figure 3.10): R_{yu}, R_{ee}, R_{uu}, and R_{ue}.

By applying the Fast Fourier Transform *(FFT)*, the spectral densities of eigen-power and reciprocal power are obtained.

$$R_{ee} \xrightarrow{\ FFT\ } S_{ee} \tag{3.33}$$

$$R_{yu} \xrightarrow{\ FFT\ } S_{yu} \tag{3.34}$$

$$R_{uu} \xrightarrow{\ FFT\ } S_{uu} \tag{3.35}$$

$$R_{ue} \xrightarrow{\ FFT\ } S_{ue} \tag{3.36}$$

Next, using the relations (3.14) and (3.18) and with the assumption in 3.32, the real parts of the spectral transmittance $P_W(\omega)$ and $P_Z(\omega)$ are calculated.

$$P_W(\omega) = real\left(\frac{S_{yu}S_{ue}}{S_{uu}S_{ee} + S_{yu}S_{ue}}\right) \tag{3.37}$$

$$P_Z(\omega) = real\left(\frac{S_{yy}S_{ue}}{S_{yy}S_{uu} + S_{uy}S_{ue}}\right) \tag{3.38}$$

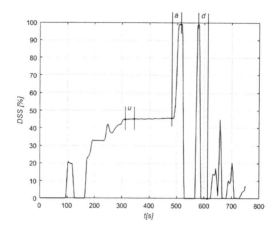

FIGURE 3.18 *DSS* displacement trend, recorded during a ground test of the turbine jet engine, with: *a*—test interval for acceleration; *d*—deceleration; *u*—steady state.

Using the transition from the frequency domain *(ω)* to the time domain *(t)* according to these Formulas:

$$y_W(t) = \frac{2}{\pi}\int_0^{\omega_n} P_W(\omega)\frac{\sin(\omega t)}{\omega}d\omega \tag{3.39}$$

$$y_Z(t) = \frac{2}{\pi}\int_0^{\omega_n} P_Z(\omega)\frac{\sin(\omega t)}{\omega}d\omega \tag{3.40}$$

The trends are obtained for step input response in the time domain from the input function applied to the controller (y_w) and from the input function applied to the object (the interferences) (y_z).

The calculations were performed out according to an algorithm (based on Formula 3.17):

$$y_W(t_i) = \sum_{n=1}^{n=\infty}\frac{2}{\pi}\cdot\frac{\sin(\omega_n\cdot t_i)}{\omega_n}P_{Wn}(\omega)\cdot\Delta\omega \tag{3.41}$$

$$y_Z(t_i) = \sum_{n=1}^{n=\infty}\frac{2}{\pi}\cdot\frac{\sin(\omega_n\cdot t_i)}{\omega_n}P_{Zn}(\omega)\cdot\Delta\omega \tag{3.42}$$

Formulas 3.41 and 3.42 allow the step response of the turbine jet engine to be determined both during the ground test (y_w) from an input function applied to the regulator and during flight (y_z) from the interferences acting directly on the object.

These calculations facilitate transition from the frequency domain, where the spectral transmittances are identified, to the time domain, which allows the determination of the determined characteristics of the engine in the time domain to permit the performance quality of the engine to be assessed in the particular test intervals shown in Figure 3.18.

3.8 TESTING THE EFFECT OF INPUT AND OUTPUT CHANGES ON THE CHARACTERISTICS OF A TURBINE JET ENGINE

3.8.1 TEST PROGRAM

- From the trends of the signals recorded during the ground tests of turbine jet engine (Figure 3.17) with a sampling rate of 1/16 s, the signals were separated (according to Figure 3.18) into 3 characteristic intervals according to the values of the displacement ratio of the engine control lever *(DSS)*. These three intervals include: acceleration, deceleration, and steady state of the engine. The division of the engine signal trends is shown in Table 3.7.

Each of the time intervals was processed as follows:

(a) the signals were normalised so that their trends ranged from the minimum value to 1;
(b) for each of the intervals, the effect of variations in the individual signals on the engine performance quality (the quality of characteristics) was calculated.

The effect of the change of signals on the engine performance quality was tested separately for each signal. Changes were made by increasing or decreasing the signal value by 5%. The changes were made according to Table 3.8.

The effect of simultaneous changes of two signals by ±5% on the engine performance quality was tested according to the scheme in Table 3.9.

TABLE 3.7

Signal Observation Intervals Used in the Engine Tests

Interval designation	DSS displacement [%]		Duration [s]
	From	To	
1. Steady state, u	37	50	33
2. Acceleration, a	36	100	33
3. Deceleration, d	100	0	33

TABLE 3.8

Test Program for Changes of a Single Signal in Set $\{m_p, n, p_2, p_4\}$

Tested parameters	m_p			p_2			n			p_4		
Parameter change method	$0.95 \cdot m_p$	m_p	$1.05 \cdot m_p$	$0.95 \cdot p_2$	p_2	$1.05 \cdot p_2$	$0.95 \cdot n$	n	$1.05 \cdot n$	$0.95 \cdot p_4$	p_4	$1.05 \cdot p_4$
Parameters unchanged	n, p_2, p_4			m_p, n, p_4			m_p, p_2, p_4			m_p, n, p_2		

TABLE 3.9

Test Program for Simultaneous Change of Two Signals in Set

Tested parameters	n, m_p	n, p_2	n, p_4	p_2, m_p	p_4, m_p	p_4, p_2
Changes of parameters	$0.95{\cdot}n,\ 1.05{\cdot}m_p$; $1.05{\cdot}n,\ 0.95{\cdot}m_p$	$0.95{\cdot}n,\ 1.05\,p_2$; $1.05{\cdot}n,\ 0.95\,p_2$	$0.95{\cdot}n,\ 1.05{\cdot}p_4$; $1.05{\cdot}n,\ 0.95\,p_4$	$0.95{\cdot}p_2,\ 1.05{\cdot}m_p$; $1.05{\cdot}p_2,\ 0.95{\cdot}m_p$	$0.95{\cdot}p_4,\ 1.05{\cdot}m_p$; $1.05{\cdot}p_4,\ 0.95{\cdot}m_p$	$0.95{\cdot}p_4,\ 1.05{\cdot}p_2$; $1.05{\cdot}p_4,\ 0.95{\cdot}p_2$
Parameters unchanged	p_2, p_4	m_p, p_4	m_p, p_2	n, p_4	n, p_2	n, m_p

(c) modulated signals $u = mp_2$ (describing the engine input) and $y = np_4$, and the signal describing the regulator input, $e = -y$ were determined;
(d) the modified signals u and y were determined and e were shaped using the Hanning window;
(e) the necessary self-correlations and cross-correlations were determined: R_{yu}, R_{ee}, R_{uu};
(f) the required eigen and reciprocal spectral densities S_{yu}, S_{ee}, S_{uu}, and S_{ue} were determined;
(g) the spectral transmittances $Hw(j\omega)$ and $H_z(j\omega)$ were determined;
(h) the real parts of spectral transmittance $P_w(\omega)$ and $P_z(\omega)$ were determined;
(i) the time responses to step inputs $y_w(t)$ and $y_z(t)$ were determined;
(j) the phase portraits of the engine with the Lyapunov functions related to the energy feed of the engine (Formula 1.25) were determined.

3.8.2 Test Results

Acceleration—a—displacement of the *DSS* lever from 45% to 100% during 33 s.
An analysis of the Figures 3.21–3.25 and the test results shown in Tables 3.10 and 3.11 reveals the following:

1. Table 3.10— changing p_4 to 0.95 p_4 results in a change from 0.585 to 0.570 (an improvement) for steady state u from setting w, yet from z there is a change from 0.590 to 0.605 (a deterioration).
2. Table 3.10— changing p_2 to 1.05 p_2 does not change the signal from w for u, but it strongly affects the change from z (change from 0.590 to 0.620).
3. Table 3.10— changing p_2 to 1.05 p_2 and m_p to 0.95 m_p results in no change of the maximum value for d from w and from z, the maximum value changes from 0.59 to 0.652.
4. Table 3.11— changing p_4 to 0.95 p_4 results in a change from 0.472 to 0.460 (an improvement) for steady state u from setting w, yet from z there is a change from 0.476 to 0.488 (a deterioration).

This means that minimal regulation errors causing random changes in p_2, p_4, m_p, and n cause mostly small changes in the "ground test" regulation quality indicators from w and mostly large changes in the "in flight" regulation quality indicators from z. It is also seen that the improvement of the "on ground" quality indicators is detrimental to the "in flight" counterparts.

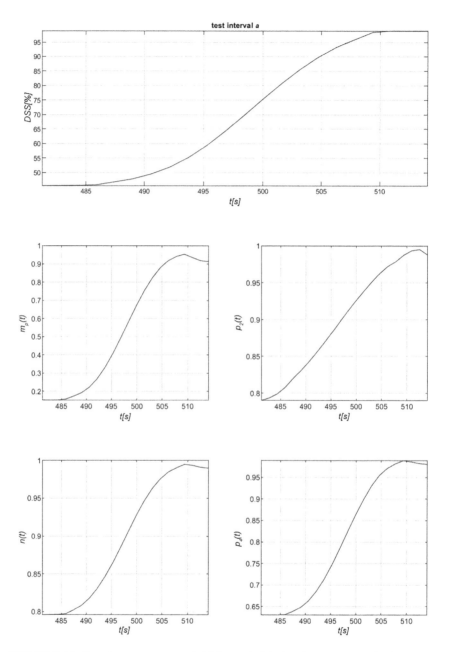

FIGURE 3.19 Signals n, m_p, p_2, p_4, and DSS recorded during the ground test for interval a.

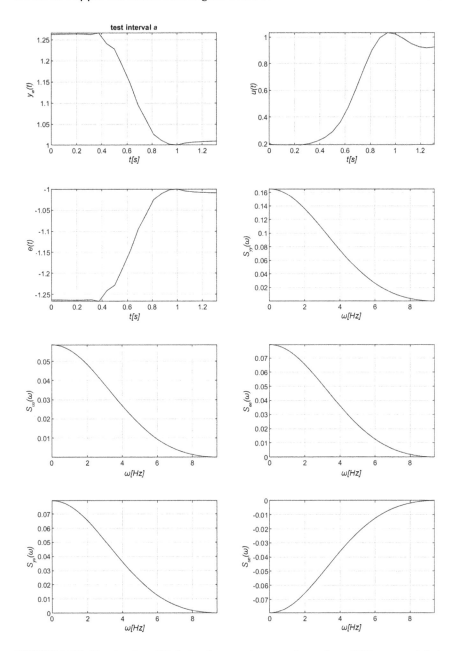

FIGURE 3.20 Trends of modified signals $u = m/p_2$, $y = n/p_4$, and $e = DSS - np_4$ and their eigen- and reciprocal power spectral densities for interval a.

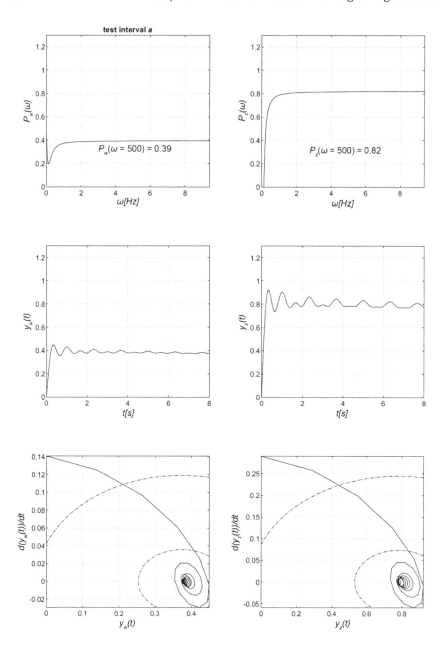

FIGURE 3.21 Trends of the amplitude gain real part $P_w(\omega)$, $P_z(\omega)$ and of responses $y_w(t)$ and $y_z(t)$ for interval a.

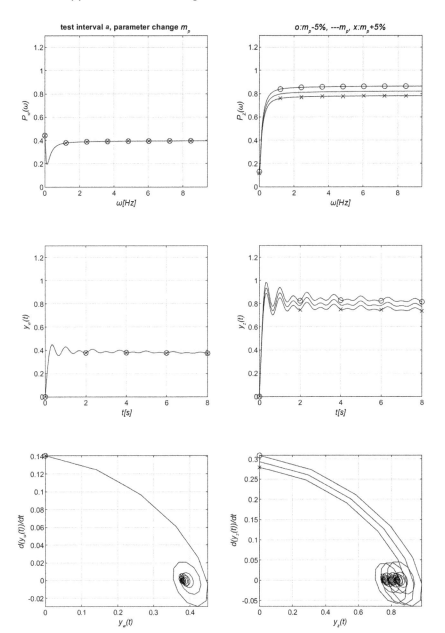

FIGURE 3.22 Effect of signal m_p changes on the trends of the amplitude gain real part $P_w(\omega)$, $P_z(\omega)$ and of responses $y_w(t)$ and $y_z(t)$ for interval a.

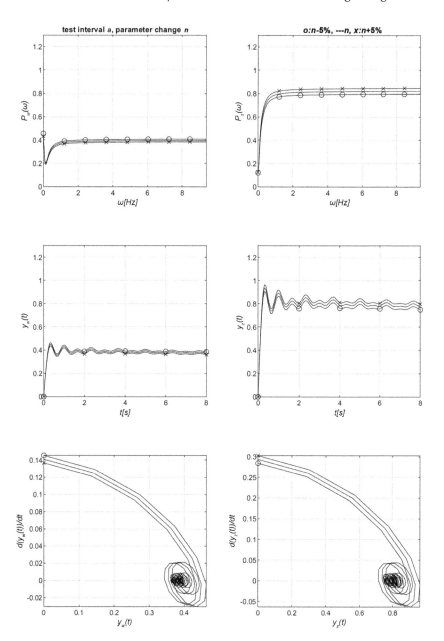

FIGURE 3.23 Effect of signal n changes on the of the amplitude gain real part $P_w(\omega)$, $P_z(\omega)$ and of responses $y_w(t)$ and $y_z(t)$ for interval a.

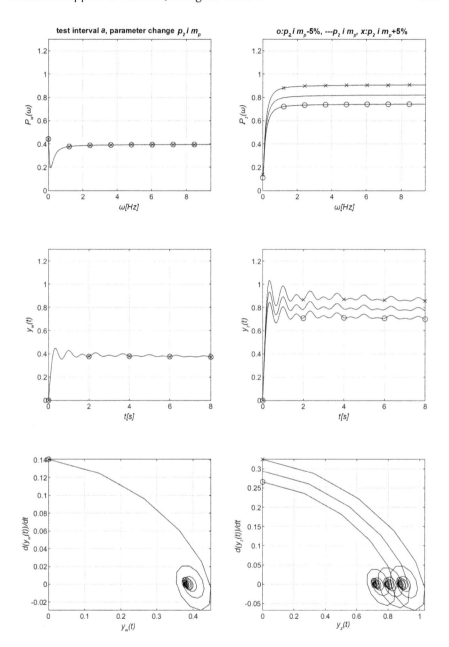

FIGURE 3.24 Effect of the simultaneous change of signals p_2 and m_p on the trends of the amplitude gain real part $P_w(\omega)$, $P_z(\omega)$ and of responses $y_w(t)$ and $y_z(t)$ for interval a.

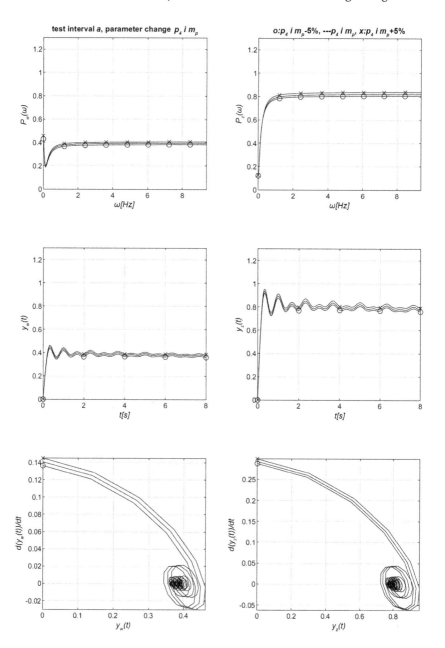

FIGURE 3.25 Effect of the simultaneous change of signals p_4 and m_p on the trends of the amplitude gain real part $P_w(\omega)$, $P_z(\omega)$ and of responses $y_w(t)$ and $y_z(t)$ for interval a.

TABLE 3.10

Summary of the Maximum Values of Signals y_w and y_z for Different Options of Single Signal Changes (per the test program in Table 3.8)

Parameter change	Maximum values from w			Maximum values from z		
	U	a	d	U	a	d
$0.95 \cdot p_4$	0.570	0.434	0.337	0.605	0.964	1.243
p_4	0.585	0.448	0.349	0.590	0.934	1.200
$1.05 \cdot p_4$	0.599	0.462	0.361	0.576	0.906	1.160
$0.95 \cdot p_2$	0.585	0.448	0.349	0.561	0.888	1.140
p_2	0.585	0.448	0.349	0.590	0.934	1.200
$1.05 \cdot p_2$	0.585	0.448	0.349	0.620	0.981	1.260
$0.95 \cdot m_p$	0.585	0.448	0.349	0.621	0.984	1.263
m_p	0.585	0.448	0.349	0.590	0.934	1.200
$1.05 \, m_p$	0.585	0.448	0.349	0.562	0.890	1.143
$0.95 \cdot n$	0.600	0.462	0.362	0.575	0.905	1.158
n	0.585	0.448	0.349	0.590	0.934	1.200
$1.05 \cdot n$	0.571	0.435	0.338	0.605	0.963	1.241
$0.95 \cdot p_4, \, 1.05 \cdot p_2$	0.570	0.434	0.337	0.636	1.013	1.305
$p_4, \, p_2$	0.585	0.448	0.349	0.590	0.934	1.200
$1.05 \cdot p_4, \, 0.95 \cdot p_2$	0.599	0.462	0.361	0.547	0.861	1.102
$0.95 \cdot p_2, \, 1.05 \cdot m_p$	0.585	0.448	0.349	0.534	0.845	1.086
$p_2, \, m_p$	0.585	0.448	0.349	0.590	0.934	1.200
$1.05 \cdot p_2, \, 0.95 \cdot m_p$	0.585	0.448	0.349	0.652	1.033	1.326
$0.95 \cdot p_4, \, 1.05 \cdot m_p$	0.570	0.434	0.337	0.576	0.919	1.183
$p_4, \, m_p$	0.585	0.448	0.349	0.590	0.934	1.200
$1.05 \cdot p_4, \, 0.95 \cdot m_p$	0.599	0.462	0.361	0.606	0.954	1.221
$0.95 \cdot n, \, 1.05 \cdot p_4$	0.614	0.476	0.374	0.561	0.877	1.119
$n, \, p_4$	0.585	0.448	0.349	0.590	0.934	1.200
$1.05 \cdot n, \, 0.95 \cdot p_4$	0.556	0.421	0.326	0.620	0.993	1.284
$0.95 \cdot n, \, 1.05 \cdot p_2$	0.600	0.462	0.362	0.604	0.950	1.216
$n, \, p_2$	0.585	0.448	0.349	0.590	0.934	1.200
$1.05 \cdot n, \, 0.95 \cdot p_2$	0.571	0.435	0.338	0.574	0.915	1.179
$0.95 \cdot n, \, 1.05 \cdot m_p$	0.600	0.462	0.362	0.548	0.862	1.103
$n, \, m_p$	0.585	0.448	0.349	0.590	0.934	1.200
$1.05 \cdot n, \, 0.95 \cdot m_p$	0.571	0.435	0.338	0.636	1.014	1.306

TABLE 3.11

Summary of the Reaction Time Values for Signals y_w and y_z for Different Options of Two Signals Changes (per the Test Program in Table 3.9)

Parameter change	Reaction times from w			Reaction times from z		
	U	a	d	U	a	d
$0.95 \cdot p_4$	0.460	0.361	0.278	0.488	0.798	1.020
p_4	0.472	0.373	0.288	0.476	0.774	0.985

(Continued)

TABLE 3.11 (*Continued*)
Summary of the Reaction Time Values for Signals y_w and y_z for Different Options of two signals Changes (per the test program in Table 3.9)

Parameter change	Reaction times from w			Reaction times from z		
	U	a	d	U	a	d
$1.05 \cdot p_4$	0.483	0.384	0.298	0.464	0.751	0.952
$0.95 \cdot p_2$	0.472	0.373	0.288	0.452	0.735	0.936
p_2	0.472	0.373	0.288	0.476	0.774	0.985
$1.05 \cdot p_2$	0.472	0.373	0.288	0.500	0.812	1.034
$0.95 \cdot m_p$	0.472	0.373	0.288	0.501	0.815	1.037
m_p	0.472	0.373	0.288	0.476	0.774	0.985
$1.05\ m_p$	0.472	0.373	0.288	0.453	0.737	0.938
$0.95 \cdot n$	0.484	0.384	0.298	0.464	0.750	0.950
N	0.472	0.373	0.288	0.476	0.774	0.985
$1.05 \cdot n$	0.460	0.362	0.278	0.487	0.797	1.018
$0.95 \cdot p_4, 1.05 \cdot p_2$	0.460	0.361	0.278	0.512	0.838	1.071
p_4, p_2	0.472	0.373	0.288	0.476	0.774	0.985
$1.05 \cdot p_4, 0.95 \cdot p_2$	0.483	0.384	0.298	0.441	0.714	0.904
$0.95 \cdot p_2, 1.05 \cdot m_p$	0.472	0.373	0.288	0.430	0.700	0.891
p_2, m_p	0.472	0.373	0.288	0.476	0.774	0.985
$1.05 \cdot p_2, 0.95 \cdot m_p$	0.472	0.373	0.288	0.526	0.855	1.088
$0.95 \cdot p_4, 1.05 \cdot m_p$	0.460	0.361	0.278	0.465	0.760	0.972
p_4, m_p	0.472	0.373	0.288	0.476	0.774	0.985
$1.05 \cdot p_4, 0.95 \cdot m_p$	0.483	0.384	0.298	0.489	0.791	1.002
$0.95 \cdot n, 1.05 \cdot p_4$	0.495	0.395	0.308	0.452	0.727	0.918
n, p_4	0.472	0.373	0.288	0.476	0.774	0.985
$1.05 \cdot n, 0.95 \cdot p_4$	0.448	0.350	0.268	0.500	0.821	1.055
$0.95 \cdot n, 1.05 \cdot p_2$	0.484	0.384	0.298	0.487	0.787	0.997
n, p_2	0.472	0.373	0.288	0.476	0.774	0.985
$1.05 \cdot n, 0.95 \cdot p_2$	0.460	0.362	0.278	0.463	0.757	0.968
$0.95 \cdot n, 1.05 \cdot m_p$	0.484	0.384	0.298	0.442	0.714	0.905
n, m_p	0.472	0.373	0.288	0.476	0.774	0.985
$1.05 \cdot n, 0.95 \cdot m_p$	0.460	0.362	0.278	0.513	0.839	1.072

3.9　SUMMARY

The regulation of aircraft jet engines is carried out during the ground test from *w*. The dynamic quality of the engine "on the ground" is determined. During the test flight of the aircraft, which follows the ground test (with the former necessary after every repair), the "in flight" engine dynamic quality is determined. The physical testing "on the ground" and "in flight" is a very complicated, labour-intensive, expensive, and risky process, because there is never enough certainty that the engine that has been correctly regulated from w ("on the ground") will also be correctly adjusted from z ("in flight").

Hence, the idea emerged to determine as accurately as possible the determined characteristics of the engine in flight from disturbance signal z based on the trends of the turbine jet engine regulation signals recorded during ground tests from setting w, input to the regulator by operating the *DSS*, and to determine the phase portraits of the engine with the time of transition of the engine state vector between its different energy states defined by Lyapunov functions.

During ground tests, signals $p_2(t)$, $m_p(t)$, $p_4(t)$, $n(t)$ are recorded, which are difficult to convert to typical engine characteristics in time t. Also, their operator forms, $p_2(s)$, $m_p(s)$, $p_4(s)$, $n(s)$ cannot be interpreted. All these difficulties are solved by moving from the time domain t to the frequency domain ω.

A modified signal, $u = m_p/p_2$ is formed from signals $p_2(t)$ and $m_p(t)$ to describe the input of the system, while a modified signal $y = n/p_4$ is formed from signals $p_4(t)$ and $n(t)$ to describe the output of the system; also, signal $e = -y$ is formed.

Using the modified signals as the inputs to determine the self and cross-correlation functions, which are used in turn to determine the spectral power functions signals $(S_{yu}, S_{ee}, S_{uu},$ and $S_{ue})$, it is finally possible to determine the required spectral transmittances $(H_W(j\omega)$ and $H_Z(j\omega))$.

Then, using the relations:

$$y_W(t) = \frac{2}{\pi}\int_0^{\omega_n} P_W(\omega)\frac{\sin(\omega t)}{\omega}d\omega \text{ and } y_Z(t) = \frac{2}{\pi}\int_0^{\omega_n} P_Z(\omega)\frac{\sin(\omega t)}{\omega}d\omega$$

the real parts $(P_W(\omega)$ and $P_Z(\omega))$ of the spectral transmittances are transformed into the responses to step input function, $y_w(t)$ and $y_z(t)$.

The step responses were determined for acceleration a, deceleration d, and operation at steady-state speed u.

Tests were carried out to investigate the effect of a $\pm 5\%$ change in inputs $(m_p$ and $p_2)$ and outputs $(p_4$ and $n)$ of the engine. From the characteristics obtained as a result of the tests, the regulation time values and the maximum values achieved by the step responses were determined (Tables 3.10 and 3.11).

The completed tests confirm that there is a real possibility that during ground tests the engine characteristics from w can be determined (as typical of operation on the ground) and that during ground tests the characteristics of the engine from z can also be determined (for operation in flight, which have not yet been determined).

The results obtained confirm that there are real and conflicting difficulties in regulation, because as the result of the regulation process of the characteristics from signal w improves (during ground tests), there is a deterioration of the engine characteristics from z (during the flight of the aircraft); it is still necessary to find the required optimal solution.

REFERENCES

1. Dzierżanowski P., Kordziński W., Łyżwiński M., Otyś J., Szczeciński S., Wiatrek R.: Turbinowe silniki odrzutowe. WKiŁ, Warszawa 1983.
2. Orkisz M.: Simulation analysis of the influence of variation in some selected design and control parameters on the acceleration time of a turbojet engine. Engineering Transactions, vol. 39, nos. 3–4, 1991.
3. Balicki W., Chachurski R., Głowacki P., Godzimirski J., Kawalec K., Kozakiewicz A., Pągowski Z., Rowiński A., Szczeciński J., Szczeciński S.: Aviation Turbine Engines. Design—Exploitation—Diagnostic: Part I. Scientific Publications of the Institute of Aviation, Warsaw 2010.
4. Balicki W., Chachurski R., Głowacki P., Godzimirski J., Kawalec K., Kozakiewicz A., Pągowski Z., Rowiński A., Szczeciński J., Szczeciński S.: Aviation Turbine Engines. Design—Exploitation—Diagnostic: Part II. Scientific Publications of the Institute of Aviation, Warsaw 2012.
5. Balicki W., Szczeciński S.: Diagnostyka lotniczych silników turbinowych. Zastosowanie symulacyjnych modeli silników do optymalizacji zbioru parametrów diagnostycznych. Biblioteka Naukowa Instytutu Lotnictwa, Warszawa 2001.
6. Lindstedt P., Golak K.: Podstawy metody oceny stanu regulacji silnika w zmiennym otoczeniu. Journal of KONBiN, vol. 1, no. 17, pp. 195–204, 2011.
7. Pawlak W.I.: Turbinowy silnik odrzutowy—elementy symulacji, sterowania i monitorowania. Biblioteka Naukowa Instytutu Lotnictwa. Seria: Napędy Lotnicze, poz. 31, Warszawa 2010.
8. Wei X., Yingqing G.: Aircraft engine sensor fault diagnostics based on estimation of engine's health degradation. Chinese Journal of Aeronautics, vol. 22, no. 1, 2009.
9. Bodner W.A.: Automatyka silników lotniczych. Wydawnictwo Ministerstwa Obrony Narodowej, Warszawa 1958.
10. Cichosz E., Kordziński W., Łyżwiński M., Szczeciński S.: Napędy lotnicze. Charakterystyka i zastosowanie napędów. WKiŁ, Warszawa 1980.
11. Golak K.: Parametryczna ocena turbinowego silnika odrzutowego w locie na podstawie jego prób naziemnych. PhD Thesis, Białystok 2016.
12. Szczeciński S.: Lotnicze silniki turbinowe. MON, Warszawa 1965.
13. Szczeciński S.: Napęd samolotu I-22 IRYDA. Wojskowy Przegląd Techniczny i Logistyczny, no. 3, 1995.
14. Шевяков А.А.: Автоматика авиационных и ракетных силовых установок. Машиностроение, Moskwa 1970.
15. Lipiński J.: Tymczasowa instrukcja użytkowania i obsługi silnika K-15, opracowanie wew. WSK Rzeszów, Warszawa 1994.
16. Pawlak W.I., Wiklik K., Morawski J.M.: Synteza i badanie układów sterowania lotniczych silników turbinowych metodami symulacji komputerowej. Biblioteka Naukowa Instytutu Lotnictwa, Warszawa 1996.
17. Balicki W., Głowacki P., Szczeciński S.: Uszkodzenia turbinowych silników odrzutowych. Przegląd Sił Powietrznych, no. 2, 2008.
18. Balicki W., Kawalec K., Szczeciński S., Chachurski R., Kozakiewicz A.: Praca niestateczna silników turbinowych—przyczyny powstania i sposoby zapobiegania. Prace Instytutu Lotnictwa, vol. 4, no 199, pp. 50–55, 2009.
19. Boliński B., Stelmaszczyk Z.: Eksploatacja silników turbinowych. Wydawnictwo Komunikacji i Łączności, Warszawa 1981.
20. Lindstedt P., Golak K., Borowczyk H.: Kompleksowa metoda predykcji właściwości użytkowych silnika turbinowego w locie na podstawie badań naziemnych. In Problemy badań i eksploatacji techniki lotniczej 8, pod red. Lewitowicz J., Cwojdziński L., Kowalski M., Szczepanik R. wyd ITWL, Warszawa 2012.

21. Lindstedt P., Golak K.: Examination of operational dependability demonstrated by turbine reactive engines. Journal of KONBiN, vol. 2/3, no. 14–15, pp. 61–76, 2010.
22. Lindstedt P.: Praktyczna regulacja maszyn i jej teoretyczne podstawy. Wydawnictwo ITWL, Warszawa 2010.
23. Piety K.R.: Method for determining rotational speed from machine vibration data. United States Patent no. 5,744,723, US 1998.
24. Golak K.: Validity check of the assessment of a jet turbine engine regulation in flight using a computer simulation. Solid State Phenomena, vol. 199, pp. 12–128, 2013.
25. Lindstedt P., Golak K.: Premises of parametrical assessment of turbojet engine in flight regulation condition during ground test. Acta Mechanica et Automatica, vol. 6, no. 1, 2012.
26. Muszyński M., Orkisz M.: Modelowanie turbinowych silników odrzutowych. Biblioteka Naukowa Instytutu Lotnictwa, Warszawa 1997 (Modelling of Turbojet Engines). Scientific Library of Institute of Aviation, Warsaw 1997.
27. Balicki W., Szczeciński S., Chachurski R., Szczeciński J.: Effect of the atmosphere on the performances of aviation turbine engines. Acta Mechanica et Automatica, vol. 8, no. 2, 2014.
28. Łukomski B.: Wrażliwość parametryczna układu automatycznej regulacji prędkości obrotowej dwuwirnikowego lotniczego turbinowego silnika odrzutowego w aspekcie diagnostyki technicznej. Zagadnienia Eksploatacji Maszyn, vol. 26, no. 2, 1976.
29. Antoniewicz J.: Automatyka. WNT, Warszawa 1973.
30. Golak K., Lindstedt P.: Analiza oceny jakości przebiegu prędkości obrotowej silnika odrzutowego od wartości zadanej i sygnału zakłócenia. Journal of KONBiN, vol. 2, 2013.
31. Pełczewski W.: Teorie sterowania. WNT, Warszawa 1980.
32. Staniszewski R.: Sterowanie zespołów napędowych. WKŁ, Warszawa 1998.
33. Bendat J.S., Piersol A.G.: Random Data: Analysis and Measurement Procedures, 4th Edition. Wiley 2010.
34. Lindstedt P.: Possibilities of Assessment of the Control Potential of Aircraft Engines. In Solid State Phenomena, Vols 147–149. Trans Tech Publications 2009, pp. 498–503.
35. Golak K.: Method of regulation condition assessment of turbine jet engine in flight basing on signals recorded during ground tests. Journal of KONES, vol. 19, no. 3, 2012.

4 Decision Support in Machine Diagnostics

4.1 INTRODUCTION

A fluid-flow machine or a turbomachine (also known as a fluid-flow machine) is a complex technical object consisting of many components: blades/vanes, bearings, discs, and the like. This object works in a complex environment, which is affected by variable loads like pressure, temperature, and vibrations. One of the basic components responsible for the reliable and safe operation of a fluid-flow machine—apart from the bearings—are the blades/vanes. They are structurally simple technical objects but difficult to operate and maintain. Practice has demonstrated that the breaking of just one blade out of several dozen or even several hundred almost always leads to a severe failure of the entire fluid-flow machine (like an axial compressor or a turbine). It is therefore important that these objects are always monitored during operation and maintenance to identify changes in the technical condition (status) and changes in the operating status, in conjunction with changes in the reliability status. Hence the great interest in methods of routine diagnostics (condition/status/health monitoring) of blades/vanes during operation.

A number of methods are currently used to diagnose the condition of blades/vanes during operation of fluid-flow machines. Diagnostic testing in these methods is based on "contactless" measurement of the values of current displacements of the blade tip in short instances, when the tip is in the sensing range of a dedicated sensor. Commonly known and used measuring systems are manufactured by companies: Hood, Aquilis, Pratt & Whitney (USA), Rolls-Royce (UK), Turbocharges (Switzerland), and MTU (Germany), as well as Russian, Chinese, and Indian companies [1–18].

In the case of Polish systems, there are systems designed, developed, and implemented by ITWL (Instytut Techniczny Wojsk Lotniczych—Air Force Institute of Technology) in Warsaw:

- blade break indicator: SPŁ—29,
- blade over-vibration indicator: SNDŁ—2b,
- microwave sensors: MUH and PIT.

They have been operated with great success on specific, operational technical objects, the SO-3 engines [19–22].

The measurements of blade action signals $y(t)$ and the blade environment $x(t)$ during fluid-flow machine operation are difficult, often impossible. This is particularly true of the environment $x(t)$, which is why it is underestimated in the

DOI: 10.1201/9781032638447-4

diagnostics of turbine blades. Therefore, it can be concluded that the existing methods for assessment of the technical condition (status) of blades in operation of fluid-flow machines do not fully satisfy the basic principle of technical diagnostics, which demands examination and analysis of the technical condition of an object in its environment; this means that the methods are not sufficiently accurate or reliable.

This problem is solved by methods of diagnosing the blade based on special diagnostic models. The models are the difference between the signal phase shift and the square of the amplitude gain of the diagnostic signal, allowing the actual, non-measurable environment to be eliminated with dedicated operations [8, 23–28].

4.2   DIAGNOSTIC OBJECT, DIAGNOSTIC SIGNAL

- The object of interest were the blades of the first axial compressor stage of the SO-3 engine. The research involved testing, which was completed on a turbojet engine test bed at ITWL in Warsaw.

Inside the turbojet engine casing, a permanently attached contactless induction sensor (Figure 4.1) was installed for the measurement of the instantaneous compressor blade tip position during operation of the engine. The output signal from the sensor was recorded with dedicated instruments and stored on a PC computer. The tests were carried out at a rotational speed of 6900 rpm. The time and value were recorded for the instantaneous signal of the compressor blade tip position during engine operation when the blade approached the sensor and when it moved away from the sensor—Figure 4.2 (time T_{01} and T_{12}, respectively).

- The movement of the tip of each blade was reflected by the sensor output signal (Figure 4.2—first tip for blade # 1, second tip for blade # 2, etc.), in the form of a time shift of the signal in relation to the expected position. By extracting this information from the sampled signal at an appropriate resolution, the task of measuring the displacement of the blade tips of the first stage axial compressor could be accomplished [8, 21, 24, 28].

Figure 4.2 shows the recorded displacement signal of four consecutive blades (out of a total of 28) [21, 22, 24, 26, 28, 30].

T_{02d}, T_{02k}—respectively, long and short intervals of observation of the blade tip presence within the sensor range; T_0, T_1, T_2—characteristic instances of observation of the blade tip within the sensor range; T_{01}, T_{12}—period of blade approach and departure from the sensor; mV—blade tip displacement signal; μs—blade displacement time [28].

The recorded blade tip displacement signal is a complex signal that contains information about the operating status of the blade, $y(t)$ in the environment $x(t)$ [21, 22, 24, 26, 28, 30].

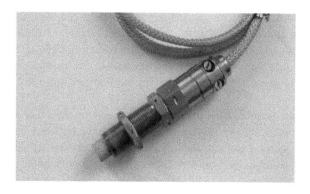

FIGURE 4.1 Contactless induction sensor [29].

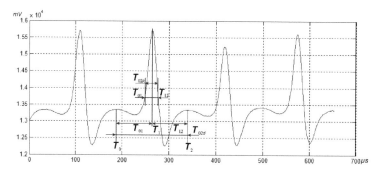

FIGURE 4.2 Induction sensor output signal [29].

The diagnostic signal, *y(t)* consists of longitudinal deformation of the blade *(Y_w)*, bending deformation of the blade *(Y_g)*, blade torsion angle *(Y_s)*; signal of different forms of vibration (bending, torsion, and longitudinal) *(Y_f)*; thermal deformation from non-uniform temperature distribution *(Y_c)*.

This signal can therefore be expressed using a function:

$$y(t) = f(Y_w, \ Y_g, \ Y_s, \ Y_f, \ Y_c) \tag{4.1}$$

On the other hand, the environment signal, *x(t)* consists of the following components: rotational speed *(n)*, centrifugal force *(F_0)*, blade aerodynamic lift force *(P_z)*, drag force *(P_x)*, rotor ring inlet gas pressure *(P_1)*, rotor ring outlet gas pressure *(P_2)*, vibration signal *(f)*, casing vibration signal *(f_{ob})*, temperature distribution signal *(c)*.

Therefore, this signal can be expressed as a function:

$$x(t) = f\left(n, F_0, P_z, P_x, P_1, P_2, f, f_{ob}, c\right) \tag{4.2}$$

Note that the source of signals includes many different, often unidentified factors. In addition, it is perceived that only one measurable—and disturbed—signal *y(t)* with a virtually unmeasurable environment signal *x(t)* (apart from signal *n*) is available to perform the blade diagnostic process.

However, having extracted the times of approach and departure of the blade tip to and from the sensor face, two parametric diagnostic methods with environment elimination can be used [26, 28].

4.3 THEORETICAL FOUNDATIONS OF OBJECT DIAGNOSTIC MODELS WITH ENVIRONMENT ELIMINATION

4.3.1 MODEL A^2_{T12T01}

It is tentatively assumed that the diagnostic signal, $y(t)$, and the environment signal, $x(t)$, are time, stochastic, and perturbed waveforms (trends). In this situation, it is reasonable to move from time space t of signals $x(t)$ and $y(t)$ to time space τ of correlation functions $R_{xx}(\tau)$ and $R_{yy}(\tau)$.

For displacement $y(t)$ in the assumed observation intervals T_{01} and T_{12}, the self-correlation functions are determined, R^{T01}_{yy} and R^{T12}_{yy}. These functions are then approximated with analytical expressions, providing a fit of more than 0.997 (this condition is satisfied for $n = 5$) [24–28, 30, 31].

$$R_{yy}(\tau) = a_n \tau^n + \ldots + a_4 \tau^4 + a_3 \tau^3 + a_2 \tau^2 + a_1 \tau + a_0 \qquad (4.3)$$

with: $a_0, a_1, (\ldots) a_n$—parameters of the self-correlation function of the diagnostic signal trends.

Then, from the obtained analytical forms of the self-correlation functions R^{T01}_{yy} and R^{T12}_{yy}, the corresponding spectral density functions of the eigenpower $S^{T01}_{yy}(j\omega)$ and $S^{T12}_{yy}(j\omega)$ are determined using the Fourier transform:

$$S^{T01}_{yy}(j\omega) = F(R^{T01}_{yy}(\tau)) \qquad (4.4)$$

$$S^{T12}_{yy}(j\omega) = F(R^{T12}_{yy}(\tau)) \qquad (4.5)$$

It is known that there is a relation between the eigenpower spectral density functions of the output and input signals of an object, and the relation is:

- the transmittance modulus:

$$|G(j\omega)|^2 = \frac{S_{yy}(j\omega)}{S_{xx}(j\omega)} \qquad (4.6)$$

- amplitude gain square:

$$A^2_{T12T01} = |G(j\omega)|^2 \qquad (4.7)$$

When considering the characteristic phases of blade movement, the following is obtained:

$$A^2_{T01} = \frac{S^{T01}_{yy}}{S^{T01}_{xx}}, \quad A^2_{T12} = \frac{S^{T12}_{yy}}{S^{T12}_{xx}} \qquad (4.8)$$

with:

A^2_{T01}— square of the amplitude gain of the signals x and y in the phase of blade approach to the sensor;

A^2_{T12}— square of the amplitude gain of the signals x and y in the phase of blade departure from the sensor.

Since the observation intervals of the signals follow each in very quick succession (short time intervals), it can be assumed that the environment in the frequency domain does not change. Hence:

$$S^{T12}_{xx} \cong S^{T01}_{xx} \tag{4.9}$$

Based on relations (4.8) and (4.9), a new physically interpretable quantity can be introduced—the amplitude gain quotient, A^2_{T12T01}:

$$A^2_{T12T01} = \frac{A^2_{T12}}{A^2_{T01}} = \frac{\dfrac{S^{T12}_{yy}}{S^{T12}_{xx}}}{\dfrac{S^{T01}_{yy}}{S^{T01}_{xx}}} \xrightarrow{S^{T12}_{xx}=S^{T01}_{xx}} \frac{S^{T12}_{yy}}{S^{T01}_{yy}} \tag{4.10}$$

The new diagnostic model can be expressed in a parameterised form, the parameters of which hold information about the technical status of the blade being diagnosed [24–26, 28, 30, 31]:

$$A^2_{T12T01} = \frac{S^{T12}_{yy}}{S^{T01}_{yy}} = \frac{M^*_0 + M^*_1 s + M^*_2 s^2 + ... + M^*_n s^n}{L^*_0 + L^*_1 s + L^*_2 s^2 + ... + L^*_n s^n} \tag{4.11}$$

with:

s— complex variable ($s \equiv j\omega$);

M_i— values of the parameters of the amplitude gain quotient numerator of the diagnostic signals;

L_i— values of the parameters of the amplitude gain quotient denominator of the diagnostic signals.

The difference in the technical status between successive blades is determined from relative changes of parameters M_0 to M_5 and L_0 to L_5.

$$\Delta \bar{L}_i = \frac{L_{i1} - L_{sr}}{L_{sr}} ; i = 1, ..., 30 \tag{4.12}$$

$$\Delta \bar{M}_i = \frac{M_{i1} - M_{sr}}{M_{sr}} ; i = 1, ..., 30 \tag{4.13}$$

with: L_{sr}, M_{sr}—average value of the parameter (the standard value is calculated from 30 arbitrarily selected revolutions from the set of 3000).

With the relative parameters calculated, the following are calculated: μ, σ, 2σ, and 3σ (the mean value and the standard deviation). To simplify interpretation, the determined relative values are mapped to specified colours:

- green, if the relative value does not exceed $\mu \pm \sigma$;
- blue, if the relative value is between $\mu \pm \sigma$ and $\mu \pm 2\sigma$;
- red if the relative value is between $\mu \pm 2\sigma$ and $\mu \pm 3\sigma$;
- black, if the relative value exceeds $\mu \pm 3\sigma$. In this way, a portrait of the blade is generated, which indicates its state of fitness. Black colour indications, if multiple are present, identify damage to the blade; red indications identify increased blade wear; and blue and green indications identify acceptable wear.

This approach provides a clear and unambiguous picture of the assessment of the damage status of the blade.

4.3.2   MODEL φ_{T12T01}

Model φ_{T12T01} is determined like to model A_{T12T01}^2 : two observation intervals of blade tip displacement are considered—T_{01} and T_{12}. It is then assumed that environment $x(t)$ is a high-power noise, represented by distribution $\delta(t, \tau)$, and that it can be correlated with signal $y(t)$ [24, 26, 28, 30].

For displacement $y(t)$ in the assumed observation intervals T_{01} and T_{12} and distribution $\delta(t, \tau)$, estimates of the cross-correlation function R_{xy}^{T01} and R_{xy}^{T12}. The functions are then approximated with analytical expressions, providing a fit of more than 0.997 (this condition is satisfied for $n = 5$) [24, 26, 28, 30].

$$R_{xy}(\tau) = a_n \tau^n + ... + a_4 \tau^4 + a_3 \tau^3 + a_2 \tau^2 + a_1 \tau + a_0 \qquad (4.14)$$

with: a_0, a_1, (. . .) a_n— parameters of the self-correlation function of the diagnostic signal trends.

Then, from the obtained analytical forms of the cross-correlation functions R_{xy}^{T01} and R_{xy}^{T12}, the corresponding spectral density functions of the power $S_{xy}^{T01}(j\omega)$ and $S_{xy}^{T12}(j\omega)$ are determined using the Fourier transform:

$$S_{xy}^{T01}(j\omega) = F(R_{xy}^{T01}(\tau)) \qquad (4.15)$$

$$S_{xy}^{T12}(j\omega) = F(R_{xy}^{T12}(\tau)) \qquad (4.16)$$

It is known that there is a relation between the spectral power density functions of the output and input signals of an object, and the relation is:

- the transmittance is:

$$G(j\omega) = \frac{S_{xy}(j\omega)}{S_{xx}(j\omega)} \qquad (4.17)$$

- the main argument is:

$$Arg(G(j\omega)) = Arg\,\frac{S_{xy}(j\omega)}{S_{xx}(j\omega)} \tag{4.18}$$

This means the following:

$$\varphi = Arg(G(j\omega)) \tag{4.19}$$

for the observation intervals and considered this can be expressed:

$$\varphi_{T01} = Arg\,\frac{S_{xy}^{T01}}{S_{xx}^{T01}}, \quad \varphi_{T12} = Arg\,\frac{S_{xy}^{T12}}{S_{xx}^{T12}} \tag{4.20}$$

with:

φ_{T01}— phase shift of signals x and y as the blade approaches the sensor;
φ_{T12}— phase shift of signals x and y as the blade departs from the sensor.

Again, the main assumption is that the observation intervals of the signals follow each in very quick succession (short time intervals), so it can be assumed that the environment in the frequency domain does not change, and thus:

$$S_{xx}^{T12} \cong S_{xx}^{T01} \text{ (see Formula 4.9)}$$

Based on relations (4.9) and (4.20), a new physically interpretable quantity can be introduced in the form of phase shift difference, φ_{T12} and φ_{T01}:

$$\varphi_{T12T01} = \varphi_{T12} - \varphi_{T01} = Arg\,\frac{\dfrac{S_{xy}^{T12}}{S_{xx}^{T12}}}{\dfrac{S_{xy}^{T01}}{S_{xx}^{T01}}} = Arg\,\frac{A_{12}e^{-j\varphi_{T12}}}{A_{01}e^{-j\varphi_{T01}}} = ArgA_{T12T01}e^{-j(\varphi_{T12}-\varphi_{T01})} = Arg\,\frac{S_{xy}^{T12}}{S_{xy}^{T01}} \tag{4.21}$$

The environment signal, x in S_{xy} can be any distribution because S_{xy}^{T12} and S_{xy}^{T01} depend on signal x, but their quotient does not. In this case, the influence of the environment is also eliminated [24, 26, 28, 30, 31].

The model can also be expressed in a parameterised form, the parameters of which hold information about the technical status of the blade being diagnosed [24, 26, 28, 30, 31]:

$$\varphi_{T12T01} = Arg\,\frac{S_{xy}^{T12}}{S_{xy}^{T01}} = Arg\,\frac{B_0^* + B_1^* s + B_2^* s^2 + ... + B_n^* s^n}{A_0^* + A_1^* s + A_1^* s^2 + ... + A_1^* s^n} \tag{4.22}$$

with:

> s— complex variable ($s \equiv j\omega$);
> B_i— estimates of the numerator parameters of the quotient of the difference of the phase shifts of the diagnostic signals;
> A_i— estimates of the denominator parameters of the quotient of the difference of the phase shifts of the diagnostic signals.

The difference in the technical status between successive blades is determined from relative changes of parameters A_0 to A_5 and B_0 to B_5.

$$\Delta \overline{A}_i = \frac{A_{i1} - A_{sr}}{A_{sr}} \; ; i = 1, \ldots, 30 \tag{4.23}$$

$$\Delta \overline{B}_i = \frac{B_{i1} - B_{sr}}{B_{sr}} \; ; i = 1, \ldots, 30 \tag{4.24}$$

with: A_{sr}, B_{sr}— average value of the parameter (the standard value is calculated from 30 arbitrarily selected revolutions from the set of 3000).

With the relative parameters calculated, the following are calculated: μ, σ, 2σ, and 3σ (the mean value and the standard deviation). To simplify interpretation, the determined relative values are mapped to specified colours:

- green, if the relative value does not exceed $\mu \pm \sigma$;
- blue, if the relative value is above $\mu \pm \sigma$ and still below $\mu \pm 2\sigma$;
- red, if the relative value is above $\mu \pm 2\sigma$ and still below $\mu \pm 3\sigma$;
- black, if the relative value exceeds $\mu \pm 3\sigma$.

In this way, a portrait of the blade is generated, which indicates its state of fitness. Black colour indications, if multiple are present, identify damage to the blade; red indications identify increased blade wear; and blue and green indications identify low wear.

Based on Formula 4.22, changes in the parameters of model φ_{T12T01} can be expected to correspond to changes in the structural features of the blade airfoil (like cracks, dents, deformations, or pitting).

4.4 DETERMINATION OF MODEL PARAMETERS FROM EXPERIMENTAL TESTS

The signal trends with Formulas 4.3–4.22 applied were transformed into relative values of the parameters of model A^2_{T12T01} and then into the relative values of the parameters of model φ_{T12T01} [24, 26, 28, 30]. Tables 4.1 to 4.4 list selected results of the performed tests and analyses (the values of parameters of models A^2_{T12T01} and φ_{T12T01}) for blades # 7 and # 20.

TABLE 4.1

Values of Blade # 7 Parameters for Model A^2_{T12T01}

	Blade # 7 parameter values											
	L_0	L_1	L_2	L_3	L_4	L_5	M_0	M_1	M_2	M_3	M_4	M_5
Cycle 1	2.125E-05	-4.932E-04	5.052E-03	-2.610E-02	1.226E-02	9.966E-01	2.083E-05	-4.849E-04	4.982E-03	-2.584E-02	1.215E-02	9.965E-01
Cycle 8	2.135E-05	-4.952E-04	5.066E-03	-2.614E-02	1.215E-02	9.967E-01	2.050E-05	-4.787E-04	4.939E-03	-2.576E-02	1.275E-02	9.959E-01
Cycle 15	2.134E-05	-4.949E-04	5.065E-03	-2.614E-02	1.219E-02	9.967E-01	2.053E-05	-4.794E-04	4.944E-03	-2.577E-02	1.269E-02	9.960E-01
Cycle 22	2.131E-05	-4.945E-04	5.061E-03	-2.613E-02	1.220E-02	9.967E-01	2.063E-05	-4.812E-04	4.956E-03	-2.579E-02	1.249E-02	9.962E-01
Cycle 29	2.132E-05	-4.946E-04	5.062E-03	-2.613E-02	1.218E-02	9.967E-01	2.061E-05	-4.809E-04	4.954E-03	-2.579E-02	1.254E-02	9.962E-01
Cycle 36	2.128E-05	-4.938E-04	5.056E-03	-2.611E-02	1.223E-02	9.967E-01	2.074E-05	-4.832E-04	4.970E-03	-2.582E-02	1.232E-02	9.964E-01
Cycle 43	2.135E-05	-4.951E-04	5.066E-03	-2.614E-02	1.217E-02	9.967E-01	2.049E-05	-4.786E-04	4.939E-03	-2.576E-02	1.278E-02	9.959E-01
Cycle 50	2.133E-05	-4.948E-04	5.064E-03	-2.614E-02	1.218E-02	9.967E-01	2.057E-05	-4.801E-04	4.949E-03	-2.578E-02	1.264E-02	9.961E-01
Cycle 57	2.126E-05	-4.934E-04	5.053E-03	-2.610E-02	1.224E-02	9.966E-01	2.081E-05	-4.845E-04	4.980E-03	-2.584E-02	1.220E-02	9.965E-01
Cycle 64	2.125E-05	-4.933E-04	5.052E-03	-2.611E-02	1.227E-02	9.966E-01	2.082E-05	-4.847E-04	4.981E-03	-2.584E-02	1.219E-02	9.965E-01
Cycle 71	2.129E-05	-4.939E-04	5.057E-03	-2.612E-02	1.223E-02	9.967E-01	2.072E-05	-4.829E-04	4.968E-03	-2.582E-02	1.237E-02	9.963E-01
Cycle 78	2.129E-05	-4.939E-04	5.057E-03	-2.612E-02	1.222E-02	9.967E-01	2.073E-05	-4.829E-04	4.968E-03	-2.581E-02	1.234E-02	9.964E-01
Cycle 85	2.128E-05	-4.939E-04	5.057E-03	-2.612E-02	1.223E-02	9.967E-01	2.072E-05	-4.827E-04	4.967E-03	-2.582E-02	1.238E-02	9.963E-01
Cycle 92	2.129E-05	-4.941E-04	5.058E-03	-2.612E-02	1.222E-02	9.967E-01	2.068E-05	-4.822E-04	4.963E-03	-2.581E-02	1.243E-02	9.963E-01
Cycle 99	2.124E-05	-4.931E-04	5.051E-03	-2.610E-02	1.228E-02	9.966E-01	2.085E-05	-4.852E-04	4.985E-03	-2.584E-02	1.213E-02	9.966E-01
Cycle 106	2.135E-05	-4.952E-04	5.066E-03	-2.614E-02	1.216E-02	9.967E-01	2.048E-05	-4.785E-04	4.938E-03	-2.576E-02	1.279E-02	9.959E-01
Cycle 113	2.128E-05	-4.939E-04	5.057E-03	-2.612E-02	1.223E-02	9.967E-01	2.072E-05	-4.828E-04	4.968E-03	-2.582E-02	1.238E-02	9.963E-01
Cycle 120	2.127E-05	-4.936E-04	5.054E-03	-2.611E-02	1.225E-02	9.966E-01	2.076E-05	-4.836E-04	4.973E-03	-2.583E-02	1.230E-02	9.964E-01
Cycle 127	2.128E-05	-4.938E-04	5.056E-03	-2.611E-02	1.224E-02	9.966E-01	2.073E-05	-4.830E-04	4.969E-03	-2.582E-02	1.236E-02	9.963E-01
Cycle 134	2.127E-05	-4.936E-04	5.054E-03	-2.611E-02	1.225E-02	9.966E-01	2.074E-05	-4.833E-04	4.972E-03	-2.583E-02	1.236E-02	9.963E-01
Cycle 141	2.130E-05	-4.941E-04	5.059E-03	-2.612E-02	1.222E-02	9.967E-01	2.065E-05	-4.815E-04	4.959E-03	-2.580E-02	1.252E-02	9.962E-01

(Continued)

TABLE 4.1 (*Continued*)
Values of Blade # 7 Parameters for Model A^2_{T12T01}

Blade # 7 parameter values

	L_0	L_1	L_2	L_3	L_4	L_5	M_0	M_1	M_2	M_3	M_4	M_5
Cycle 148	2.132E-05	-4.946E-04	5.062E-03	-2.613E-02	1.220E-02	9.957E-01	2.058E-05	-4.803E-04	4.950E-03	-2.579E-02	1.262E-02	9.961E-01
Cycle 155	2.129E-05	-4.940E-04	5.058E-03	-2.612E-02	1.223E-02	9.957E-01	2.067E-05	-4.819E-04	4.962E-03	-2.581E-02	1.249E-02	9.962E-01
Cycle 162	2.136E-05	-4.953E-04	5.067E-03	-2.615E-02	1.216E-02	9.957E-01	2.044E-05	-4.778E-04	4.933E-03	-2.576E-02	1.290E-02	9.958E-01
Cycle 169	2.127E-05	-4.937E-04	5.055E-03	-2.611E-02	1.225E-02	9.956E-01	2.071E-05	-4.827E-04	4.967E-03	-2.582E-02	1.242E-02	9.963E-01
Cycle 176	2.133E-05	-4.948E-04	5.064E-03	-2.614E-02	1.219E-02	9.957E-01	2.052E-05	-4.792E-04	4.944E-03	-2.578E-02	1.277E-02	9.959E-01
Cycle 183	2.129E-05	-4.939E-04	5.057E-03	-2.612E-02	1.223E-02	9.957E-01	2.067E-05	-4.820E-04	4.963E-03	-2.581E-02	1.249E-02	9.962E-01
Cycle 190	2.129E-05	-4.941E-04	5.058E-03	-2.612E-02	1.223E-02	9.957E-01	2.064E-05	-4.813E-04	4.958E-03	-2.581E-02	1.257E-02	9.961E-01
Cycle 197	2.125E-05	-4.932E-04	5.051E-03	-2.610E-02	1.227E-02	9.956E-01	2.079E-05	-4.842E-04	4.979E-03	-2.585E-02	1.231E-02	9.964E-01
Cycle 204	2.130E-05	-4.943E-04	5.060E-03	-2.613E-02	1.222E-02	9.957E-01	2.061E-05	-4.809E-04	4.956E-03	-2.580E-02	1.261E-02	9.961E-01
Cycle 211	2.125E-05	-4.932E-04	5.052E-03	-2.610E-02	1.226E-02	9.956E-01	2.078E-05	-4.840E-04	4.977E-03	-2.584E-02	1.231E-02	9.964E-01
Cycle 218	2.124E-05	-4.931E-04	5.051E-03	-2.610E-02	1.228E-02	9.956E-01	2.080E-05	-4.844E-04	4.980E-03	-2.585E-02	1.229E-02	9.964E-01
Cycle 225	2.128E-05	-4.938E-04	5.056E-03	-2.612E-02	1.224E-02	9.966E-01	2.067E-05	-4.821E-04	4.964E-03	-2.582E-02	1.253E-02	9.962E-01
Cycle 232	2.127E-05	-4.936E-04	5.054E-03	-2.611E-02	1.224E-02	9.966E-01	2.073E-05	-4.831E-04	4.971E-03	-2.583E-02	1.241E-02	9.963E-01
Cycle 239	2.128E-05	-4.938E-04	5.056E-03	-2.612E-02	1.224E-02	9.966E-01	2.068E-05	-4.821E-04	4.964E-03	-2.582E-02	1.251E-02	9.962E-01
Cycle 246	2.132E-05	-4.946E-04	5.062E-03	-2.613E-02	1.218E-02	9.967E-01	2.054E-05	-4.796E-04	4.947E-03	-2.579E-02	1.278E-02	9.959E-01

Source: cycle = full revolution

TABLE 4.2

Values of Blade # 20 Parameters for Model A^2_{T12T01}

						Blade # 20 parameter values					
	L_0	L_1	L_2	L_3	L_4	L_5	M_0	M_1	M_2	M_3	M_4	M_5
Cycle 1	2.135E-05	-4.951E-04	5.066E-03	-2.614E-02	1.217E-02	9.967E-01	2.098E-05	-4.876E-04	5.001E-03	-2.588E-02	1.196E-02	9.967E-01
Cycle 8	2.135E-05	-4.951E-04	5.066E-03	-2.614E-02	1.216E-02	9.967E-01	2.099E-05	-4.878E-04	5.003E-03	-2.589E-02	1.193E-02	9.968E-01
Cycle 15	2.135E-05	-4.951E-04	5.066E-03	-2.614E-02	1.218E-02	9.967E-01	2.098E-05	-4.876E-04	5.001E-03	-2.588E-02	1.193E-02	9.968E-01
Cycle 22	2.132E-05	-4.946E-04	5.062E-03	-2.613E-02	1.219E-02	9.967E-01	2.105E-05	-4.890E-04	5.011E-03	-2.590E-02	1.180E-02	9.969E-01
Cycle 29	2.134E-05	-4.950E-04	5.065E-03	-2.614E-02	1.217E-02	9.967E-01	2.099E-05	-4.879E-04	5.004E-03	-2.589E-02	1.193E-02	9.968E-01
Cycle 36	2.141E-05	-4.963E-04	5.075E-03	-2.617E-02	1.209E-02	9.968E-01	2.074E-05	-4.833E-04	4.972E-03	-2.583E-02	1.236E-02	9.963E-01
Cycle 43	2.140E-05	-4.961E-04	5.073E-03	-2.616E-02	1.213E-02	9.968E-01	2.077E-05	-4.837E-04	4.975E-03	-2.583E-02	1.231E-02	9.964E-01
Cycle 50	2.138E-05	-4.957E-04	5.070E-03	-2.615E-02	1.213E-02	9.968E-01	2.089E-05	-4.860E-04	4.990E-03	-2.586E-02	1.211E-02	9.966E-01
Cycle 57	2.142E-05	-4.965E-04	5.076E-03	-2.617E-02	1.210E-02	9.968E-01	2.072E-05	-4.828E-04	4.968E-03	-2.582E-02	1.241E-02	9.963E-01
Cycle 64	2.141E-05	-4.963E-04	5.075E-03	-2.617E-02	1.211E-02	9.968E-01	2.074E-05	-4.832E-04	4.971E-03	-2.583E-02	1.236E-02	9.963E-01
Cycle 71	2.134E-05	-4.949E-04	5.064E-03	-2.614E-02	1.219E-02	9.967E-01	2.098E-05	-4.877E-04	5.002E-03	-2.589E-02	1.195E-02	9.968E-01
Cycle 78	2.134E-05	-4.950E-04	5.065E-03	-2.614E-02	1.217E-02	9.967E-01	2.098E-05	-4.876E-04	5.002E-03	-2.588E-02	1.194E-02	9.968E-01
Cycle 85	2.137E-05	-4.956E-04	5.069E-03	-2.615E-02	1.213E-02	9.968E-01	2.090E-05	-4.861E-04	4.991E-03	-2.586E-02	1.208E-02	9.966E-01
Cycle 92	2.140E-05	-4.961E-04	5.073E-03	-2.616E-02	1.213E-02	9.968E-01	2.076E-05	-4.836E-04	4.974E-03	-2.583E-02	1.235E-02	9.964E-01
Cycle 99	2.139E-05	-4.960E-04	5.073E-03	-2.616E-02	1.213E-02	9.968E-01	2.079E-05	-4.842E-04	4.978E-03	-2.584E-02	1.228E-02	9.964E-01
Cycle 106	2.136E-05	-4.953E-04	5.067E-03	-2.615E-02	1.216E-02	9.967E-01	2.092E-05	-4.866E-04	4.995E-03	-2.587E-02	1.206E-02	9.966E-01
Cycle 113	2.139E-05	-4.958E-04	5.071E-03	-2.616E-02	1.213E-02	9.968E-01	2.083E-05	-4.849E-04	4.983E-03	-2.585E-02	1.219E-02	9.965E-01
Cycle 120	2.134E-05	-4.949E-04	5.064E-03	-2.614E-02	1.218E-02	9.967E-01	2.099E-05	-4.877E-04	5.003E-03	-2.589E-02	1.195E-02	9.968E-01
Cycle 127	2.133E-05	-4.949E-04	5.064E-03	-2.614E-02	1.219E-02	9.967E-01	2.100E-05	-4.879E-04	5.004E-03	-2.589E-02	1.194E-02	9.968E-01
Cycle 134	2.132E-05	-4.946E-04	5.062E-03	-2.613E-02	1.219E-02	9.967E-01	2.104E-05	-4.888E-04	5.010E-03	-2.590E-02	1.186E-02	9.969E-01
Cycle 141	2.133E-05	-4.948E-04	5.064E-03	-2.614E-02	1.217E-02	9.967E-01	2.100E-05	-4.880E-04	5.004E-03	-2.589E-02	1.193E-02	9.968E-01

(Continued)

TABLE 4.2 (Continued)
Values of Blade # 20 Parameters for Model A^2_{T12T01}

	Blade # 20 parameter values											
	L_0	L_1	L_2	L_3	L_4	L_5	M_0	M_1	M_2	M_3	M_4	M_5
Cycle 148	2.134E-05	-4.949E-04	5.065E-03	-2.614E-02	1.218E-02	9.967E-01	2.096E-05	-4.874E-04	5.000E-03	-2.588E-02	1.199E-02	9.967E-01
Cycle 155	2.140E-05	-4.962E-04	5.074E-03	-2.617E-02	1.212E-02	9.968E-01	2.074E-05	-4.833E-04	4.972E-03	-2.583E-02	1.239E-02	9.963E-01
Cycle 162	2.134E-05	-4.950E-04	5.065E-03	-2.614E-02	1.218E-02	9.967E-01	2.097E-05	-4.874E-04	5.001E-03	-2.589E-02	1.201E-02	9.967E-01
Cycle 169	2.135E-05	-4.952E-04	5.066E-03	-2.614E-02	1.216E-02	9.957E-01	2.093E-05	-4.868E-04	4.997E-03	-2.588E-02	1.206E-02	9.966E-01
Cycle 176	2.138E-05	-4.958E-04	5.071E-03	-2.616E-02	1.214E-02	9.958E-01	2.081E-05	-4.846E-04	4.981E-03	-2.585E-02	1.227E-02	9.964E-01
Cycle 183	2.132E-05	-4.946E-04	5.062E-03	-2.613E-02	1.221E-02	9.957E-01	2.100E-05	-4.880E-04	5.005E-03	-2.590E-02	1.197E-02	9.967E-01
Cycle 190	2.132E-05	-4.947E-04	5.063E-03	-2.613E-02	1.219E-02	9.957E-01	2.102E-05	-4.884E-04	5.008E-03	-2.590E-02	1.193E-02	9.968E-01
Cycle 197	2.135E-05	-4.952E-04	5.067E-03	-2.614E-02	1.216E-02	9.957E-01	2.091E-05	-4.865E-04	4.994E-03	-2.588E-02	1.210E-02	9.966E-01
Cycle 204	2.134E-05	-4.950E-04	5.065E-03	-2.614E-02	1.219E-02	9.957E-01	2.093E-05	-4.867E-04	4.997E-03	-2.589E-02	1.211E-02	9.966E-01
Cycle 211	2.139E-05	-4.959E-04	5.072E-03	-2.616E-02	1.213E-02	9.958E-01	2.078E-05	-4.841E-04	4.978E-03	-2.585E-02	1.233E-02	9.964E-01
Cycle 218	2.135E-05	-4.952E-04	5.067E-03	-2.615E-02	1.217E-02	9.957E-01	2.092E-05	-4.865E-04	4.995E-03	-2.588E-02	1.211E-02	9.966E-01
Cycle 225	2.134E-05	-4.950E-04	5.066E-03	-2.614E-02	1.219E-02	9.957E-01	2.093E-05	-4.868E-04	4.997E-03	-2.588E-02	1.209E-02	9.966E-01
Cycle 232	2.142E-05	-4.965E-04	5.076E-03	-2.617E-02	1.209E-02	9.958E-01	2.068E-05	-4.821E-04	4.964E-03	-2.583E-02	1.255E-02	9.962E-01
Cycle 239	2.140E-05	-4.962E-04	5.074E-03	-2.616E-02	1.212E-02	9.958E-01	2.071E-05	-4.828E-04	4.969E-03	-2.583E-02	1.248E-02	9.962E-01
Cycle 246	2.139E-05	-4.959E-04	5.072E-03	-2.616E-02	1.214E-02	9.968E-01	2.074E-05	-4.833E-04	4.973E-03	-2.584E-02	1.244E-02	9.963E-01

Source: cycle = full revolution

TABLE 4.3
Values of Blade # 7 Parameters for Model φ_{T12T01}

	Blade # 7 parameter values											
	L_0	L_1	L_2	L_3	L_4	L_5	M_0	M_1	M_2	M_3	M_4	M_5
Cycle 1	1.966E-05	-4.616E-04	4.794E-03	-2.524E-02	1.298E-02	9.956E-01	2.023E-05	-4.767E-04	4.980E-03	-2.655E-02	1.823E-02	9.937E-01
Cycle 8	1.972E-05	-4.625E-04	4.796E-03	-2.519E-02	1.253E-02	9.958E-01	2.011E-05	-4.739E-04	4.951E-03	-2.639E-02	1.770E-02	9.939E-01
Cycle 15	1.971E-05	-4.623E-04	4.795E-03	-2.519E-02	1.255E-02	9.958E-01	2.012E-05	-4.743E-04	4.955E-03	-2.641E-02	1.778E-02	9.938E-01
Cycle 22	1.970E-05	-4.621E-04	4.795E-03	-2.520E-02	1.269E-02	9.957E-01	2.016E-05	-4.752E-04	4.963E-03	-2.646E-02	1.794E-02	9.938E-01
Cycle 29	1.970E-05	-4.621E-04	4.795E-03	-2.520E-02	1.266E-02	9.957E-01	2.016E-05	-4.750E-04	4.962E-03	-2.645E-02	1.791E-02	9.938E-01
Cycle 36	1.968E-05	-4.618E-04	4.794E-03	-2.522E-02	1.282E-02	9.957E-01	2.020E-05	-4.760E-04	4.972E-03	-2.651E-02	1.810E-02	9.938E-01
Cycle 43	1.972E-05	-4.624E-04	4.796E-03	-2.519E-02	1.252E-02	9.958E-01	2.010E-05	-4.737E-04	4.948E-03	-2.637E-02	1.764E-02	9.939E-01
Cycle 50	1.971E-05	-4.623E-04	4.796E-03	-2.520E-02	1.262E-02	9.957E-01	2.013E-05	-4.745E-04	4.957E-03	-2.643E-02	1.783E-02	9.938E-01
Cycle 57	1.967E-05	-4.616E-04	4.794E-03	-2.523E-02	1.292E-02	9.957E-01	2.022E-05	-4.765E-04	4.977E-03	-2.654E-02	1.818E-02	9.937E-01
Cycle 64	1.966E-05	-4.615E-04	4.793E-03	-2.523E-02	1.293E-02	9.956E-01	2.023E-05	-4.766E-04	4.978E-03	-2.654E-02	1.819E-02	9.937E-01
Cycle 71	1.968E-05	-4.619E-04	4.795E-03	-2.522E-02	1.281E-02	9.957E-01	2.019E-05	-4.758E-04	4.970E-03	-2.650E-02	1.805E-02	9.938E-01
Cycle 78	1.969E-05	-4.619E-04	4.795E-03	-2.522E-02	1.280E-02	9.957E-01	2.019E-05	-4.758E-04	4.970E-03	-2.650E-02	1.803E-02	9.938E-01
Cycle 85	1.968E-05	-4.618E-04	4.794E-03	-2.521E-02	1.280E-02	9.957E-01	2.019E-05	-4.757E-04	4.969E-03	-2.649E-02	1.804E-02	9.938E-01
Cycle 92	1.969E-05	-4.619E-04	4.795E-03	-2.521E-02	1.276E-02	9.957E-01	2.018E-05	-4.754E-04	4.966E-03	-2.648E-02	1.798E-02	9.938E-01
Cycle 99	1.965E-05	-4.614E-04	4.792E-03	-2.523E-02	1.295E-02	9.956E-01	2.024E-05	-4.767E-04	4.979E-03	-2.655E-02	1.820E-02	9.937E-01
Cycle 106	1.972E-05	-4.623E-04	4.795E-03	-2.518E-02	1.249E-02	9.958E-01	2.010E-05	-4.737E-04	4.948E-03	-2.637E-02	1.763E-02	9.939E-01
Cycle 113	1.968E-05	-4.618E-04	4.794E-03	-2.521E-02	1.279E-02	9.957E-01	2.018E-05	-4.756E-04	4.967E-03	-2.648E-02	1.798E-02	9.938E-01
Cycle 120	1.967E-05	-4.617E-04	4.794E-03	-2.522E-02	1.289E-02	9.957E-01	2.020E-05	-4.761E-04	4.973E-03	-2.651E-02	1.810E-02	9.938E-01
Cycle 127	1.968E-05	-4.618E-04	4.794E-03	-2.522E-02	1.282E-02	9.957E-01	2.019E-05	-4.757E-04	4.969E-03	-2.649E-02	1.801E-02	9.938E-01
Cycle 134	1.967E-05	-4.617E-04	4.794E-03	-2.523E-02	1.290E-02	9.957E-01	2.019E-05	-4.757E-04	4.968E-03	-2.648E-02	1.797E-02	9.938E-01
Cycle 141	1.969E-05	-4.620E-04	4.795E-03	-2.522E-02	1.278E-02	9.957E-01	2.015E-05	-4.749E-04	4.960E-03	-2.643E-02	1.782E-02	9.938E-01
Cycle 148	1.970E-05	-4.621E-04	4.795E-03	-2.520E-02	1.266E-02	9.957E-01	2.014E-05	-4.745E-04	4.957E-03	-2.642E-02	1.781E-02	9.938E-01

(Continued)

TABLE 4.3 (Continued)
Values of Blade # 7 Parameters for Model φ_{T12T01}

	Blade # 7 parameter values											
	L_0	L_1	L_2	L_3	L_4	L_5	M_0	M_1	M_2	M_3	M_4	M_5
Cycle 155	1.969E-05	-4.619E-04	4.795E-03	-2.522E-02	1.280E-02	9.957E-01	2.016E-05	-4.751E-04	4.962E-03	-2.645E-02	1.787E-02	9.938E-01
Cycle 162	1.972E-05	-4.625E-04	4.797E-03	-2.519E-02	1.253E-02	9.958E-01	2.007E-05	-4.730E-04	4.940E-03	-2.632E-02	1.744E-02	9.939E-01
Cycle 169	1.968E-05	-4.618E-04	4.795E-03	-2.523E-02	1.289E-02	9.957E-01	2.018E-05	-4.755E-04	4.967E-03	-2.648E-02	1.797E-02	9.938E-01
Cycle 176	1.971E-05	-4.623E-04	4.796E-03	-2.520E-02	1.263E-02	9.957E-01	2.010E-05	-4.737E-04	4.948E-03	-2.637E-02	1.760E-02	9.939E-01
Cycle 183	1.968E-05	-4.619E-04	4.795E-03	-2.522E-02	1.282E-02	9.957E-01	2.016E-05	-4.751E-04	4.962E-03	-2.645E-02	1.788E-02	9.938E-01
Cycle 190	1.969E-05	-4.621E-04	4.797E-03	-2.523E-02	1.283E-02	9.957E-01	2.015E-05	-4.747E-04	4.957E-03	-2.642E-02	1.774E-02	9.939E-01
Cycle 197	1.966E-05	-4.616E-04	4.795E-03	-2.525E-02	1.303E-02	9.956E-01	2.020E-05	-4.758E-04	4.969E-03	-2.648E-02	1.794E-02	9.938E-01
Cycle 204	1.970E-05	-4.621E-04	4.797E-03	-2.522E-02	1.278E-02	9.957E-01	2.013E-05	-4.744E-04	4.955E-03	-2.640E-02	1.771E-02	9.939E-01
Cycle 211	1.966E-05	-4.615E-04	4.793E-03	-2.523E-02	1.296E-02	9.956E-01	2.020E-05	-4.758E-04	4.969E-03	-2.649E-02	1.797E-02	9.938E-01
Cycle 218	1.966E-05	-4.616E-04	4.795E-03	-2.525E-02	1.306E-02	9.956E-01	2.020E-05	-4.760E-04	4.971E-03	-2.649E-02	1.799E-02	9.938E-01
Cycle 225	1.968E-05	-4.619E-04	4.797E-03	-2.524E-02	1.291E-02	9.957E-01	2.015E-05	-4.748E-04	4.958E-03	-2.642E-02	1.775E-02	9.939E-01
Cycle 232	1.968E-05	-4.619E-04	4.797E-03	-2.525E-02	1.299E-02	9.956E-01	2.017E-05	-4.752E-04	4.963E-03	-2.644E-02	1.782E-02	9.939E-01
Cycle 239	1.968E-05	-4.620E-04	4.797E-03	-2.524E-02	1.292E-02	9.957E-01	2.015E-05	-4.748E-04	4.958E-03	-2.642E-02	1.775E-02	9.939E-01
Cycle 246	1.971E-05	-4.623E-04	4.797E-03	-2.522E-02	1.273E-02	9.957E-01	2.009E-05	-4.734E-04	4.944E-03	-2.634E-02	1.748E-02	9.939E-01

Source: cycle = full revolution

TABLE 4.4
Values of Blade # 20 Parameters for Model φ_{T12T01}

	L_0	L_1	L_2	L_3	L_4	L_5	M_0	M_1	M_2	M_3	M_4	M_5
						Blade # 20 parameter values						
Cycle 1	1.971E-05	-4.622E-04	4.793E-03	-2.517E-02	1.243E-02	9.958E-01	2.030E-05	-4.785E-04	5.002E-03	-2.672E-02	1.892E-02	9.934E-01
Cycle 8	1.971E-05	-4.622E-04	4.793E-03	-2.516E-02	1.241E-02	9.958E-01	2.030E-05	-4.786E-04	5.002E-03	-2.672E-02	1.894E-02	9.934E-01
Cycle 15	1.971E-05	-4.622E-04	4.793E-03	-2.516E-02	1.243E-02	9.958E-01	2.030E-05	-4.786E-04	5.003E-03	-2.673E-02	1.895E-02	9.934E-01
Cycle 22	1.970E-05	-4.620E-04	4.793E-03	-2.518E-02	1.253E-02	9.958E-01	2.033E-05	-4.791E-04	5.008E-03	-2.676E-02	1.904E-02	9.934E-01
Cycle 29	1.971E-05	-4.622E-04	4.793E-03	-2.517E-02	1.244E-02	9.958E-01	2.030E-05	-4.786E-04	5.003E-03	-2.673E-02	1.896E-02	9.934E-01
Cycle 36	1.975E-05	-4.628E-04	4.795E-03	-2.514E-02	1.217E-02	9.959E-01	2.022E-05	-4.768E-04	4.985E-03	-2.663E-02	1.867E-02	9.935E-01
Cycle 43	1.974E-05	-4.626E-04	4.794E-03	-2.514E-02	1.219E-02	9.959E-01	2.022E-05	-4.769E-04	4.986E-03	-2.664E-02	1.870E-02	9.935E-01
Cycle 50	1.973E-05	-4.624E-04	4.794E-03	-2.515E-02	1.229E-02	9.958E-01	2.027E-05	-4.778E-04	4.995E-03	-2.668E-02	1.882E-02	9.935E-01
Cycle 57	1.975E-05	-4.627E-04	4.794E-03	-2.512E-02	1.209E-02	9.959E-01	2.021E-05	-4.765E-04	4.983E-03	-2.662E-02	1.863E-02	9.935E-01
Cycle 64	1.975E-05	-4.627E-04	4.794E-03	-2.513E-02	1.213E-02	9.959E-01	2.022E-05	-4.768E-04	4.986E-03	-2.664E-02	1.871E-02	9.935E-01
Cycle 71	1.970E-05	-4.620E-04	4.792E-03	-2.516E-02	1.241E-02	9.958E-01	2.030E-05	-4.785E-04	5.002E-03	-2.672E-02	1.893E-02	9.934E-01
Cycle 78	1.971E-05	-4.622E-04	4.794E-03	-2.517E-02	1.245E-02	9.958E-01	2.030E-05	-4.785E-04	5.002E-03	-2.673E-02	1.895E-02	9.934E-01
Cycle 85	1.973E-05	-4.625E-04	4.795E-03	-2.516E-02	1.235E-02	9.958E-01	2.027E-05	-4.779E-04	4.996E-03	-2.669E-02	1.885E-02	9.935E-01
Cycle 92	1.974E-05	-4.626E-04	4.794E-03	-2.514E-02	1.219E-02	9.959E-01	2.021E-05	-4.766E-04	4.983E-03	-2.662E-02	1.861E-02	9.935E-01
Cycle 99	1.974E-05	-4.626E-04	4.794E-03	-2.514E-02	1.221E-02	9.959E-01	2.023E-05	-4.770E-04	4.987E-03	-2.664E-02	1.869E-02	9.935E-01
Cycle 106	1.972E-05	-4.624E-04	4.794E-03	-2.517E-02	1.240E-02	9.958E-01	2.028E-05	-4.781E-04	4.998E-03	-2.670E-02	1.888E-02	9.934E-01
Cycle 113	1.974E-05	-4.626E-04	4.795E-03	-2.515E-02	1.230E-02	9.958E-01	2.025E-05	-4.775E-04	4.993E-03	-2.668E-02	1.882E-02	9.935E-01
Cycle 120	1.971E-05	-4.622E-04	4.793E-03	-2.517E-02	1.247E-02	9.958E-01	2.030E-05	-4.785E-04	5.002E-03	-2.672E-02	1.892E-02	9.934E-01
Cycle 127	1.971E-05	-4.622E-04	4.794E-03	-2.518E-02	1.250E-02	9.958E-01	2.030E-05	-4.785E-04	5.002E-03	-2.672E-02	1.894E-02	9.934E-01
Cycle 134	1.970E-05	-4.620E-04	4.793E-03	-2.518E-02	1.255E-02	9.958E-01	2.032E-05	-4.789E-04	5.005E-03	-2.674E-02	1.896E-02	9.934E-01
Cycle 141	1.971E-05	-4.621E-04	4.793E-03	-2.517E-02	1.250E-02	9.958E-01	2.030E-05	-4.785E-04	5.001E-03	-2.671E-02	1.890E-02	9.935E-01
Cycle 148	1.971E-05	-4.622E-04	4.794E-03	-2.517E-02	1.248E-02	9.958E-01	2.029E-05	-4.782E-04	4.998E-03	-2.670E-02	1.883E-02	9.935E-01

(Continued)

TABLE 4.4 (Continued)
Values of Blade # 20 Parameters for Model φ_{T12T01}

	Blade ≠ 20 parameter values											
	L_0	L_1	L_2	L_3	L_4	L_5	M_0	M_1	M_2	M_3	M_4	M_5
Cycle 155	1.975E-05	-4.628E-04	4.795E-03	-2.514E-02	1.221E-02	9.959E-01	2.021E-05	-4.764E-04	4.980E-03	-2.660E-02	1.853E-02	9.936E-01
Cycle 162	1.971E-05	-4.622E-04	4.794E-03	-2.517E-02	1.247E-02	9.958E-01	2.029E-05	-4.782E-04	4.998E-03	-2.670E-02	1.883E-02	9.935E-01
Cycle 169	1.972E-05	-4.623E-04	4.795E-03	-2.517E-02	1.246E-02	9.958E-01	2.027E-05	-4.779E-04	4.995E-03	-2.668E-02	1.879E-02	9.935E-01
Cycle 176	1.974E-05	-4.626E-04	4.796E-03	-2.516E-02	1.233E-02	9.958E-01	2.023E-05	-4.770E-04	4.987E-03	-2.664E-02	1.867E-02	9.935E-01
Cycle 183	1.970E-05	-4.621E-04	4.794E-03	-2.519E-02	1.257E-02	9.958E-01	2.029E-05	-4.782E-04	4.997E-03	-2.669E-02	1.877E-02	9.935E-01
Cycle 190	1.970E-05	-4.621E-04	4.794E-03	-2.519E-02	1.258E-02	9.958E-01	2.030E-05	-4.784E-04	5.000E-03	-2.670E-02	1.884E-02	9.935E-01
Cycle 197	1.972E-05	-4.624E-04	4.795E-03	-2.517E-02	1.246E-02	9.958E-01	2.027E-05	-4.778E-04	4.994E-03	-2.668E-02	1.878E-02	9.935E-01
Cycle 204	1.971E-05	-4.622E-04	4.793E-03	-2.517E-02	1.247E-02	9.958E-01	2.026E-05	-4.777E-04	4.993E-03	-2.667E-02	1.874E-02	9.935E-01
Cycle 211	1.974E-05	-4.626E-04	4.795E-03	-2.516E-02	1.230E-02	9.958E-01	2.022E-05	-4.766E-04	4.982E-03	-2.661E-02	1.855E-02	9.936E-01
Cycle 218	1.972E-05	-4.624E-04	4.796E-03	-2.518E-02	1.248E-02	9.958E-01	2.026E-05	-4.776E-04	4.992E-03	-2.666E-02	1.869E-02	9.935E-01
Cycle 225	1.972E-05	-4.624E-04	4.796E-03	-2.519E-02	1.253E-02	9.958E-01	2.027E-05	-4.777E-04	4.993E-03	-2.666E-02	1.870E-02	9.935E-01
Cycle 232	1.976E-05	-4.629E-04	4.797E-03	-2.515E-02	1.220E-02	9.959E-01	2.017E-05	-4.757E-04	4.973E-03	-2.655E-02	1.838E-02	9.936E-01
Cycle 239	1.975E-05	-4.628E-04	4.796E-03	-2.515E-02	1.225E-02	9.959E-01	2.018E-05	-4.759E-04	4.974E-03	-2.656E-02	1.840E-02	9.936E-01
Cycle 246	1.974E-05	-4.627E-04	4.797E-03	-2.517E-02	1.234E-02	9.958E-01	2.019E-05	-4.761E-04	4.977E-03	-2.657E-02	1.844E-02	9.936E-01

Source: cycle = full revolution

4.5   GRAPHIC TECHNICAL STATUS PORTRAITS FOR BLADES

A direct interpretation of the results in Tables 4.1 to 4.4 is difficult. This requires a presentation of the results in the form of colour-coded portraits.

These graphical portraits of the technical condition (status) of blades # 7 and # 20 of the first stage compressor in the SO-3 engine are shown in Figures 4.3 and 4.4.

The portraits of the diagnosed blades clearly show different external and internal wear between them. The analysis should be carried out comprehensively. An expert diagnostician should consider the portraits generated for

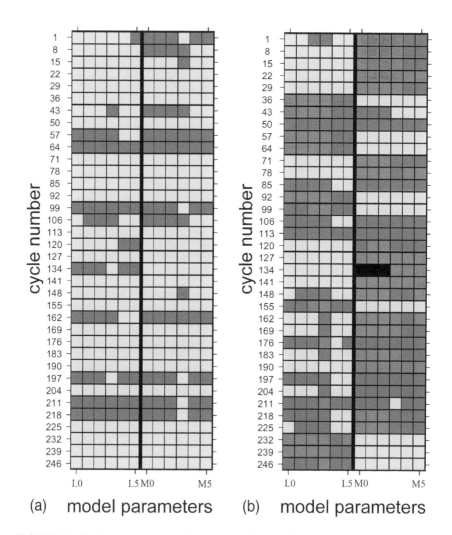

FIGURE 4.3 Technical status portrait for model A^2_{T12TOI} of blades (a) # 7 and (b) # 20.

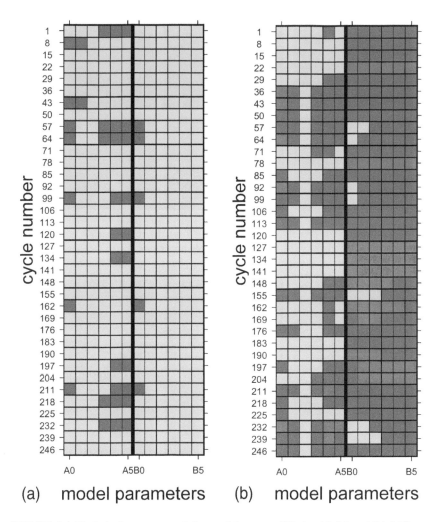

(a) model parameters (b) model parameters

FIGURE 4.4 Technical status portrait for model φ_{T12T01} of blades (a) # 7 and (b) # 20.

different rotational speeds, models, and the overruns of successive diagnostic thresholds, the values of the thresholds, and severities. Analysing the generated blade portraits, it can be concluded that blade # 20 is in a much worse technical condition than blade # 7. Blade # 20 demands increasing attention in further diagnostic tests.

The results of the diagnostics based on the technical status portraits (Figures 4.3 and 4.4) were verified using direct (endoscopic) methods. Figures 4.5 and 4.6 show photographs of the blades with their defects and damage. There is full compliance between the diagnostic test results and the endoscopic examination results.

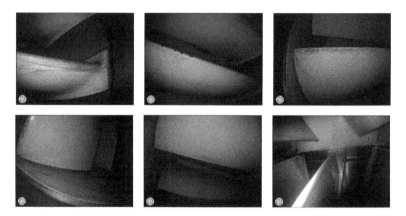

FIGURE 4.5 Endoscopic photographs of the blade # 7 (a), (b), (c) the leading edge, from the locking piece to the apex seen from the upper surface, (d) the apex, (e), (f) the trailing edge from the apex to the locking pieces, seen from the upper surface [29].

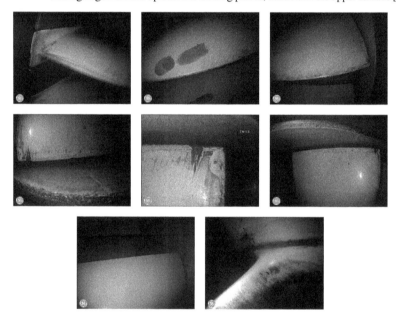

FIGURE 4.6 Endoscopic photographs of the blade # 20 (a), (b), (c) the leading edge, from the locking piece to the apex seen from the upper surface, (d), (e) the apex, (f), (g), (h) the trailing edge from the apex to the locking pieces, seen from the upper surface [29].

4.6 NON-PARAMETRIC METHOD OF BLADE TECHNICAL STATUS ASSESSMENT

The inverse of Formulas 4.10 and 4.21 can be regarded as abstract virtual operator transmittances of the blade, $H(s)$ [25]. The input signal is therefore the movement of the blade when air is flowing onto it (time T_{01}), and the output signal is the blade movement when air is flowing off the blade (time T_{12}). It means that $j\omega$ should be inserted after s in the resulting transmittances. The result is a conventional spectral transmittance, $H(j\omega)$. The real part $P(\omega)$ of this transmittance should be determined. $P(\omega)$ allows the determination of step response $h(t)$ and pulse response $g(t)$.

$$g(t) = \frac{2}{\pi}\int_0^\infty P(\omega)\cdot\omega\frac{\cos\omega t}{\omega}d\omega \qquad (4.24)$$

$$h(t) = \frac{2}{\pi}\int_0^\infty P(\omega)\frac{\sin\omega t}{\omega}d\omega \qquad (4.25)$$

Using the data in Tables 4.1 and 4.2 for model A^2_{T12T0P} the pulse and step responses were determined for all the cycles (revolutions) tested with both blade # 7 and blade # 20. The trends of the responses to pulse and step input function for selected revolution cycles of model A^2_{T12T0I} are shown in Figures 4.7 (blade # 7) and 4.8 (blade # 20).

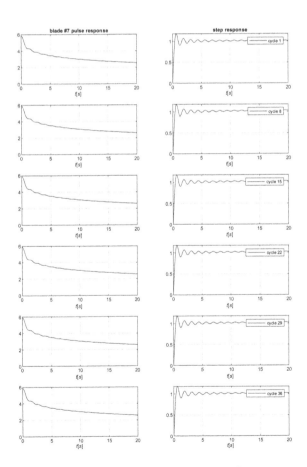

FIGURE 4.7 Step and pulse responses determined for model A^2_{T12T0I} for different revolution cycles of blade # 7.

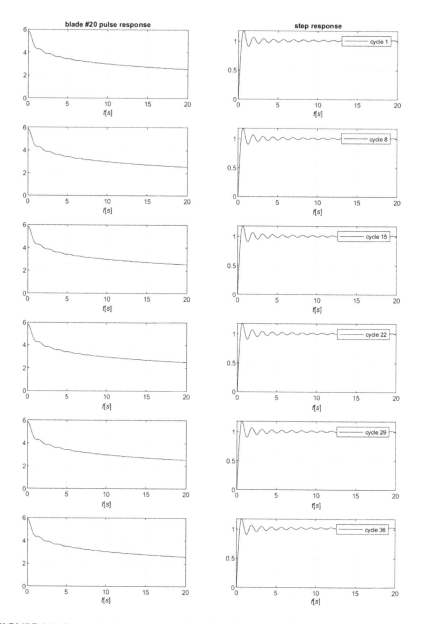

FIGURE 4.8 Step and pulse responses determined for model A^2_{T12T01} for different revolution cycles of blade # 20.

These calculations were repeated for the data in Table 4.4 for model φ_{T12T01}. The trends of the responses to pulse and step input function for selected revolution cycles of model φ_{T12T01} are shown in Figures 4.9 (blade # 7) and 4.10 (blade # 20).

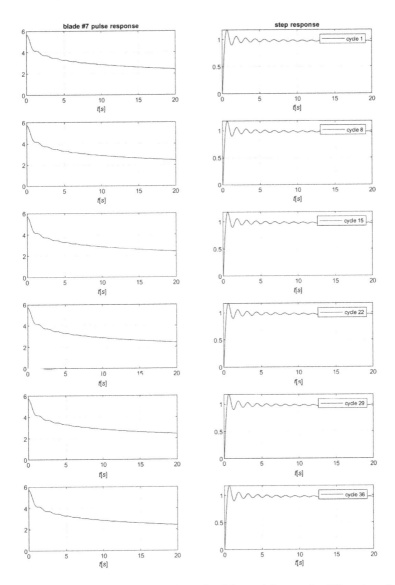

FIGURE 4.9 Step and pulse responses determined for model φ_{T12T01} for different revolution cycles of blade # 7.

For the obtained responses to step and impulse input functions in models A^2_{T12T01} and φ_{T12T01}, the maximum values and overrun calculated from threshold $\mu \pm 20\% \mu$ were determined. They are listed in Table 4.5.

The regulation times [s], calculated as the time after which the step response does not exceed the stable value of $\pm 2\%$, were also determined for the generated responses to step input function in models A^2_{T12T01} and φ_{T12T01}. The regulation times are listed in Table 4.6.

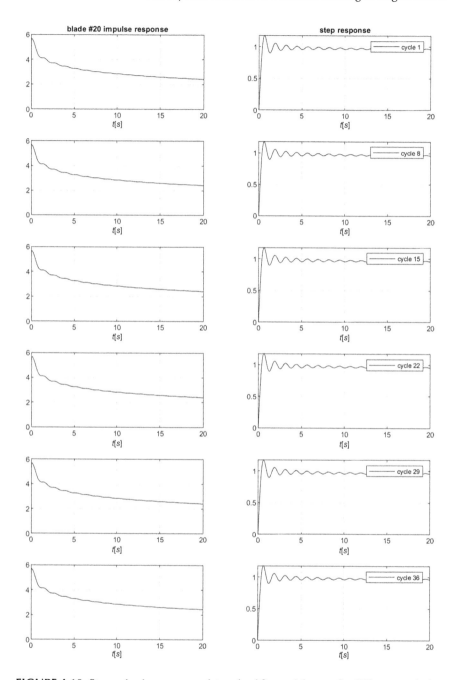

FIGURE 4.10 Step and pulse responses determined for model φ_{T12T01} for different revolution cycles of blade # 20.

TABLE 4.5

Maximum Values of Step Responses for Blade # 7 and Blade # 20

Cycle #	Blade # 7				Blade # 20			
	Model A^2_{T12T01}		Model φ_{T12T01}		Model A^2_{T12T01}		Model φ_{T12T01}	
	Pulse response	Step response	Pulse response	Step response	Pulse response	Step response	Pulse response	Step response
1	5.859	1.180	5.685	1.177	5.851	1.180	5.682	1.177
8	5.935	1.182	5.716	1.178	5.849	1.180	5.681	1.177
15	5.926	1.182	5.712	1.178	5.851	1.180	5.681	1.177
22	5.904	1.181	5.703	1.178	5.834	1.180	5.675	1.177
29	5.909	1.181	5.705	1.178	5.847	1.180	5.680	1.177
36	5.880	1.181	5.693	1.177	5.902	1.181	5.701	1.178
43	5.935	1.182	5.717	1.178	5.895	1.181	5.699	1.178
50	5.918	1.182	5.710	1.178	5.871	1.180	5.690	1.177
57	5.864	1.180	5.687	1.177	5.908	1.181	5.703	1.178
64	5.861	1.180	5.686	1.177	5.902	1.181	5.700	1.178
71	5.884	1.181	5.695	1.177	5.848	1.180	5.680	1.177
78	5.884	1.181	5.696	1.177	5.850	1.180	5.681	1.177
85	5.885	1.181	5.695	1.177	5.869	1.180	5.689	1.177
92	5.892	1.181	5.699	1.177	5.897	1.181	5.701	1.178
99	5.854	1.180	5.683	1.177	5.890	1.181	5.697	1.177
106	5.937	1.182	5.717	1.178	5.862	1.180	5.687	1 177
113	5.885	1.181	5.696	1.177	5.882	1.181	5.693	1.177
120	5.874	1.181	5.691	1.177	5.848	1.180	5.681	1.177
127	5.882	1.181	5.695	1.177	5.846	1.180	5.681	1.177
134	5.877	1.181	5.694	1.177	5.836	1.180	5.676	1.177
141	5.899	1.181	5.703	1.178	5.845	1.180	5.680	1.177
148	5.915	1.182	5.708	1.178	5.852	1.180	5.683	1.177
155	5.895	1.181	5.701	1.177	5.901	1.181	5.703	1.178
162	5.945	1.182	5.723	1.178	5.852	1.180	5.684	1.177
169	5.884	1.181	5.697	1.177	5.859	1.180	5.687	1.177
176	5.927	1.182	5.715	1.178	5.885	1.181	5.697	1.177
183	5.893	1.181	5.701	1.177	5.843	1.180	5.682	1.177
190	5.900	1.181	5.705	1.178	5.840	1.180	5.680	1.177
197	5.865	1.180	5.691	1.177	5.863	1.180	5.688	1.177
204	5.906	1.181	5.708	1.178	5.858	1.180	5.687	1.177
211	5.867	1.180	5.691	1.177	5.891	1.181	5.700	1.178
218	5.863	1.180	5.690	1.177	5.862	1.180	5.690	1.177
225	5.891	1.181	5.703	1.177	5.858	1.180	5.688	1.177
232	5.879	1.181	5.698	1.177	5.915	1.182	5.710	1.178
239	5.891	1.181	5.703	1.177	5.906	1.181	5.708	1.178
246	5.922	1.182	5.717	1.178	5.898	1.181	5.705	1.178

TABLE 4.6

Percentage Changes of the Maximum Values of Step Responses for Blade # 7 and Blade # 20

Cycle #	Blade # 7		Blade # 20	
	Model A^2_{T12T01}	Model φ_{T12T01}	Model A^2_{T12T01}	Model φ_{T12T01}
1	7.62	7.58	9.49	9.42
8	10.15	7.57	8.24	9.44
15	10.12	7.58	8.25	9.44
22	8.91	6.37	8.28	9.48
29	8.92	6.41	8.28	9.45
36	8.83	8.91	9.44	8.25
43	10.15	8.89	8.24	8.26
50	10.09	7.65	8.26	8.28
57	7.64	8.92	9.48	8.24
64	7.63	8.91	9.49	8.25
71	8.85	7.56	8.3	9.45
78	8.85	7.57	8.3	9.44
85	8.85	7.65	8.3	8.29
92	8.88	8.89	8.29	8.25
99	7.6	8.87	9.5	8.26
106	10.15	7.63	8.24	8.29
113	8.85	8.84	8.3	8.27
120	7.66	7.56	9.46	9.45
127	8.84	6.41	9.43	9.45
134	7.67	6.38	9.45	9.48
141	8.9	6.41	8.28	9.45
148	8.94	7.59	8.27	9.43
155	8.89	8.9	8.29	8.25
162	10.17	7.59	8.22	8.3
169	8.85	7.62	8.3	8.29
176	10.12	8.85	8.25	8.27
183	8.88	6.4	8.29	9.46
190	8.9	6.39	8.28	9.47
197	7.64	7.63	9.48	8.29
204	8.92	7.62	8.28	8.3
211	7.65	8.87	9.48	8.26
218	7.63	7.63	9.48	8.29
225	8.88	7.61	8.29	8.3
232	8.83	10.05	9.44	8.23
239	8.88	8.92	8.29	8.24
246	10.11	8.9	8.26	8.25

The maximum values of the step input function responses in Table 4.5 are shown in the form of bar graphs in Figures 4.11–4.14.

The values of the regulation time of the response of model A^2_{T12T01} and φ_{T12T01} to the step input function (Table 4.6). are shown in the form of bar graphs in Figures 4.15–4.18.

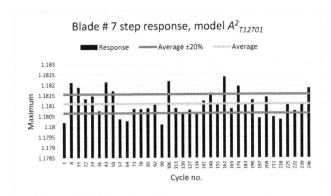

FIGURE 4.11 Maximum values of the pulse response, their average, and the threshold for blade # 7 in model A^2_{T12T01} for individual cycles.

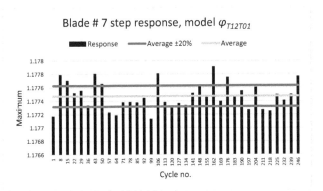

FIGURE 4.12 Maximum values of the step response, their average, and the threshold for blade # 7 in model φ_{T12T01} for individual cycles.

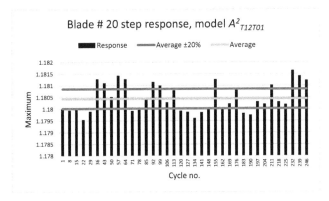

FIGURE 4.13 Maximum values of the pulse response, their average, and the threshold for blade # 20 in model A^2_{T12T01} for individual cycles.

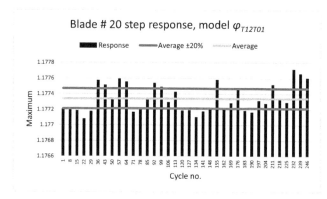

FIGURE 4.14 Maximum values of the step response, their average, and the threshold for blade # 20 in model φ_{T12T01} for individual cycles.

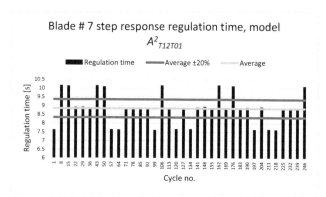

FIGURE 4.15 Regulation time values of the step response, their average, and the threshold for blade # 7 in model A^2_{T12T01} for individual cycles.

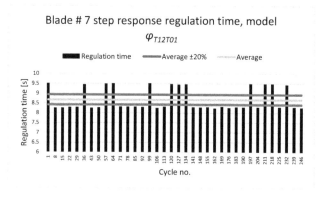

FIGURE 4.16 Regulation time values of the step response, their average, and the threshold for blade # 7 in model φ_{T12T01} for individual cycles.

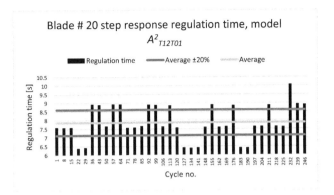

FIGURE 4.17 Regulation time values of the step response, their average, and the threshold for blade # 20 in model A^2_{T12T01} for individual cycles.

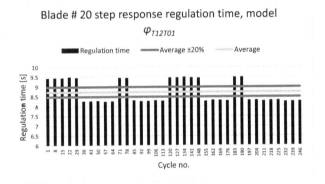

FIGURE 4.18 Regulation time values of the step response, their average, and the threshold for blade # 20 in model φ_{T12T01} for individual cycles.

According to the principles of automation (by observing overshoot (χ) and its lower deviations from the average, and regulation time (t_r) and its lower deviations from the average), it is evident that the performance of blade # 7 is better than that of blade # 20.

Based on the model, changes in parameters (with parametric methods) or other features of the model (with non-parametric methods) can be tested.

Parametric methods require statistical (imprecise) diagnostic thresholds, while non-parametric methods do not require the thresholds because they are defined by determined principles of automation ($\chi < 20\%$, t_r—short).

Probabilistic thresholds are determined from full statistical knowledge of the diagnostic object and its environment. The thresholds require many sets of measurements of specific quantities (at least a dozen or more) performed during diagnostic tests, for which statistics are determined: arithmetic mean, median, standard deviation, distribution density function, significance level, expected lifetime, and expected lifetime between failures. The thresholds may have a fixed value and a value that depends on the number of measurements produced during diagnostic testing or during operation of the object. The thresholds are decided by experts/ diagnosticians, taking into consideration the differences between the parameter values guaranteed by the manufacturer and the parameter values obtained during tests in the process of operation.

Non-parametric (determined) thresholds are determined from full, determined statistical and dynamic knowledge of the diagnostic object and its environment. Detailed information on the intended use of the object and its operating conditions are required for this. The knowledge applied in the design of the object is needed and must include the design assumptions, laboratory test results, assumed performance quality and reliability characteristics, and the knowledge arising directly from production of the object. The static and dynamic characteristics, which are expressly defined for all regulation systems, are important in this regard.

By comparing the step response trends for the individual blades, it is possible to see the differences in performance between the blades in different duty cycles. By examining the quality indicators determined by the principles of automation for all systems (overshoots, maximum values, and regulation time) of step and pulse responses for individual blade cycles, the operating status of the blades can be assessed and the technical condition (status) of the blades can be inferred.

4.7 SUMMARY

The method of running assessment of changes in the technical condition (status) of blades based on the analysis of the diagnostic models of the blades is an innovative method of diagnosing blades in the environment without measuring the environment signals.

A characteristic of models A^2_{T12T01} i φ_{T12T01} is that no measurement of environment signals is required to determine the models. A characteristic feature of this method is the determination of a diagnostic model as a quotient of mathematical models that link diagnostic and environment signals with technical condition (status) parameters.

It is possible to eliminate the environment from the model thanks to appropriate implementation of diagnostic tests, which—in their basic version—must include measurement of the environment signals, $x(t)$, and the diagnostic signals, $y(t)$. The elimination of signals $x(t)$ from the model that defines the relations between $x(t)$ and $y(t)$ can be performed by, for example, an appropriate organisation of tests. Hence, during the observation time $\{T\}$ (Figure 4.2), two observation intervals T_{12} and T_{01} are distinguished [2, 4, 5, 6]. Signal $x(t)$ is assumed to remain unchanged in intervals T_{12} and T_{01}. Therefore, the respective blade models in the frequency domain for intervals T_{12} and T_{01}, which are the amplitude gain A^2 (Formula 4.7) and the difference of phase shifts $\Delta\varphi$ (Formula 4.19), can be reduced to new diagnostic models in the form of the ratio of amplitude gains A^2_{T12} to A^2_{T01} (Formula 4.9) and the difference of phase shifts φ_{T12} to φ_{T01} (Formula 4.20). This leads to elimination of the environment from the diagnostic model. Parameters A^2 and $\Delta\varphi$ are observed in the diagnostic inference process. Their changes are related to changes in the technical condition (status) of the blade of interest (parametric diagnostics), or the blade portraits.

The use of the proposed parametric methods can additionally expand the diagnostician's knowledge with information about the internal condition of the blade of interest (through the analysis of the blade portraits in particular cycles of its operation). The methods used here clearly showed that the technical condition of blade # 7 was different from the technical condition of blade # 20.

Also note that parametric methods should not be used with small numbers of data as the methods require the determination of diagnostic thresholds from statistical operations. The methods can only be used if it is feasible to record at least a dozen [32, 33] blade passes under the sensor, so that the diagnostic threshold determined is reliable.

Formulas 4.9 and 4.20 can be considered operator transmittances and can be reduced to spectral transmittances. The output signal in these transmittances is "air flow off the blade—time T_{12}", and the input signal is "air flow to the blade—time T_{01}".

This way, the operator transmittance and the spectral transmittance take the form of the inverse of Formulas 4.9 and 4.20. By distinguishing the real part $P(\omega)$ from the transmittance, it is possible to determine the pulse and step response of the blade (Formulas 4.11 and 4.12), which reduces the testing of the blade driven by the principles of statistics to testing driven by the principles of automation. All test results are mutually verified and confirmed.

REFERENCES

1. Abdelrhman A.M., Hee L.M., Leong M.S., Al-Obaidi S.: Condition monitoring of blade in turbomachinery: a review. Advances in Mechanical Engineering, vol. 6, no. 210717, pp. 1–10, 2014.
2. Al-Badour F., Sunar M., Cheded L.: Vibration analysis of rotating machinery using time-frequency analysis and wavelet techniques. Mechanical Systems and Signal Processing, vol. 25, no. 6, pp. 2083–2101, 2011.
3. Al-Obaidi S., Leong M.S., Hamzah R., Abdelrhman A.M.: A review of acoustic emission technique for machinery condition monitoring: defects detection and diagnostic. Applied Mechanics and Materials, vol. 229, pp. 1476–1480, 2012.
4. Aretakis N., Mathioudakis K.: Wavelet analysis for gas turbine fault diagnostics. ASME Journal of Engineering for Gas Turbines and Power, vol. 119, no. 4, pp. 870–875, 1997.
5. Bai Z., Chen S., Jia L., Zeng Z.: Phased array ultrasonic signal compressive detection in low-pressure turbine disc. NDT&E International, vol. 89, pp. 1–13, 2017.
6. Barragan J.M.: Engine vibration monitoring and diagnosis based on on-board captured data, DTIC Document ADP014124. MTU Aero Engines GmBH, Munich 2013.
7. Battiato G., Firrone C.M., Berruti T.M.: Forced response of rotating bladed disks: blade tip-timing measurements. Mechanical Systems and Signal Processing, vol. 85, pp. 912–926, 2017.

8. Blachnio J.: Capabilities to assess health/maintenance status of gas turbine blades with non-destructive methods. Polish Maritime Research, vol. 4, no. 84, pp. 41–47, 2014.
9. Chang C., Chen L.: Damage detection of cracked thick rotating blades by a spatial wavelet based approach. Applied Acoustics, vol. 65, no. 11, pp. 1095–1111, 2004.
10. Chatfield C.: The analysis of time series—an introduction. Chapman and Hall, London 2003.
11. Chen Z., Yang Y., Xie Y., Guo B., Hu Z.: Non-contact crack detection of high-speed blades based on principal component analysis and Euclidian angles using optical-fiber sensors. Sensors and Actuators A: Physical, vol. 201, pp. 66–72, 2013.
12. Freund O., Montgomery M., Mittelbach M., Seume J.R.: Non-contact test set-up for aeroelasticity in a rotating turbomachine combining a novel acoustic excitation system with tip-timing. Measurement Science and Technology, vol. 25, no. 035008, 2014.
13. Guo H., Duan F., Zhang J.: Blade resonance parameter identification based on tip-timing method without the once-per revolution sensor. Mechanical Systems and Signal Processing, vol. 66, pp. 625–639, 2016.
14. Lackner M.: Vibration and crack detection in gas turbine engine compressor blades using eddy current sensors, M.Sc. Thesis, Massachusetts Institute of Technology 2003.
15. Lim M.H., Leong M.S.: Detection of early faults in rotating machinery based on wavelet analysis. Advances in Mechanical Engineering, vol. 5, no. 625863, pp. 1–8, 2013.
16. Madhavan S., Jain R., Sujatha C., Sekhar A.S.: Vibration based damage detection of rotor blades in a gas turbine engine. Engineering Failure Analysis, vol. 46, pp. 26–39, 2014.
17. Neumann M., Dreier F., Gunther P., Wilke U., Fischer A., Buttner L., Holzinger F., Schiffer H.P., Czarske J.: A laser-optical sensor system for blade vibration detection of high-speed compressors. Mechanical Systems and Signal Processing, vol. 64, pp. 337–346, 2015.
18. Simmons H.R., Michalsky D.L., Brewer K.E., Smalley A.J.: Measuring rotor and blade dynamics using an optical blade tip sensor. Proceedings of the 35th ASME International Gas Turbine and Aeroengine Congress and Exposition, Brussels, June 11–14, 1990.
19. Przysowa R., Rokicki E.: Inductive sensors for blade tip-timing in gas turbines. Journal of KONBiN, vol. 4, no. 36, pp. 147–164, 2015.
20. Randall R., Sawalhi N.: Use of cepstrum to remove selected discrete frequency components from a time signal. Rotating Machinery, Structural Health Monitoring, Shock and Vibration, vol. 5, pp. 451–461, 2011.
21. Rokicki E., Spychala J., Szczepanik R., Majewski P.: Induction sensor to measure vibrations of a turbo-machine rotor blade. US Patent no. 8,240,212 B2. Washington, DC: U.S. Patent and Trademark Office, 2012.
22. Rzadkowski R., Rokicki E., Piechowski L., Szczepanik R.: Analysis of middle bearing failure in rotor jet engine using tip-timing and tip-clearance techniques. Mechanical Systems and Signal Processing, vol. 76, pp. 213–227, 2016.
23. Golak K., Lindstedt P., Gradzki R.: Studies of the jet engine control quality based on its response to the disturbance inflicted on the object, designated from its response to the set point inflicted to the controller. Proceedings of the European Safety and Reliability Conference: Methodology and Applications 2014 (ESREL'14), Wroclaw, September 14–18, pp. 137–140.

24. Gradzki R.: Influence of diagnostic signal sampling frequency on rotor blade technical condition images determined from phase shift difference. Journal of KONES Powertrain and Transport, vol. 19, no. 2, pp. 181–189, 2012.
25. Grądzki R., Golak K., Lindstedt P.: Parametric and nonparametric diagnostic models for blades in the rotating machinery with environment elimination. Journal of KONES, vol. 23, no. 2, pp. 137–145, 2016.
26. Lindstedt P., Gradzki R.: Premises and the example of parametric method of evaluation of technical condition of the turbomachine blade with elimination of its immeasurable environment. Journal of KONBiN, vol. 1, no. 17, pp. 179–194, 2011.
27. Lindstedt P., Kotowski A.: Basics for innovations in vibroacoustic diagnostics of transport machines rotor blades. The Archives of Transport, vol. 16, no. 4, pp. 47–61, 2004.
28. Lindstedt P., Gradzki R.: Parametrical models of working rotor machine blade diagnostics with its unmeasurable environment elimination. Acta Mechanica et Automatica, vol. 4, no. 4, pp. 56–63, 2010.
29. Gradzki R.: Parametryczne modele diagnostyczne łopatki pracującej maszyny wirnikowej z eliminacją niemierzalnych sygnałów otoczenia [Parametric diagnostic models of a blade in an operating rotor machine, with the elimination of unmeasurable ambient signals]. Doctoral Dissertation, Bialystok University of Technology 2012.
30. Gradzki R.: The influence of diagnostic signal measurement period on blades technical condition images determined from phase shift difference. Solid State Phenomena, vol. 199, pp. 67–72, 2013.
31. Kotowski A., Lindstedt P.: The using of signals of impulse acoustic response in test of rotor blades in stationary conditions. The International Symposium on Stability Control of Rotating Machinery, ISCORMA 4, Calgary, AB, 2007.
32. Jiang H., Li C., Li H.: An improved EEMD with multiwavelet packet for rotating machinery multi-fault diagnosis. Mechanical Systems and Signal Processing, vol. 36, pp. 225–239, 2013.
33. Hoskins R.F.: Delta functions. Introduction to generalised functions, 2nd Edition. Woodhead Publishing, Sawston, Cambridge 2009.

5 Test Method for Reliability of a Bus in Various Operating Conditions

5.1 INTRODUCTION

Running reliability testing of technical objects is an important and ever-present problem (see Section 1.1.4). This is particularly the case when dealing with small sets of objects (including two or three objects) or single objects, and small sets of failures of these objects. The method of failure identification becomes an important part of the process of reliability testing. The map of catastrophic, parametric, and transient failures is fundamental for the determination of reliability characteristics and parameters [1–16].

Currently, catastrophic failures, which are dangerous to the existence of a single object being an element of a given set of objects, are primarily used to determine the reliability characteristics and parameters. Parametric and transient failures are not used widely, but they are not as absolutely hazardous to the existence of the object of interest. The theory of reliability features this formula [17–21]:

$$R(t) = R_a(t) R_b(t) R_c(t) \tag{5.1}$$

with:

$R(t)$— probability of correct performance/operation of the object (a machine, an equipment unit, or a system);
$R_a(t)$— probability of correct performance/operation due to catastrophic failure;
$R_b(t)$— probability of correct performance/operation due to parametric failure;
$R_c(t)$— probability of correct performance/operation due to transient failure.

It follows from Formula 5.1 that the number of catastrophic failures $m_a(t)$, parametric failures $m_b(t)$, and transient failures $m_c(t)$—and hence, the number of estimators $R_a^*(t)$, $R_b^*(t)$, and $R_c^*(t)$ (Formula 1.129)—are required to determine the reliability (the probability of correct operation of an object as an element of a set

DOI: 10.1201/9781032638447-5

of the number of n objects—Formula 1.135). Since it is virtually always difficult to determine $m_b(t)$ and $m_c(t)$, the reliability characteristics are usually determined only from the number of catastrophic failures $m_a(t)$ for a sufficiently large set of objects. The disadvantages of this method, which is currently used to calculate the reliability characteristics, are that it is based on continuously hazardous catastrophic failures (the parametric failures can be partially taken into account) and that it can be implemented best on a large set of n objects (a dozen, 18, 19, and more). In these circumstances, the reliability formula is:

$$R(t) = R_a(t) \cdot 1 \cdot 1 \qquad (5.2)$$

Operating practice imposes increasingly difficult tasks on maintenance. It is required that reliability characteristics be determined, preferably before the occurrence of dangerous catastrophic failures and for small sets of (individual) objects. In this case, the reliability formula is expressed like so

$$R(t) = 1 \cdot R_b(t) \cdot R_c(t) \qquad (5.3)$$

The execution of this task is complex. It is because it requires the identification of parametric failures $m_b(t)$ and transient failures $m_c(t)$—a difficult task, as said before—and has been the reason for that up to now, reliability characteristics are often determined only from catastrophic failures $m_a(t)$.

5.2 THEORETICAL FOUNDATION FOR PARAMETRIC AND TRANSIENT FAILURE IDENTIFICATION FROM EQUATIONS OF INTERACTION

It is assumed that each technical object can be described by two correlated equations of status (condition) (which are equations of interaction—Formula 1.30). It can be expressed in two forms: without or with initial conditions. There is a view expressed that the most appropriate approach to failure identification is the use of equations that include initial conditions (the unknown past service life of the object), and in-service testing of the object should be based on these conditions [18, 22–26].

- The technical object being tested (a bus vehicle) is described by two autonomous, interrelated equations of state (equations of interaction), which include the initial conditions:

$$\frac{dD}{d\theta} = a_T D + b_{T1} U + b_{T0} \qquad (5.4)$$

$$\frac{dU}{d\theta} = a_R U + b_{R1} D + b_{R0} \qquad (5.5)$$

where:

D— complex diagnostic signal of the bus;

U— complex performance quality signal (the signal of use—environment);

a_R— operating status parameter, which first depends on the bus performance, U and the effect of the object diagnostic signals D on the performance;

a_T— technical status parameter of the bus, which depends on the diagnostic signals and the environmental effect signals;

b_{TI}, b_{T0}, b_{RI}, b_{R0}— the parameters of the effect of the performance signals U and the diagnostic signals D, and their initial conditions on the technical status or the operating status;

θ— operating time.

These equations are based on the obvious observation that the utility value of an object U depends on its technical status (physical wear), D and the technical status D depends on the severity of use U. This means that the technical status D is the environment for the operating status U, and the operating status U is the environment for the technical status D, and both statuses are autonomous [17, 18, 23, 27–29].

The consideration of initial conditions is very important because each technical object is always different at the beginning of its life and therefore has different initial conditions from other technical objects.

Formulas 5.4 and 5.5 can also be expressed in a simplified form.

$$\frac{\Delta D}{\Delta \theta} = a_T D + a_T \hat{a}_{T1} U + a_T \hat{a}_{T0} \tag{5.6}$$

$$\frac{\Delta D}{\Delta \theta} = a_T (D + \hat{a}_{T1} U + \hat{a}_{T0}) \tag{5.7}$$

$$\frac{\Delta U}{\Delta \theta} = a_R U + a_R \hat{a}_{R1} D + a_R \hat{a}_{R0} \tag{5.8}$$

$$\frac{\Delta U}{\Delta \theta} = a_R (U + \hat{a}_{R1} D + \hat{a}_{R0}) \tag{5.9}$$

According to the static identification principles $\dot{D} = 0$ and assuming that $\Delta \theta$ is sufficiently small, Formulas 5.4 and 5.7 yield [18–20, 30, 31]:

$$\hat{a}_{T1} = \frac{n \sum_{i=1}^{n} D_i U_i - \sum_{i=1}^{n} D_i \sum_{i=1}^{n} U_i}{n \sum_{i=1}^{n} U_i^2 - \sum_{i=1}^{n} U_i \sum_{i=1}^{n} U_i} \tag{5.10}$$

$$\hat{a}_{T0} = \frac{\sum_{i=1}^{n} D_i \sum_{i=1}^{n} U_i^2 - \sum_{i=1}^{n} D_i U_i \sum_{i=1}^{n} U_i}{n \sum_{i=1}^{n} U_i^2 - \sum_{i=1}^{n} U_i \sum_{i=1}^{n} U_i} \tag{5.11}$$

and ultimately, the sought technical status parameter:

$$a_T = \frac{\Delta D}{\Delta\theta(D + \hat{a}_{T_1}U + \hat{a}_{T0})} \tag{5.12}$$

Parameter a_T characterises the technical condition (status) of the object. It depends on diagnostic signals (D), the signals resulting from the effects of the environment (U), and the initial conditions $\hat{a}_{T0}$.

Considering the second case of the equations of interaction for $\dot{U} = 0$ and assuming that $\Delta\theta$ is sufficiently small, Formulas 5.5 and 5.8 provide the following:

$$\hat{a}_{R1} = \frac{n\sum_{i=1}^{n}D_iU_i - \sum_{i=1}^{n}D_i\sum_{i=1}^{n}U_i}{n\sum_{i=1}^{n}D_i^2 - \sum_{i=1}^{n}D_i\sum_{i=1}^{n}D_i} \tag{5.13}$$

$$\hat{a}_{R0} = \frac{\sum_{i=1}^{n}U_i\sum_{i=1}^{n}D_i^2 - \sum_{i=1}^{n}D_iU_i\sum_{i=1}^{n}D_i}{n\sum_{i=1}^{n}D_i^2 - \sum_{i=1}^{n}D_i\sum_{i=1}^{n}D_i} \tag{5.14}$$

and ultimately, the sought operating (use) status:

$$a_R = \frac{\Delta U}{\Delta\theta(U + \hat{a}_{R1}D + \hat{a}_{R0})} \tag{5.15}$$

Parameter a_R characterises the operating status of the object. It depends on the performance (use/utility) signals U resulting from the conditions of operation and the effects of the environment, on the diagnostic signals D resulting from the technical condition (status) of the object, and on the initial conditions $\hat{a}_{R0}$.

It follows from the relations (5.12 and 5.15) that at any instant $\theta i + \Delta\theta$ ($\Delta\theta$ is low enough and larger than zero, which is produced by referencing $\Delta\theta$ to θ_{res}), the instantaneous values of a_T and a_R can be calculated. These values are the basis for a quantitative assessment of the technical status and the regulation status. Moreover, the trends of sequences of the values of $a_T(\theta)$ and $a_R(\theta)$ can drive the identification of parametric and transient failures, and thus the identification of reliability characteristics (before catastrophic failures occur).

A notable feature of this method of failure identification is the observation that sufficiently large instantaneous changes of parameter a_T can be considered a symptom of parametric failure, while sufficiently large changes of parameter a_R can be considered a symptom of transient (instantaneous) failure.

- The way to identify the number of failures $m_b(t)$ and $m_c(t)$ is as follows:

1. Measure the technical status (condition) signals $D_1, D_2, D_3, \ldots$ and calculate the complex diagnostic signal, D:

$$D = \sqrt{\bar{D}_1^2 + \bar{D}_2^2 + \ldots \bar{D}_n^2} \qquad (5.16)$$

$\bar{D}_i$ — relative value of the successive diagnostic signal $\bar{D} = \dfrac{D_i}{D_{idop}}$;

D_{idop} — acceptable signal value specified by the manufacturer (or other decision-maker).

2. Measure the operating (utility) signals $U_1, U_2, U_3, \ldots$ and calculate the complex environment signal, U:

$$U = \sqrt{\bar{U}_1^2 + \bar{U}_2^2 + \ldots \bar{U}_n^2} \qquad (5.17)$$

with:

$\bar{U}_i$ — relative value of the successive operating signal $\bar{U} = \dfrac{U_i}{U_{idop}}$;

U_{idop} — acceptable signal value specified by the manufacturer (or other decision-maker).

3. The trends in values of the technical status parameters a_T and regulation status a_R, their average values μ_{a_T} and μ_{a_R} their standard deviations σ_{a_T} and σ_{a_R} are determined from the autonomous equations of state (5.12 and 5.15).

4. Determine the number of conventional parametric and transient failures $m_b(t)$ and $m_c(t)$, assuming that failure occurs when the current values of parameters a_T and a_R are greater than the determined threshold values and also when these values change their sign.

Therefore, the determination of diagnostic thresholds for the technical status parameter a_T and operating status parameter a_R poses a serious problem.

A significant change in parameters a_T and a_R is considered to occur when the value of a_T or a_R reaches or exceeds a statistical threshold, for example, $\mu \pm 0.25\sigma$, $\mu \pm 0.5\sigma$, $\mu \pm 0.75\sigma$, or $\mu \pm \sigma$, where μ is the average value (the statistic) of a_T or a_R and σ is the standard deviation (a statistic) of a_T or a_R [30, 32–35]. The numbers of overruns of $m_b(t)$ and $m_c(t)$ of the statistical thresholds adopted like so facilitate identification of the failure of interest.

The numbers of failures determined facilitate determination of the reliability characteristics of each individual object. These characteristics can be determined before a catastrophic failure occurs. In this case, failure $m_b(t)$ and $m_c(t)$ are also the forecasts of catastrophic failure, $m_a(t)$.

In terms of reliability (according to PN-77/N-04010), a bus vehicle is: a repairable object (2), operating until reaching the limit status (2), operating with regular operating breaks (2) and incapable of continued operation after a failure (2). Hence, the bus is identified (according to Table 1.6) with code 2222. Further, for the objects with code 2222 (according to Table 1.7), it is established that the basic bus reliability characteristic is $R(t)$—the reliability function (Formula 1.117).

5.3 IN-SERVICE TESTING OF BUSES

The objects of testing were two buses, No. 301 and No. 303, operated by Komunalne Przedsiębiorstwo Komunikacji Miejskiej (KPKM) in Białystok, Poland, in two consecutive years, 2012 and 2013.

The following devices and personnel were used to produce diagnostic data:

- smoke metre—for testing the smoke opacity [1/m];
- sound level metre—for noise level testing [dB];
- diagnostic bench (a vehicle chassis dyno)—for fuel consumption testing [1/100 km];
- expert knowledge (of the operator and the maintenance).

The collected information, which was determined (measurable), probabilistic, and heuristic (expert), was divided into two subsets:

- technical status signals, D (Table 5.1);
- effect signals for the effects of maintenance, the operator, and the environment, U (Table 5.2).

One of the standard tests in motor vehicle engine diagnostics is the testing of smoke opacity by light obscuration metering. Smoke opacity is the result of the presence of particulates (soot) and other components (CO_2, CO, HC, and NO_x) in exhaust gas. Smoke tests with a smoke metre help identify engine failure in advance. Increased emissions of rich combustion or unburnt fuel indicate combustion abnormalities, which can be caused by poor mixture—for example, due to damaged injectors, incorrect setting of the start of discharge, or increased engine oil consumption. Combustion disturbances can lead to increased exhaust gas smoke (smog), which takes on a corresponding colour in all engine operating conditions. By identifying the colour of the smoke, it can be determined whether increased smoke is due to the presence of soot particles, engine oil, fuel, and/or coolant (water).

Another indicator used in the operating process is noise, which is the characteristic sound emitted by the different parts of the motor vehicle in motion. The predominant factor in the general noise of internal combustion engines (with the exhaust gas outlet sufficiently away from the engine assembly) is noise of mechanical origin. The aerodynamic noise components caused by fuel combustion, air intake, and exhaust systems are generally obscured by interference from piston impacts on cylinder walls, vehicle body vibrations, and the performance of the valve timing gear and fuel injection mechanisms; it is therefore important to properly place the testing microphone at different engine components. Noise is measured using a Class 0 or Class 1 sound level metre with correction curve "a" and the metre time constant "F".

Fuel consumption is another indication of the technical condition of the motor vehicle engine. Engine wear is measured on a diagnostic bench (which is a vehicle chassis dyno) during simulated urban and highway driving over a predetermined distance, with preset driving speeds and accelerations that emulate the actual environment of operation of the tested vehicle. Fuel consumption is calculated not by weight but from the heat balance, expressed as the quantity of CO_2 and converted to [dm^3 per 100 km].

A particular form of information is expert knowledge from, for example, the driver of the motor vehicle. The driver may notice various engine abnormalities (knocking, stuttering, stalling in idle, etc.). Additional information can be obtained from the driver's observations of the condition of the road on which the vehicle is operated: whether the road is in good repair or features many potholes and ruts, what is the traffic density at different times of the bus journey, what is the number of bus passengers on different legs of the bus route, and so on.

Another no less important piece of information is the mental and physical condition of the driver, which characterises that person's driving training, driving style, seniority of work, etc.

All this information, when formulated in an appropriate way into a coherent whole, provides the necessary information about the bus and about the effects of the environment on the tested vehicle, and thus on its engine.

Sets of diagnostic and environment signals are defined:

The diagnostic signals selected include:

D_{M1}— average fuel consumption without Diesel fuel-fed cabin heating [1/100 km];

D_{M2}— average fuel consumption with Diesel fuel-fed cabin heating [1/100 km];

D_{M3}— scavenge smoke opacity [1/m];

D_{M4}— smoke opacity during engine operation [1/m];

D_{M5}— peak noise level [dB],

D_{M6}— average noise level [dB],

D_{M7}— front axle left wheel braking force [kN];

D_{M8}— front axle right wheel braking force [kN];

D_{M9}— percentage difference between DM7 and DM8 [%];

D_{M10}— rear axle left wheel braking force [kN];

D_{M11}— rear axle right wheel braking force [kN];

D_{M12}— percentage difference between DM10 and DM11 [%];

D_{E1}— knocking;

D_{E2}— spontaneous stalling (in idle);

D_{E3}— stalling (in operation at higher rpms);

D_{E4}— bus mileage.

The operating (environment) status signals include:

U_{K1}— driver's seniority [years];

U_{K2}— hours worked monthly [h];

U_{K3}— smoothness of driving (braking and acceleration);

U_{D1}— number of stops;

U_{D2}— route length;
U_{D3}— road surface and terrain shape;
U_{P1}— ambient temperature;
U_{P2}— wind;
U_{P3}— atmospheric pressure;
U_{P4}— rainfall.

The following tests were performed to determine signals D_{M1} to D_{M12} and D_{E1} to D_{E4}:

- smoke opacity—with the AT600L smoke metre. The smoke opacity was measured at an engine temperature of 80 °C. The first measurement was made with the engine scavenge, and the second was the average of the values measured at different engine speeds. The maximum smoke opacity limit for the type of bus tested is 2.51 [1/m].
- the average fuel consumption test is a calculation performed at the end of each month by dividing the product of the number of litres refuelled and 100 by the number of kilometres the bus travelled.
- noise, which was measured using the AS-200 vehicle sound level meter. The peak noise value and the average value of the three measurements were measured. The maximum permissible noise level is 98 dB.
- braking force measurement, performed on the dyno bench.

Environment signals U_{K1} to U_{K3} were acquired directly after surveying the bus drivers using questionnaires.

To obtain environment signals $U_{D1} \div U_{D4}$, the route along which the bus travels was examined. The route was then identified with the bus line number (there were four lines). Each route was divided into legs: 1—route with many downhill sections with good asphalt pavement; 2—route with straight sections with good asphalt pavement; 3—route with many uphill sections with good asphalt pavement; 4—route with many downhill sections with poor asphalt pavement; 5—route with straight sections with poor asphalt pavement; 6—route with many uphill sections with poor asphalt pavement. The next step was to calculate the percentage of the legs in relation to the entire length of the bus route, followed by the calculation of a single value showing the condition of the route along the entire section.

Signals U_{P1} to U_{P4} were obtained from a meteorological data logging service.

All diagnostic and environment signals presented here vary in their physical nature. To determine the complex diagnostic signal, D, and the complex environment signal, U, the component signals had to be reduced to conventional point values. The method of importing changes in the diagnostic and environment signal values was based on a score scale, modelled on the methodology that was applied in the process of diagnosing the SH-2G helicopter (USA). Failure was identified, and a corresponding number of points was assigned to it. The failure severity was determined (minor—severity 1, medium—severity 3, and critical—severity 6). The global number of points was then calculated. In this method, if the global number of points (for the object being the helicopter) exceeds a certain threshold value, then the helicopter should be referred for an overhaul [18, 25, 28, 34, 36].

By reducing the signals to their point form, complex signals can be determined (Formulas 5.16 and 5.17).

The first step in the conversion of physical values into point values was to determine the signal weights (significance) [17, 19, 23]. For this purpose, questionnaire surveys were conducted among the bus drivers and diagnosticians.

The survey was conducted with a group of 20 experts with a minimum of 5 years of work experience (seniority) as bus drivers. Table 5.1 is s summary table with the significance information D and U, expressed by the expert weight scores for the assessment of the engine condition and its environment obtained from the bus driver (initial assessments) and the diagnostician (Ewp).

TABLE 5.1
Expert Weights for the Assessment of the Condition of the Engine, the Operator, the Driver, and the Environment (with the Driver and the Diagnosticians Being the Experts)

Signals	Signal description	Group significance	Group assessment	Ewp (expert weight score)
D_{M1}	Average fuel consumption without Diesel fuel-fed cabin heating [l/100km]		5	15
D_{M2}	Average fuel consumption with Diesel fuel-fed cabin heating [l/100km]		5	15
D_{M3}	Scavenge smoke opacity [l/m]		4	10
D_{M4}	Smoke opacity during engine operation [l/m]		4	10
D_{M5}	Peak noise level [dB]	5	3	5
D_{M6}	Average noise level [dB]		3	5
D_{M9}	Braking force percentage difference between front axle left and right wheels [%]		5	15
D_{M12}	Braking force percentage difference between rear axle left and right wheels [%]		5	15
D_{E1}	Knocks		4	8
D_{E2}	Spontaneous stalling	4	2	4
D_{E3}	Stalling		5	12
D_{E4}	Bus mileage		3	4
U_{K1}	Driver's seniority [years]		2	3
U_{K2}	Hours worked monthly [h]	3	3	6
U_{K3}	Smoothness of driving (braking and acceleration)		4	9
U_{D1}	Number of stops		2	4
U_{D2}	Route length	2	1	2
U_{D3}	Road surface and terrain shape		3	6
U_{P1}	Ambient temperature		1	1
U_{P2}	Wind		1	1
U_{P3}	Atmospheric pressure	1	1	1
U_{P4}	Rainfall		1	1

TABLE 5.2

Expert Scores for the Evaluation of the Engine, the Operator, and the Environmental Conditions

Signals	Signal description	Ewp	N	N + 5%	N + 10%	N + 15%	N + 20%
D_{M1}	Average fuel consumption without Diesel fuel-fed cabin heating [l/100 km]	15	15	30	45	60	75
D_{M2}	Average fuel consumption with Diesel fuel-fed cabin heating [l/100 km]	15	15	30	45	60	75
D_{M3}	Scavenge smoke opacity [1/m]	10	10	20	30	40	50
D_{M4}	Smoke opacity during engine operation [1/m]	10	10	20	30	40	50
D_{M5}	Peak noise level [dB]	5	5	10	15	20	25
D_{M6}	Average noise level [dB]	5	5	10	15	20	25

Signals	Signal description	Ewp	<1%	1–10%	10–20%	20–30%	>30%
D_{M7}	Front axle left wheel braking force [kN]	–	–	–	–	–	–
D_{M8}	Front axle right wheel braking force [kN]	–	–	–	–	–	–
D_{M9}	Percentage difference between DM7 and DM8 [%]	15	15	30	45	60	75
D_{M10}	Rear axle left wheel braking force [kN]	–	–	–	–	–	–
D_{M11}	Rear axle right wheel braking force [kN]	–	–	–	–	–	–
D_{M12}	Percentage difference between DM10 and DM11 [%]	15	15	30	45	60	75

Signals	Signal description	Ewp	1–2	2–5	>5
D_{E1}	Knocks	8	8	16	24
D_{E2}	Spontaneous stalling (in idle)	4	4	8	12
D_{E3}	Stalling (in operation at higher rpms)	12	12	24	36

Signals	Signal description	Ewp	< 500 k	500 k–1 M	>1 M
D_{E4}	Bus mileage	4	4	8	12

(Continued)

TABLE 5.2 (Continued)
Expert Scores for the Evaluation of the Engine, the Operator, and the Environmental Conditions

Signals	Signal description	Ewp						
U_{K1}	Driver's seniority [years]	Ewp	<5 years — 3	5–12 years — 6	>12 years — 9			
U_{K2}	Hours worked monthly [h]	Ewp	<140 h — 6	140–180 h — 12	>180 h — 18			
U_{K3}	Smoothness of driving (braking and acceleration)	Ewp	<10 — 9	10–15 — 18	>15 — 27			
U_{D1}	Number of stops	Ewp	<15 — 4	15–30 — 8	>30 — 12			
U_{D2}	Route length	Ewp	<4 km — 2	4–8 km — 4	> 8 km — 6			
U_{D3}	Road surface and terrain shape	Ewp	Good pavement — 6	Acceptable pavement — 12	Poor pavement — 18			
U_{P1}	Ambient temperature	Ewp	< -10 °C — 3	-10–10 °C — 2	10–20 °C — 1	20–30 °C — 2	>30 °C — 3	
U_{P2}	Wind	Ewp	<28.4 km/h — 1	28.4–61.56 km/h — 2	>61.56 km/h — 3			
U_{P3}	Atmospheric pressure	Ewp	<994.66 hPa — 1	996.66–1020 hPa — 2	>1020 hPa — 3			
U_{P4}	Rainfall	Ewp	without rainfall — 1	without significant rainfall — 2	light rainfall — 3	Rainfall — 4	Light snow — 5	Snow — 6

TABLE 5.3

Summary of the Diagnostic and Environment Signals in the Physical Form for No. 301 Bus in 2012

Signals	Operating signals											
	I	II	III	IV	V	VI	VII	VIII	IX	X	XI	XII
D_{M1}	35.7	35.7	35.7	35.7	35.7	35.7	33.66	33.66	33.66	35.1	35.1	35.1
D_{M2}	35.7	35.7	35.7	35.7	35.7	35.7	33.66	33.66	33.66	35.1	35.1	35.1
D_{M3}	0.37	0.37	0.37	0.37	0.37	0.37	0.45	0.45	0.45	0.42	0.42	0.42
D_{M4}	0.02	0.02	0.02	0.02	0.02	0.02	0.03	0.03	0.03	0.03	0.03	0.03
D_{M5}	95	95	95	95	95	95	94	94	94	91.9	91.9	91.9
D_{M6}	92	92	92	92	92	92	90	90	90	91	91	91
D_{M7}	12	12	12	12	12	12	11.4	11.4	11.4	8.8	8.8	8.8
D_{M8}	13.2	13.2	13.2	13.2	13.2	13.2	12	12	12	12.6	12.6	12.6
D_{M9}	9.09	9.09	9.09	9.09	9.09	5.09	5	5	5	30.16	30.16	30.16
D_{M10}	15.8	15.8	15.8	15.8	15.8	15.8	12.5	12.5	12.5	11.9	11.9	11.9
D_{M11}	14.7	14.7	14.7	14.7	14.7	14.7	12.3	12.3	12.3	13.3	13.3	13.3
D_{M12}	6.96	6.96	6.96	6.96	6.96	6.96	1.6	1.6	1.6	10.53	10.53	10.53
D_{E1}	0	0	0	0	1	0	0	0	0	3	0	0
D_{E2}	0	1	0	0	0	3	0	0	0	3	0	0
D_{E3}	0	0	0	2	0	0	0	0	0	0	0	0
D_{E4}	215582	217982	220102	222669	225125	227358	229758	232273	234571	236699	239047	241392

(Continued)

TABLE 5.3 *(Continued)*
Summary of the Diagnostic and Environment Signals in the Physical Form for No. 301 Bus in 2012

Signals	Environment signal											
	I	II	III	IV	V	VI	VII	VIII	IX	X	XI	XII
U_{K1}	4	24	24	10	10	16	16	16	16	4	4	4
U_{K2}	125	164	160	179	146	187	110	144	170	144	154	185
U_{K3}	5	5	5	5	5	6	6	4	4	4	7	7
U_{D1}	33	21	21	21	40	40	40	40	40	29	29	29
U_{D2}	15	9.4	9.4	9.4	16.9	16.9	16.9	16.9	16.9	14.6	14.6	14.6
U_{D3}	2	1	1	1	2	2	2	2	2	2	2	2
U_{P1}	–	–	–	–	–	–	–	–	–	–	–	–
U_{P2}	–	–	–	–	–	–	–	–	–	–	–	–
U_{P3}	–	–	–	–	–	–	–	–	–	–	–	–
U_{P4}	–	–	–	–	–	–	–	–	–	–	–	–

Table 5.2 lists the expert scores for evaluation of the engine, the operator, and the environment, considering the operating changes of the object (the bus) and its environment.

A summary of the measured and recorded diagnostic and environment signals in the physical form for No. 301 bus is shown in Table 5.3 for 2012 and in Table 5.4 for 2013. Subsequently, the converted physical signals into point signals with the weights included in Tables 5.1 and 5.2 are presented in Table 5.5 for 2012 and in Table 5.6 for 2013.

Tables 5.7 and 5.8 show the data from Tables 5.4 and 5.5, respectively, which was reduced to relative values (the maximum value is determined by the decision-maker from the observations of the whole operating process of interest).

TABLE 5.4
Summary of the Diagnostic and Environment Signals in the Physical Form for No. 301 Bus in 2013

Signals	I	II	III	IV	V	VI	VII	VIII	IX	X	XI	XII
					Operating signals							
D_{M1}	37.2	37.2	37.2	37.2	37.2	37.2	34.1	34.1	34.1	36.2	36.2	36.2
D_{M2}	37.2	37.2	37.2	37.2	37.2	37.2	34.1	34.1	34.1	36.2	36.2	36.2
D_{M3}	0.42	0.42	0.42	0.42	0.42	0.42	0.47	0.47	0.47	0.45	0.45	0.45
D_{M4}	0.03	0.03	0.03	0.03	0.03	0.03	0.05	0.05	0.05	0.03	0.03	0.03
D_{M5}	96	96	96	96	96	96	93	93	93	94.4	94.4	94.4
D_{M6}	93	93	93	93	93	93	91	91	91	92	92	92
D_{M7}	14	14	14	14	14	14	12.6	12.6	12.6	11.9	11.9	11.9
D_{M8}	14.8	14.8	14.8	14.8	14.8	14.8	13.3	13.3	13.3	12.3	12.3	12.3
D_{M9}	5.41	5.41	5.41	5.41	5.41	5.41	5.26	5.26	5.26	3.25	3.25	3.25
D_{M10}	16.2	16.2	16.2	16.2	16.2	16.2	14.8	14.8	14.8	13.3	13.3	13.3
D_{M11}	15.3	15.3	15.3	15.3	15.3	15.3	14.5	14.5	14.5	15.7	15.7	15.7
D_{M12}	5.56	5.56	5.56	5.56	5.56	5.56	2.03	2.03	2.03	15.29	15.29	15.29
D_{E1}	1	0	2	0	1	0	0	0	0	0	0	0
D_{E2}	0	0	0	3	0	0	0	1	0	0	3	0
D_{E3}	0	0	0	0	0	1	0	0	0	0	2	0
D_{E4}	243747	246125	248577	250992	253490	255855	258256	260695	263183	265524	267835	270190
					Environment signal							
U_{K1}	4	4	4	4	24	24	24	24	24	24	24	24
U_{K2}	141	148	151	165	165	168	153	153	174	182	157	153
U_{K3}	3	3	4	4	8	8	4	4	5	5	5	6
U_{D1}	4	4	4	4	21	21	21	21	21	21	21	21
U_{D2}	14.6	14.6	14.6	14.6	9.4	9.4	9.4	9.4	9.4	9.4	9.4	9.4
U_{D3}	2	2	2	2	1	1	1	1	1	1	1	1
U_{P1}	–	–	–	–	–	–	–	–	–	–	–	–
U_{P2}	–	–	–	–	–	–	–	–	–	–	–	–
U_{P3}	–	–	–	–	–	–	–	–	–	–	–	–
U_{P4}	–	–	–	–	–	–	–	–	–	–	–	–

TABLE 5.5

Summary of the Diagnostic and Environment Signals in the Point Form for No. 301 Bus in 2012

	Operating signals											
Signals	I	II	III	IV	V	VI	VII	VIII	IX	X	XI	XII
D_{M1P}	15	15	15	15	15	15	15	15	15	15	15	15
D_{M2P}	15	15	15	15	15	15	15	15	15	15	15	15
D_{M3P}	10	10	10	10	10	10	10	10	10	10	10	10
D_{M4P}	10	10	10	10	10	10	10	10	10	10	10	10
D_{M5P}	5	5	5	5	5	5	5	5	5	5	5	5
D_{M6P}	5	5	5	5	5	5	5	5	5	5	5	5
D_{M9P}	30	30	30	30	30	30	30	30	30	75	75	75
D_{M12P}	30	30	30	30	30	30	30	30	30	45	45	45
D_{E1P}	–	–	–	–	8	–	–	–	–	16	–	–
D_{E2P}	–	4	–	–	–	8	–	–	–	8	–	–
D_{E3P}	–	–	–	12	–	–	–	–	–	–	–	–
D_{E4P}	4	4	4	4	4	4	4	4	4	4	4	4
	Environment signal											
Signals	I	II	III	IV	V	VI	VII	VIII	IX	X	XI	XII
U_{K1P}	3	9	9	6	6	9	9	9	9	3	3	3
U_{K2P}	6	12	12	12	12	18	6	12	12	12	12	18
U_{K3P}	9	9	9	9	9	9	9	9	9	9	9	9
U_{D1P}	12	12	12	12	12	12	12	12	12	12	12	12
U_{D2P}	4	2	2	2	6	6	6	6	6	4	4	4
U_{D3P}	12	6	6	6	12	12	12	12	12	12	12	12
U_{P1P}	2.03	2.25	1.58	1.43	1.65	1.80	2.35	1.97	1.47	1.29	1.77	2.03
U_{P2P}	1	1.07	1.13	1.03	1	1	1	1.03	1.03	1.06	1	1.06
U_{P3P}	1.55	1.61	1.77	1.17	1.71	1.33	1.52	1.65	1.67	1.45	1.53	1.55
U_{P4P}	2.32	2.89	2.06	2.1	2.26	2.73	1.94	1.97	1.40	1.55	1.33	2.03

TABLE 5.6

Summary of the Diagnostic and Environment Signals in the Point Form for No. 301 Bus in 2013

	Operating signals											
Signals	I	II	III	IV	V	VI	VII	VIII	IX	X	XI	XII
D_{M1P}	15	15	15	15	15	15	15	15	15	15	15	15
D_{M2P}	15	15	15	15	15	15	15	15	15	15	15	15
D_{M3P}	10	10	10	10	10	10	10	10	10	10	10	10
D_{M4P}	10	10	10	10	10	10	10	10	10	10	10	10
D_{M5P}	5	5	5	5	5	5	5	5	5	5	5	5
D_{M6P}	5	5	5	5	5	5	5	5	5	5	5	5

(Continued)

TABLE 5.6 (*Continued*)
Summary of the Diagnostic and Environment Signals in the Point Form for No. 301 Bus in 2013

D_{M9P}	30	30	30	30	30	30	30	30	30	30	30	30
D_{M12P}	30	30	30	30	30	30	30	30	30	45	45	45
D_{EIP}	8	–	8	–	8	–	–	8	–	–	–	–
D_{E2P}	–	–	–	8	–	–	–	4	–	8	–	–
D_{E3P}	–	–	–	–	–	12	–	–	–	–	12	–
D_{E4P}	4	4	4	4	4	4	4	4	4	4	4	4

	Environment signal											
Signals	**I**	**II**	**III**	**IV**	**V**	**VI**	**VII**	**VIII**	**IX**	**X**	**XI**	**XII**
U_{KIP}	3	3	3	3	9	9	9	9	9	9	9	9
U_{K2P}	12	12	12	12	12	12	12	12	12	18	12	12
U_{K3P}	9	9	9	9	9	9	9	9	9	9	9	9
U_{DIP}	4	4	4	4	12	12	12	12	12	12	12	12
U_{D2P}	4	4	4	4	2	2	2	2	2	2	2	2
U_{D3P}	12	12	12	12	6	6	6	6	6	6	6	6
U_{PIP}	2	2	2	1.6	1.71	2.07	2.16	2.26	1.33	1.13	1.77	2
U_{P2P}	1	1	1.03	1	1	1	1	1	1	1	1	1
U_{P3P}	1.32	1.54	1.39	1.57	1.23	1.43	2.00	2.13	2.13	1.77	1.37	1.68
U_{P4P}	2.84	2.75	3.03	2.27	2.32	2.53	2.06	1.84	2.67	1.57	2.23	1.77

TABLE 5.7
Summary of the Relative Diagnostic and Environment Signals in the Point Form for No. 301 Bus in 2012

	Operating signals											
Signals	**I**	**II**	**III**	**IV**	**V**	**VI**	**VII**	**VIII**	**IX**	**X**	**XI**	**XII**
D_{M1P}	0.2	0.2	0.2	0.2	0.2	0.2	0.2	0.2	0.2	0.2	0.2	0.2
D_{M2P}	0.2	0.2	0.2	0.2	0.2	0.2	0.2	0.2	0.2	0.2	0.2	0.2
D_{M3P}	0.2	0.2	0.2	0.2	0.2	0.2	0.2	0.2	0.2	0.2	0.2	0.2
D_{M4P}	0.2	0.2	0.2	0.2	0.2	0.2	0.2	0.2	0.2	0.2	0.2	0.2
D_{M5P}	0.2	0.2	0.2	0.2	0.2	0.2	0.2	0.2	0.2	0.2	0.2	0.2
D_{M6P}	0.2	0.2	0.2	0.2	0.2	0.2	0.2	0.2	0.2	0.2	0.2	0.2
D_{M9P}	0.4	0.4	0.4	0.4	0.4	0.4	0.4	0.4	0.4	1	1	1
D_{M12P}	0.4	0.4	0.4	0.4	0.4	0.4	0.4	0.4	0.4	0.6	0.6	0.6
D_{EIP}	–	–	–	–	0.33	–	–	–	–	0.67	–	–
D_{E2P}	–	0.33	–	–	–	0.67	–	–	–	0.67	–	–
D_{E3P}	–	–	–	0.33	–	–	–	–	–	–	–	–
D_{E4P}	0.33	0.33	0.33	0.33	0.33	0.33	0.33	0.33	0.33	0.33	0.33	0.33

(Continued)

TABLE 5.7 (*Continued*)
Summary of the Relative Diagnostic and Environment Signals in the Point Form for No. 301 Bus in 2012

Signals		I	II	III	IV	V	VI	VII	VIII	IX	X	XI	XII
						Environment signal							
U_{K1P}		0.33	1	1	0.67	0.67	1	1	1	1	0.33	0.33	0.33
U_{K2P}		0.33	0.67	0.67	0.67	0.67	1	0.33	0.67	0.67	0.67	0.67	1
U_{K3P}		0.33	0.33	0.33	0.33	0.33	0.33	0.33	0.33	0.33	0.33	0.33	0.33
U_{D1P}		1	1	1	1	1	1	1	1	1	1	1	1
U_{D2P}		0.67	0.33	0.33	0.33	1	1	1	1	1	0.67	0.67	0.67
U_{D3P}		0.67	0.33	0.33	0.33	0.67	0.67	0.67	0.67	0.67	0.67	0.67	0.67
U_{P1P}		0.68	0.75	0.53	0.48	0.55	0.60	0.78	0.66	0.49	0.43	0.59	0.68
U_{P2P}		0.33	0.36	0.38	0.34	0.33	0.33	0.33	0.34	0.34	0.35	0.33	0.35
U_{P3P}		0.52	0.54	0.59	0.39	0.57	0.44	0.51	0.55	0.56	0.48	0.51	0.52
U_{P4P}		0.39	0.48	0.34	0.35	0.38	0.46	0.32	0.33	0.23	0.26	0.22	0.34

TABLE 5.8
Summary of the Relative Diagnostic and Environment Signals in the Point Form for No. 301 Bus in 2013

Signals	I	II	III	IV	V	VI	VII	VIII	IX	X	XI	XII
					Operating signals							
D_{M1P}	0.2	0.2	0.2	0.2	0.2	0.2	0.2	0.2	0.2	0.2	0.2	0.2
D_{M2P}	0.2	0.2	0.2	0.2	0.2	0.2	0.2	0.2	0.2	0.2	0.2	0.2
D_{M3P}	0.2	0.2	0.2	0.2	0.2	0.2	0.2	0.2	0.2	0.2	0.2	0.2
D_{M4P}	0.2	0.2	0.2	0.2	0.2	0.2	0.2	0.2	0.2	0.2	0.2	0.2
D_{M5P}	0.2	0.2	0.2	0.2	0.2	0.2	0.2	0.2	0.2	0.2	0.2	0.2
D_{M6P}	0.2	0.2	0.2	0.2	0.2	0.2	0.2	0.2	0.2	0.2	0.2	0.2
D_{M9P}	0.4	0.4	0.4	0.4	0.4	0.4	0.4	0.4	0.4	0.4	0.4	0.4
D_{M12P}	0.4	0.4	0.4	0.4	0.4	0.4	0.4	0.4	0.4	0.6	0.6	0.6
D_{E1P}	0.33	–	0.33	–	0.33	–	–	0.33	–	–	–	–
D_{E2P}	–	–	–	0.67	–	–	–	0.33	–	–	0.67	–
D_{E3P}	–	–	–	–	–	0.33	–	–	–	–	0.33	–
D_{E4P}	0.33	0.33	0.33	0.33	0.33	0.33	0.33	0.33	0.33	0.33	0.33	0.33
					Environment signal							
Signals	**I**	**II**	**III**	**IV**	**V**	**VI**	**VII**	**VIII**	**IX**	**X**	**XI**	**XII**
U_{K1P}	0.33	0.33	0.33	0.33	1	1	1	1	1	1	1	1
U_{K2P}	0.67	0.67	0.67	0.67	0.67	0.67	0.67	0.67	0.67	1	0.67	0.67
U_{K3P}	0.33	0.33	0.33	0.33	0.33	0.33	0.33	0.33	0.33	0.33	0.33	0.33
U_{D1P}	0.33	0.33	0.33	0.33	1	1	1	1	1	1	1	1
U_{D2P}	0.67	0.67	0.67	0.67	0.33	0.33	0.33	0.33	0.33	0.33	0.33	0.33
U_{D3P}	0.67	0.67	0.67	0.67	0.33	0.33	0.33	0.33	0.33	0.33	0.33	0.33
U_{P1P}	0.67	0.67	0.67	0.53	0.57	0.69	0.72	0.75	0.44	0.38	0.59	0.67
U_{P2P}	0.33	0.33	0.34	0.33	0.33	0.33	0.33	0.33	0.33	0.33	0.33	0.33
U_{P3P}	0.44	0.51	0.46	0.52	0.41	0.48	0.67	0.71	0.71	0.59	0.46	0.56
U_{P4P}	0.47	0.46	0.51	0.38	0.39	0.42	0.34	0.31	0.44	0.26	0.37	0.3

The next step of the calculation is to determine the technical status and regulation parameters according to Formulas 5.12 and 5.15. The calculation results for No. 301 bus in 2012 are shown in Table 5.9. Items 6, 9, and 13 for the case of $\Delta D = 0$ were calculated with Formula 5.7, assuming that $\Delta D/\Delta\theta = 1$. The calculation results for No. 301 bus in 2013 are shown in Table 5.10.

TABLE 5.9
Calculation Results for the Technical Status Parameters a_T and the Operating Status a_R of No. 301 Bus in 2012

Month	Operating time θ	D	U	$\Delta\theta$	ΔD	ΔU	a_T	a_R
1	213429	0.87	1.89	2200	0.87	1.89		
2	215582	0.82	1.79	2153	−0.05	−0.10	−2.88	−2.56
3	217982	0.88	2.00	2400	0.07	0.21	3.06	4.32
4	220102	0.82	1.91	2120	−0.07	−0.08	−3.68	−2.07
5	222669	0.88	1.69	2567	0.07	−0.23	2.92	−5.02
6	225125	0.88	2.08	2456	0.00	0.39	0.57	8.01
7	227358	1.06	2.33	2233	0.17	0.25	7.48	4.86
8	229758	0.82	2.18	2400	−0.24	−0.15	−11.35	−3.08
9	232273	0.82	2.23	2515	0.00	0.05	0.58	0.88
10	234571	0.82	2.17	2298	0.00	−0.05	0.59	−1.12
11	236699	1.61	1.78	2128	0.79	−0.39	28.56	−10.17
12	239047	1.31	1.82	2348	−0.30	0.04	−11.08	1.00
13	241392	1.31	2.02	2345	0.00	0.20	0.44	4.24

TABLE 5.10
Calculation Results for the Technical Status Parameters a_T and the Operating Status a_R of No. 301 Bus in 2013

Month	Operating time θ	D	U	$\Delta\theta$	ΔD	ΔU	a_T	a_R
1	241392	1.31	2.02	2345	0.00	0.20	0.44	4.24
2	243747	0.88	1.62	2355	−0.42	−0.39	−21.39	−10.27
3	246125	0.82	1.64	2378	−0.07	0.02	−3.37	0.44
4	248577	0.88	1.64	2452	0.07	0.00	3.14	0.03
5	250992	1.06	1.57	2415	0.17	−0.07	7.72	−1.61
6	253490	0.88	1.88	2498	−0.17	0.30	−7.54	6.96
7	255855	0.88	1.94	2365	0.00	0.06	0.54	1.48
8	258256	0.82	1.99	2401	−0.07	0.05	−3.01	1.21
9	260695	0.95	2.01	2439	0.13	0.02	5.33	0.44
10	263183	0.82	1.95	2488	−0.13	−0.07	−5.72	−1.53
11	265524	0.93	2.00	2341	0.11	0.05	5.10	1.21
12	267835	1.19	1.89	2311	0.26	−0.11	10.62	−2.22
13	270190	0.93	1.93	2355	−0.26	0.04	−11.75	0.91

A summary of failures for different diagnostic thresholds of No. 301 bus is listed in Table 5.11 for 2012 and Table 5.12 for 2013. If the trend of threshold parameters a_T and a_R is exceeded, it is considered to be failure $m(t)$. In the case considered, parametric failure $m_b(t)_{aT}$ is linked with the trend of a_T and transient damage $m_c(t)_{aR}$ is linked to the trend of a_R). The failure map (Table 5.13 for 2012 and Table 5.14 for 2013) is the foundation for the determination of the reliability characteristics of the bus in operation.

TABLE 5.11

Average Values μ and the Standard Deviation σ of Parameters a_T and a_R for No. 301 Bus in 2012

	a_T	a_R
Average μ	1.64	0.17
Deviation σ	10.61	5.19
Diagnostic threshold $\mu + 0.5\sigma$	6.95	2.76
Diagnostic threshold $\mu + 2\sigma$	12.25	5.36
Diagnostic threshold $\mu + 3\sigma$	22.87	10.55

TABLE 5.12

Average Values μ and the Standard Deviation σ of Parameters a_T and aR for No. 301 Bus in 2013

	a_T	a_R
Average μ	0.10	0.67
Deviation σ	6.96	2.44
Diagnostic threshold $\mu + 0.5\sigma$	3.58	1.89
Diagnostic threshold $\mu + 2\sigma$	7.06	3.11
Diagnostic threshold $\mu + 3\sigma$	14.02	5.55

TABLE 5.13

Failure Map for No. 301 Bus in 2012, at Different Values of Standard Deviation σ (Different Diagnostic Thresholds)

θ [h]	$\theta_{obs.}$ [h]	$m_b(t)\, a_T$			$m_c(t)_{aR}$		
		Threshold $\mu + 0.5\sigma$	Threshold $\mu + \sigma$	Threshold $\mu + 2\sigma$	Threshold $\mu + 0.5\sigma$	Threshold $\mu + \sigma$	Threshold $\mu + 2\sigma$
213429	0						
215582	2153						
217982	4553	1	1	1	1	1	1
220102	6673	1	1	1	1	1	1
222669	9240	1	0	0	1	1	1

(Continued)

TABLE 5.13 (*Continued*)
Failure Map for No. 301 Bus in 2012, at Different Values of Standard Deviation σ (Different Diagnostic Thresholds)

θ [h]	$\theta_{obs.}$ [h]	$m_b(t)\,a_T$			$m_c(t)\,_{aR}$		
		Threshold $\mu + 0.5\sigma$	Threshold $\mu + \sigma$	Threshold $\mu + 2\sigma$	Threshold $\mu + 0.5\sigma$	Threshold $\mu + \sigma$	Threshold $\mu + 2\sigma$
225125	11696	0	0	0	1	1	0
227358	13929	1	1	0	1	0	0
229758	16329	1	1	1	1	1	1
232273	18844	0	0	0	0	0	0
234571	21142	0	0	0	1	1	1
236699	23270	1	1	1	1	1	1
239047	25618	1	1	1	0	0	0
241392	27963	1	1	1	1	0	0

TABLE 5.14
Failure Map for No. 301 Bus in 2013, at Different Values of Standard Deviation σ (Different Diagnostic Thresholds)

θ [h]	$\theta_{obs.}$ [h]	$m_b(t)\,a_T$			$m_c(t)\,_{aR}$		
		Threshold $\mu + 0.5\sigma$	Threshold $\mu + \sigma$	Threshold $\mu + 2\sigma$	Threshold $\mu + 0.5\sigma$	Threshold $\mu + \sigma$	Threshold $\mu + 2\sigma$
241392	0						
243747	2355						
246125	4733	1	1	1	1	1	1
248577	7185	1	0	0	1	1	1
250992	9600	1	1	1	1	1	1
253490	12098	1	1	1	1	1	1
255855	14463	0	0	0	0	0	0
258256	16864	1	1	1	0	0	0
260695	19303	1	1	1	1	1	1
263183	21791	1	1	1	1	1	1
265524	24132	1	1	1	0	0	0
267835	26443	1	1	1	1	1	1
270190	28798	1	1	1	0	0	0

The in-service testing of No. 301 bus was performed in the same way on No. 303 bus. The test results for No. 303 bus are shown in Tables 5.15 and 5.16. After performing the appropriate operations on the signals in Tables 5.15 and 5.16 (identical to those for No. 301 bus), the failure maps for No. 303 bus were obtained and are shown in Tables 5.17 and 5.18. The failure maps for No. 301 bus (Tables 5.13 and 5.14) and No. 303 bus (Tables 5.17 and 5.18) are the basis for the determination of the reliability characteristics.

TABLE 5.15

Summary of the Diagnostic and Environment Signals in the Physical Form for No. 303 Bus in 2012

	Operating signals											
Signals	I	II	III	IV	V	VI	VII	VIII	IX	X	XI	XII
D_{M1}	35.9	35.9	35.9	35.9	35.9	35.9	34.53	34.53	34.53	35.1	35.1	35.1
D_{M2}	35.9	35.9	35.9	35.9	35.9	35.9	34.53	34.53	34.53	35.1	35.1	35.1
D_{M3}	0.34	0.34	0.34	0.34	0.34	0.34	0.13	0.13	0.13	0.42	0.42	0.42
D_{M4}	0.03	0.03	0.03	0.03	0.03	0.03	0.06	0.06	0.06	0.03	0.03	0.03
D_{M5}	94	94	94	94	94	94	107.3	107.3	107.3	95.4	95.4	95.4
D_{M6}	93	93	93	93	93	93	107	107	107	94.8	94.8	94.8
D_{M7}	10.2	10.2	10.2	10.2	10.2	10.2	11.7	11.7	11.7	12	12	12
D_{M8}	10.5	10.5	10.5	10.5	10.5	10.5	12.6	12.6	12.6	13.9	13.9	13.9
D_{M9}	2.86	2.86	2.86	2.86	2.86	2.86	7.14	7.14	7.14	13.67	13.67	13.67
D_{M10}	21.3	21.3	21.3	21.3	21.3	21.3	20	20	20	15.4	15.4	15.4
D_{M11}	16	16	16	16	16	16	18.3	18.3	18.3	16.6	16.6	16.6
D_{M12}	24.88	24.88	24.88	24.88	24.88	24.88	8.50	8.50	8.50	7.23	7.23	7.23
D_{E1}	–	1	–	–	1	–	–	–	–	–	–	–
D_{E2}	–	1	–	–	–	–	–	–	–	–	–	–
D_{E3}	–	–	–	–	–	–	1	–	–	1	–	–
D_{E4}	208928	211052	213208	215729	218085	220518	223018	225392	227630	229875	232473	234829

	Environment signal											
Signals	I	II	III	IV	V	VI	VII	VIII	IX	X	XI	XII
U_{K1}	26	26	26	26	15	15	18	18	18	18	8	8
U_{K2}	110	130	160	160	160	160	155	155	155	150	160	145
U_{K3}	10	16	10	10	8	14	12	5	8	10	12	12
U_{D1}	22	22	22	22	23	23	26	26	26	26	21	21
U_{D2}	9.8	9.8	9.8	9.8	18.1	18.1	13.3	13.3	13.3	13.3	9.4	9.4
U_{D3}	1	1	1	1	2	2	3	3	3	3	1	1
U_{P1}	–	–	–	–	–	–	–	–	–	–	–	–
U_{P2}	–	–	–	–	–	–	–	–	–	–	–	–
U_{P3}	–	–	–	–	–	–	–	–	–	–	–	–
U_{P4}	–	–	–	–	–	–	–	–	–	–	–	–

TABLE 5.16

Summary of the Diagnostic and Environment Signals in the Physical Form for No. 303 Bus in 2013

	Operating signals											
Signals	I	II	III	IV	V	VI	VII	VIII	IX	X	XI	XII
D_{M1}	37.3	37.3	35.9	35.9	35.9	35.9	35.2	35.2	35.2	35.5	35.5	35.5
D_{M2}	37.3	37.3	35.9	35.9	35.9	35.9	35.2	35.2	35.2	35.5	35.5	35.5
D_{M3}	0.29	0.29	0.18	0.18	0.18	0.18	0.13	0.13	0.13	0.22	0.22	0.22

(Continued)

TABLE 5.16 (*Continued*)
Summary of the Diagnostic and Environment Signals in the Physical Form for No. 303 Bus in 2013

					Operating signals							
Signals	I	II	III	IV	V	VI	VII	VIII	IX	X	XI	XII
D_{M4}	0.03	0.03	0.04	0.04	0.04	0.04	0.06	0.06	0.06	0.04	0.04	0.04
D_{M5}	96	96	95	95	95	95	93.2	93.2	93.2	94.3	94.3	94.3
D_{M6}	95.2	95.2	94.8	94.8	94.8	94.8	93	93	93	93.2	93.2	93.2
D_{M7}	11.3	11.3	13.5	13.5	13.5	13.5	11.8	11.8	11.8	13.1	13.1	13.1
D_{M8}	11.7	11.7	12.4	12.4	12.4	12.4	12.2	12.2	12.2	12.8	12.8	12.8
D_{M9}	3.42	3.42	0	0	0	0	0.85	0.85	0.85	2.29	2.29	2.29
D_{M10}	11.4	11.4	11.9	11.9	11.9	11.9	14.3	14.3	14.3	15.3	15.3	15.3
D_{M11}	12.1	12.1	13.1	13.1	13.1	13.1	14.9	14.9	14.9	14.5	14.5	14.5
D_{M12}	5.79	5.79	0	0	0	0	4.03	4.03	4.03	5.23	5.23	5.23
D_{E1}	–	–	–	2	–	1	–	–	3	–	–	–
D_{E2}	–	–	–	–	–	–	1	–	–	–	–	–
D_{E3}	3	–	–	2	–	–	3	–	–	2	–	–
D_{E4}	237141	2399320	241674	244085	246430	248809	251108	253470	255883	258328	260829	263225
					Environment signal							
Signals	I	II	III	IV	V	VI	VII	VIII	IX	X	XI	XII
U_{K1}	15	15	15	8	8	8	8	18	18	6	6	6
U_{K2}	160	155	160	160	140	140	160	160	24	145	145	160
U_{K3}	7	6	6	8	10	3	6	2	7	7	10	11
U_{D1}	23	23	23	21	21	21	21	26	26	22	22	22
U_{D2}	18.1	18.1	18.1	9.4	9.4	9.4	9.4	13.3	13.3	9.8	9.8	9.8
U_{D3}	2	2	2	1	1	1	1	3	3	1	1	1
U_{P1}	–	–	–	–	–	–	–	–	–	–	–	–
U_{P2}	–	–	–	–	–	–	–	–	–	–	–	–
U_{P3}	–	–	–	–	–	–	–	–	–	–	–	–
U_{P4}	–	–	–	–	–	–	–	–	–	–	–	–

TABLE 5.17
Failure Map for No. 303 Bus in 2012, at Different Values of Standard Deviation σ (Different Diagnostic Thresholds)

θ [h]	$\theta_{obs.}$ [h]	$m_b(t)\,a_T$			$m_c(t)\,_{aR}$		
		Threshold $\mu + 0.5\sigma$	Threshold $\mu + \sigma$	Threshold $\mu + 2\sigma$	Threshold $\mu + 0.5\sigma$	Threshold $\mu + \sigma$	Threshold $\mu + 2\sigma$
206775	0						
208928	2153						
211052	4277	1	1	1	1	1	1

(Continued)

TABLE 5.17 (*Continued*)

Failure Map for No. 303 Bus in 2012, at Different Values of Standard Deviation σ (Different Diagnostic Thresholds)

θ [h]	$\theta_{obs.}$ [h]	$m_b(t)\,a_T$			$m_c(t)_{aR}$		
		Threshold $\mu + 0.5\sigma$	Threshold $\mu + \sigma$	Threshold $\mu + 2\sigma$	Threshold $\mu + 0.5\sigma$	Threshold $\mu + \sigma$	Threshold $\mu + 2\sigma$
213208	6433	1	1	1	1	1	1
215729	8954	1	0	0	1	1	1
218085	11310	0	0	0	1	1	0
220518	13743	0	0	0	0	0	0
223018	16243	1	1	1	1	1	1
225392	18617	1	1	1	1	1	1
227630	20855	1	1	1	1	1	1
229875	23100	1	1	1	1	1	1
232473	25698	1	1	1	1	1	1
234829	28054	0	0	0	0	0	0

TABLE 5.18

Failure Map for No. 303 Bus in 2013, at Different Values of Standard Deviation σ (Different Diagnostic Thresholds)

θ [h]	$\theta_{obs.}$ [h]	$m_b(t)\,a_T$			$m_c(t)_{aR}$		
		Threshold $\mu + 0.5\sigma$	Threshold $\mu + \sigma$	Threshold $\mu + 2\sigma$	Threshold $\mu + 0.5\sigma$	Threshold $\mu + \sigma$	Threshold $\mu + 2\sigma$
234829	0						
237141	2312						
239320	4491	1	1	1	1	1	1
241674	6845	1	0	0	1	1	1
244085	9256	0	0	0	1	1	1
246430	11601	0	0	0	0	0	0
248809	13980	0	0	0	0	0	0
251108	16279	1	1	1	0	0	0
253470	18641	0	0	0	0	0	0
255883	21054	1	1	1	1	1	1
258328	23499	0	0	0	1	1	1
260829	26000	0	0	0	0	0	0
263225	28396	1	1	1	0	0	0

5.4 METHOD FOR CONVERSIONS OF OPERATING DATA (NUMBER OF FAILURES, SET SIZE, AND FAILURE INSTANCE) INTO RELIABILITY PARAMETERS

The failure instance, $\Delta\theta$, the number of failures, $m(t)$ (Table 5.7), and the total size of the failure set, n (Formula 1.21) are the basis for the determination of the corresponding fallibility estimators, $F^*(t)$, and the reliability estimators, $R^*(t)$, followed by the determination of the reliability characteristics $R(t)$ for each of the two buses tested in sequence. The reliability estimators are determined from Formulas 1.129 to 1.134. The size of the test set of buses, n, is determined from Formula 1.135, which is a result of the ergodicity of the failure stream of a single bus (a sufficiently long observation of one bus is equivalent to the observation of a large set of buses).

Reliability characteristic $R(t)$ is the basis for the determination of reliability parameters $E(T)$ and $\sigma_{E(T)}$ with the following relation:

$$E(T) = \int_0^\infty R(t)dt \tag{5.18}$$

$$E(T^2) = 2\int_0^\infty t \cdot R(t)dt \tag{5.19}$$

$$\sigma_{E(T)} = \sqrt{E(T^2) - [E(T)]^2} \tag{5.20}$$

The expected lifetime, $E(T)$, and the expected lifetime standard deviation, $\sigma_{E(T)}$, are the reliability parameters that facilitate observation of different objects and comparison of these objects with one another in different operating periods.

When characteristic $R(t)$ is determined before a catastrophic failure $R_R(t)=1$, then (see Formula 5.3):

$$R(t) = R_b(t) R_c(t) \tag{5.21}$$

and their estimators are (see Formula 1.129):

$$R^*(t) = R_b^*(t) R_c^*(t) \tag{5.22}$$

Example calculations of reliability parameters $R^*(t)$, $E(T)$, and $\sigma_{E(T)}$ of No. 301 bus in 2012 and 2013 are shown in Tables 5.19 and 5.20, respectively.

TABLE 5.19

Results of Calculations of Reliability Parameters $R^*(t)$, $E(T)$, and $\sigma E(T)$ for No. 301 Bus in 2012

θ [h]	$\theta_{obs.}$ [h]	$R_b^*(t)$	$R_c^*(t)$	$R^*(t)$	Diagnostic threshold	$E(T)$	$\sigma_{E(T)}$
213429	0	1.00	1.00	1.00			
215582	2153	1.00	1.00	1.00			
217982	4553	0.88	0.90	0.79			
220102	6673	0.77	0.79	0.61			
222669	9240	0.65	0.69	0.45			
225125	11696	0.65	0.59	0.38			
227358	13929	0.54	0.48	0.26	$\mu + 0.5\sigma$	10460.21	6576.32
229758	16329	0.42	0.38	0.16			
232273	18844	0.42	0.38	0.16			
234571	21142	0.42	0.28	0.12			
236699	23270	0.30	0.18	0.05			
239047	25618	0.19	0.18	0.03			
241392	27963	0.07	0.07	0.01			
213429	0	1.00	1.00	1.00			
215582	2153	1.00	1.00	1.00			
217982	4553	0.87	0.89	0.77			
220102	6673	0.74	0.78	0.57			
222669	9240	0.74	0.67	0.49			
225125	11696	0.74	0.56	0.41			
227358	13929	0.60	0.56	0.34	$\mu + \sigma$	11122.19	7341.96
229758	16329	0.47	0.45	0.21			
232273	18844	0.47	0.45	0.21			
234571	21142	0.47	0.34	0.16			
236699	23270	0.34	0.23	0.08			
239047	25618	0.21	0.23	0.05			
241392	27963	0.07	0.23	0.02			
213429	0	1.00	1.00	1.00			
215582	2153	1.00	1.00	1.00			
217982	4553	0.85	0.87	0.74			
220102	6673	0.69	0.74	0.51			
222669	9240	0.69	0.61	0.42			
225125	11696	0.69	0.61	0.42			
227358	13929	0.69	0.61	0.42	$\mu + 2\sigma$	11313.01	7962.27
229758	16329	0.54	0.49	0.26			
232273	18844	0.54	0.49	0.26			
234571	21142	0.54	0.36	0.19			
236699	23270	0.38	0.23	0.09			
239047	25618	0.23	0.23	0.05			
241392	27963	0.07	0.23	0.02			

TABLE 5.20

Results of Calculations of Reliability Parameters $R^*(t)$, $E(T)$, and $\sigma_{E(T)}$ for No. 301 Bus in 2013

θ [h]	$\theta_{obs.}$ [h]	$R_b^*(t)$	$R_c^*(t)$	$R^*(t)$	Diagnostic threshold	$E(T)$	$\sigma_{E(T)}$
241392	0	1.00	1.00	1.00			
243747	2355	1.00	1.00	1.00			
246125	4733	0.85	0.86	0.73			
248577	7185	0.69	0.74	0.51			
250992	9600	0.69	0.61	0.42			
253490	12098	0.54	0.61	0.33			
255855	14463	0.54	0.61	0.33	$\mu + 0.5\sigma$	12066.93	7587.76
258256	16864	0.38	0.61	0.24			
260695	19303	0.38	0.49	0.19			
263183	21791	0.23	0.36	0.08			
265524	24132	0.23	0.36	0.08			
267835	26443	0.23	0.23	0.05			
270190	28798	0.08	0.23	0.02			
241392	0	1.00	1.00	1.00			
243747	2355	1.00	1.00	1.00			
246125	4733	0.82	0.86	0.70			
248577	7185	0.82	0.74	0.61			
250992	9600	0.82	0.61	0.50			
253490	12098	0.63	0.61	0.39			
255855	14463	0.63	0.61	0.39	$\mu + \sigma$	12676.10	7641.12
258256	16864	0.45	0.61	0.27			
260695	19303	0.45	0.49	0.22			
263183	21791	0.26	0.36	0.09			
265524	24132	0.26	0.36	0.09			
267835	26443	0.26	0.23	0.06			
270190	28798	0.08	0.23	0.02			
241392	0	1.00	1.00	1.00			
243747	2355	1.00	1.00	1.00			
246125	4733	0.82	0.86	0.70			
248577	7185	0.82	0.74	0.61			
250992	9600	0.82	0.61	0.50			
253490	12098	0.63	0.61	0.39			
255855	14463	0.63	0.61	0.39	$\mu + 2\sigma$	12676.10	7641.12
258256	16864	0.45	0.61	0.27			
260695	19303	0.45	0.49	0.22			
263183	21791	0.26	0.36	0.09			
265524	24132	0.26	0.36	0.09			
267835	26443	0.26	0.23	0.06			
270190	28798	0.08	0.23	0.02			

Example calculations of reliability parameters $R^*(t)$, $E(T)$, and $\sigma_{E(T)}$ of No. 303 are shown in Tables 5.21 and 5.22.

TABLE 5.21

Results of Calculations of Reliability Parameters $R^*(t)$, $E(T)$, and $\sigma_{E(T)}$ for No. 303 Bus in 2012

θ [h]	$\theta_{obs.}$ [h]	$R_b^*(t)$	$R_c^*(t)$	$R^*(t)$	Diagnostic threshold	$E(T)$	$\sigma_{E(T)}$
206775	0	1.00	1.00	1.00			
208928	2153	1.00	1.00	1.00			
211052	4277	0.89	0.91	0.81			
213208	6433	0.79	0.81	0.64			
215729	8954	0.68	0.72	0.49			
218085	11310	0.68	0.62	0.42			
220518	13743	0.68	0.62	0.42	$\mu + 0.5\sigma$	11442.42	7165.91
223018	16243	0.58	0.53	0.30			
225392	18617	0.47	0.43	0.20			
227630	20855	0.36	0.34	0.12			
229875	23100	0.26	0.24	0.06			
232473	25698	0.15	0.15	0.02			
234829	28054	0.15	0.15	0.02			
206775	0	1.00	1.00	1.00			
208928	2153	1.00	1.00	1.00			
211052	4277	0.88	0.91	0.80			
213208	6433	0.76	0.81	0.61			
215729	8954	0.76	0.72	0.54			
218085	11310	0.76	0.62	0.47			
220518	13743	0.76	0.62	0.47	$\mu + \sigma$	11873.20	7352.24
223018	16243	0.64	0.53	0.34			
225392	18617	0.51	0.43	0.22			
227630	20855	0.39	0.34	0.13			
229875	23100	0.27	0.24	0.07			
232473	25698	0.15	0.15	0.02			
234829	28054	0.15	0.15	0.02			
206775	0	1.00	1.00	1.00			
208928	2153	1.00	1.00	1.00			
211052	4277	0.88	0.89	0.79			
213208	6433	0.76	0.79	0.60			
215729	8954	0.76	0.68	0.52			
218085	11310	0.76	0.68	0.52			
220518	13743	0.76	0.68	0.52	$\mu + 2\sigma$	12104.73	7564.41
223018	16243	0.64	0.58	0.37			
225392	18617	0.51	0.47	0.24			
227630	20855	0.39	0.36	0.14			
229875	23100	0.27	0.26	0.07			
232473	25698	0.15	0.15	0.02			
234829	28054	0.15	0.15	0.02			

TABLE 5.22

Results of Calculations of Reliability Parameters $R^*(t)$, $E(T)$, and $\sigma_{E(T)}$ for No. 303 Bus in 2013

θ [h]	$\theta_{obs.}$ [h]	$R_b^*(t)$	$R_c^*(t)$	$R^*(t)$	Diagnostic threshold	$E(T)$	$\sigma_{E(T)}$
234829	0	1.00	1.00	1.00			
237141	2312	1.00	1.00	1.00			
239320	4491	0.82	0.85	0.69			
241674	6845	0.63	0.79	0.50			
244085	9256	0.63	0.68	0.43			
246430	11601	0.63	0.68	0.43			
248809	13980	0.63	0.68	0.43	$\mu + 0.5\sigma$	11681.15	8660.52
251108	16279	0.45	0.68	0.30			
253470	18641	0.45	0.68	0.30			
255883	21054	0.26	0.58	0.15			
258328	23499	0.26	0.47	0.12			
260829	26000	0.26	0.47	0.12			
263225	28396	0.08	0.47	0.04			
234829	0	1.00	1.00	1.00			
237141	2312	1.00	1.00	1.00			
239320	4491	0.77	0.85	0.65			
241674	6845	0.77	0.79	0.61			
244085	9256	0.77	0.68	0.52			
246430	11601	0.77	0.68	0.52			
248809	13980	0.77	0.68	0.52	$\mu + \sigma$	12988.60	8909.57
251108	16279	0.54	0.68	0.37			
253470	18641	0.54	0.68	0.37			
255883	21054	0.31	0.58	0.18			
258328	23499	0.31	0.47	0.14			
260829	26000	0.31	0.47	0.14			
263225	28396	0.08	0.47	0.04			
234829	0	1.00	1.00	1.00			
237141	2312	1.00	1.00	1.00			
239320	4491	0.77	0.85	0.65			
241674	6845	0.77	0.79	0.61			
244085	9256	0.77	0.68	0.52			
246430	11601	0.77	0.68	0.52			
248809	13980	0.77	0.68	0.52	$\mu + 2\sigma$	12988.60	8909.57
251108	16279	0.54	0.68	0.37			
253470	18641	0.54	0.68	0.37			
255883	21054	0.31	0.58	0.18			
258328	23499	0.31	0.47	0.14			
260829	26000	0.31	0.47	0.14			
263225	28396	0.08	0.47	0.04			

Based on the results in Tables 5.19 and 5.20, Figures 5.1 and 5.2 were made, which show the trends of reliability function estimators in time t in the function of the adopted diagnostic thresholds.

Based on the results in Tables 5.21 and 5.22, Figures 5.3 and 5.4 were made for time t in the function of the adopted diagnostic thresholds.

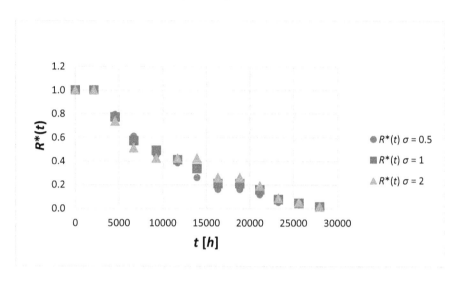

FIGURE 5.1 Estimator $R^*(t)$ trends for No. 301 bus in 2012 at different diagnostic thresholds.

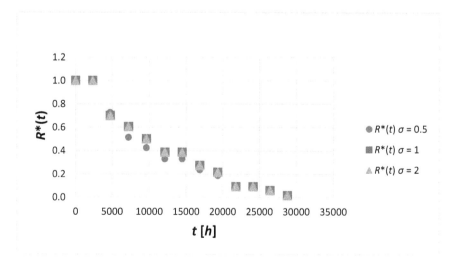

FIGURE 5.2 Estimator $R^*(t)$ trends for No. 301 bus in 2013 at different diagnostic thresholds.

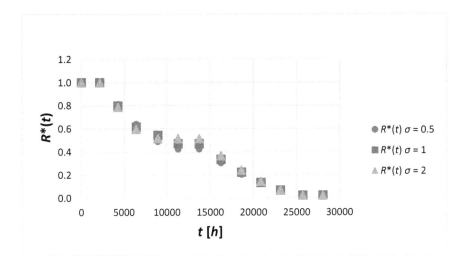

FIGURE 5.3 Estimator $R^*(t)$ trends for No. 303 bus in 2012 at different diagnostic thresholds.

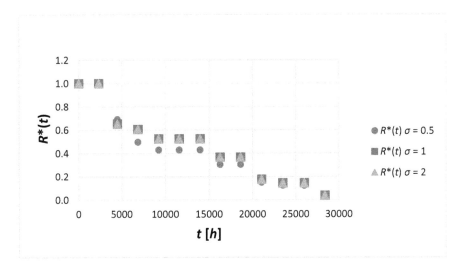

FIGURE 5.4 Estimator $R^*(t)$ trends for No. 303 bus in 2013 at different diagnostic thresholds.

The important information for maintenance is the expected lifetime $E(T)$ and the standard deviation $\sigma_{E(t)}$, and the resulting expected minimum lifetime $E(T)_{MIN} = E(T) - \sigma_{E(T)}$. A low value of this time indicates a low status of machine's reliability.

TABLE 5.23

Summary of the Results for the Reliability Parameters, $E(T)$, $\sigma_{E(T)}$, $E(T)_{MIN}$ of No. 301 Bus in 2012 and 2013

Diagnostic threshold	No. 301 bus observation period					
	Y 2012			Y 2013		
	$E(T)$	$\sigma_{E(T)}$	$E(T)_{MIN}$	$E(T)$	$\sigma_{E(T)}$	$E(T)_{MIN}$
$\mu + 0.5\sigma$	10460.21	6576.32	3883.89	12066.93	7587.76	4479.17
$\mu + \sigma$	11122.19	7341.96	3780.23	12676.10	7641.12	5034.98
$\mu + 2\sigma$	11313.01	7962.27	3350.74	12676.10	7641.12	5034.98

TABLE 5.24

Summary of the Results for the Reliability Parameters, $E(T)$, $\sigma_{E(T)}$, $E(T)_{MIN}$ of No. 303 Bus in 2012 and 2013

Diagnostic threshold	No. 303 bus observation period					
	Y 2012			Y 2013		
	$E(T)$	$\sigma_{E(T)}$	$E(T)_{MIN}$	$E(T)$	$\sigma_{E(T)}$	$E(T)_{MIN}$
$\mu + 0.5\sigma$	11442.42	7165.91	4276.51	11681.15	8660.52	3020.63
$\mu + \sigma$	11873.20	7352.24	4520.96	12988.60	8909.57	4079.03
$\mu + 2\sigma$	12104.73	7564.41	4540.32	12988.60	8909.57	4079.03

Tables 5.23 and 5.24 show the expected minimum uptime of the buses. For No. 301 bus, the time was 3350.74 in the year 2012 and 4479.17 in the year 2013. This means that at the turn of 2012/2013, the technical repair and regulation service was carried out, improving the technical condition (status) of the bus. Hence, its reliability status improved in 2013 compared to 2012. For No. 303 bus, the time was 4276.51 in the year 2012 and 3020.63 in the year 2013. Therefore, it can be surmised that the reliability of No. 303 bus in 2012 was better than in 2013. It can also be seen that No. 301 bus had a worse reliability status than No. 303 bus in 2012. It is most likely what drove the decision to overhaul No. 301.

5.5 SUMMARY

Currently, the basis for calculating the reliability characteristics and parameters of any single technical object in the process of its operation and maintenance are the symptoms of catastrophic, parametric, and transient failures, $R(t) = R_a * R_b * R_c(t)$. Reliability characteristics are usually calculated from easily identifiable catastrophic failures, $R(t)=R_a(t)$.

This approach is applied because of the sheer difficulty in determining parametric and transient faults, $m_b(t)$ and $m_c(t)$.

A particularly preferable piece of information needed, therefore, is the reliability indicators determined from only relatively minor parametric failures m_b (t) and transient failures $m_c(t)$: $R(t) = R_b(t)R_c(t)$, from which the reliability parameters, $E(T)$ and $\sigma_{E(T)}$ are determined. It is then assumed that $R_a(t) = 1$, which means that the characteristic—and this is particularly important—is determined before a catastrophic failure occurs. The characteristics are therefore determined only on the basis of parametric and transient failures, which is safe for the technical object in operation.

The identification of failures $m_b(t)$ and $m_c(t)$ can be done by the appropriate use of coupled autonomous equations of state (Formulas 5.4 and 5.5). Complex diagnostic signals D and complex operating signals U were determined by suitable transformation of their instantaneous values D_i and U_i into universal unified points.

Parameters a_T and a_R (Formulas 5.12 and 5.15) determined at different instances of operation allow the number of failures m_b and m_c (which vary with the diagnostic thresholds) to be determined, and so the facilitated determination of estimates R_b^* and R_c^* (Formulas 1.129 to 1.134, and the n needed from Formula 1.135).

The value of parameters $E(T)$ and $\sigma_{E(T)}$ (Formulas 5.18 to 5.20) at any instance of operation over a period of operation long enough (which results from the ergodicity of the failure stream) can be considered to be useful information about the reliability status of a single object (here, the bus).

REFERENCES

1. Gołda I., Izdebski M., Podviezko A.: Assessment of efficiency of assignment of vehicles to tasks in supply chains: a case study of a municipal company. Transport, vol. 32, no. 3, pp. 243–251, 2017.
2. Günther H.: Diagnozowanie silników wysokoprężnych. Wydawnictwo Komunikacji i Łączności, Warszawa 2006.
3. Jaźwiński J., Klimaszewski S., Żurek J.: Metoda prognozowania stanu obiektu w oparciu o badania kontrolne. Zagadnienia Eksploatacji Maszyn, vol. 38, no. 2, pp. 33–44, 2003.
4. Konior J: Overdurability and technical wear of materials used in the construction of old buildings. Materials, vol. 14, no. 2, 2021.
5. Konior J., Rejment M.: Correlation between defects and technical wear of materials used in traditional construction. Materials, vol. 14, no. 10, 2021.
6. Konior J., Sawicki M., Szostak M.: Intensity of the formation of defects in residential buildings with regards to changes in their reliability. Applied Sciences, vol. 10, no. 19, 2020.
7. Rymarz J., Niewczas A., Krzyzak A.: Comparison of operational availability of public city buses by analysis of variance. Eksploatacja i Niezawodnosc—Maintenance and Reliability, vol. 18, no. 3, pp. 373–378, 2016. http://doi.org/10.17531/ein.2016.3.8.
8. Rymarz J., Niewczas A., Stoklosa J.: Reliability evaluation of the city transport buses under actual conditions. Transport and Telecommunication, vol. 16, no. 4, pp. 259–266, 2015. http://doi.org/10.1515/ttj-2015-0023

9. Sarangaa H., Knezevicb J.: Reliability prediction for condition-based maintained systems. Reliability Engineering & System Safety, vol. 71, no. 2, pp. 219–224, 2001.
10. Staszak Z., Grzes Z., Rybacki P.: A method of comparative studies on checkup sets to evaluate the technical condition of tractors. Eksploatacja i Niezawodnosc—Maintenance and Reliability, vol. 20, no. 3, pp. 450–454, 2018.
11. Sudakowski T.: Premises of operational method of calculation of reliability of machines on the base of parametric and momentary symptoms of damage. Acta mechanica et automatica, vol. 3, no. 4, pp. 73–79, 2009.
12. Szpytko J., Kocerba A.: Przyczynowo-skutkowa metodyka oceny stanu technicznego środków transportu. XXXIII Zimowa Szkoła Niezawodności PAN "Metody badań przyczyn i skutków uszkodzeń". Szczyrk 10, 2005, pp. 520–526.
13. Tylicki H., Żółtowski B.: Zmiana stanu maszyny w procesie eksploatacji. XXXIII Zimowa Szkoła Niezawodności PAN "Metody badań przyczyn i skutków uszkodzeń". Szczyrk 10, 2005, pp. 551–561.
14. Woropay M., Muślewski Ł., Ślęzak M., Szubartowski M.: Assessment of the impact of human on safety of transportation system operation. Journal of KONBiN, vol. 1, no. 25, pp. 97–106, 2013.
15. Zio E.: Reliability engineering: old problems and new challenges. Reliability Engineering and System Safety, vol. 94, no. 2, pp. 125–141, 2009.
16. Żółtowski B.: Metody diagnostyki technicznej w ocenie destrukcji maszyn. XXXV Zimowa Szkoła Niezawodności PAN "Problemy niezawodności systemów". Szczyrk 2007, pp. 587–599.
17. Grądzki R., Lindstedt P.: Determination of parameters of a technical and control states of the bus engine by using its discretized operation information. Journal of KONBIN, vol. 2, pp. 97–108, 2013.
18. Grądzki R., Lindstedt P.: Method of assessment of technical object aptitude in environment of exploitation and service conditions. Eksploatacja i Niezawodnosc—Maintenance and Reliability, vol. 1, pp. 54–63, 2015.
19. Grądzki R., Lindstedt P., Golak K.: Premises of evaluation of the technical object suitability with including the quality of its maintenance and operation, and their initial conditions. Safety and Reliability: Methodology and Applications—Proceedings of the European Safety and Reliability Conference, Chapter 44, 2015, pp. 319–326.
20. Lindstedt P., Sudakowski T.: The method of assessment of suitability of the bearing system based on parameters of technical and adjustment state. Solid State Phenomena Mechatronic Systems and Materials V, pp. 73–78, 2013.
21. Sotskow B.S.: Niezawodność elementów i urządzeń automatyki. WNT, Warszawa 1973.
22. Bukowski L.: Prognozowanie niezawodności i bezpieczeństwa systemów zautomatyzowanych. Materiały XXXI Szkoły Niezawodności, Szczyrk 2003.
23. Cempel C.: Teoria i inżynieria. Wydawnictwo Naukowe Instytutu Technologii Eksploatacyjnej PIB, Poznań 2006.
24. Jardine A.K.S., Lin D., Banjevic D.: A review on machinery diagnostics and prognostics implementing condition-based maintenance. Mechanical Systems and Signal Processing, vol. 20, no. 7, pp. 1483–1510, 2006.
25. Lindstedt P.: The method of complex worthness assessment of an engineering object in the process of its use and service. Solid State Phenomena, vol. 144, pp. 45–52, 2009.
26. Szczepaniak C.: Podstawy modelowania sytemu człowiek—pojazd—otoczenie. PWN, Warszawa 1999.

27. Cempel C., Natke H.G.: Damage Evolution and Diagnosis in Operating Systems. In Safety Evaluation Based on Identification Approaches Related to Time-Variant and Nonlinear Structures. Springer 1993, pp. 44–61.
28. Szawłowski S.: Przegląd kontrolny ASPA w systemie obsługiwania śmigłowca pokładowego SH-2G. 8 Międzynarodowa konferencja AIRDIAG, Warszawa 2005.
29. Zając M.: Wykorzystanie badań ankietowych do oszacowania niezawodności systemu transportu intermodalnego. XXXIV Zimowa Szkoła Niezawodności PAN "Niekonwencjonalne metody oceny trwałości i niezawodności". Szczyrk 9, 2006, pp. 390–397.
30. Mańczak K.: Metody identyfikacji wielowymiarowych obiektów sterowania. WNT, Warszawa 1971.
31. Niederliński A.: Systemy komputerowe automatyki przemysłowej. Tom 2 Zastosowanie. WNT, Warszawa 1985.
32. Filipczyk J.: Faults of duty vehicles in the aspects of securing safety. Transport Problems, vol. 6, no. 1, pp. 105–110, 2011.
33. Jaźwiński J., Szpytko J.: Zasady wyznaczania zespołu ekspertów w badaniach niezawodności i bezpieczeństwa urządzeń technicznych. XXXIV Zimowa Szkoła Niezawodności PAN "Niekonwencjonalne metody oceny trwałości i niezawodności". Szczyrk, pp. 157–167, 2006.
34. Lindstedt P.: Reliability and its relation to regulation and diagnostics in the machinery exploitation systems. Journal of KONBiN, vol. 1, no. 2, pp. 317–330, 2006.
35. Smalko Z: Podstawy eksploatacji technicznej pojazdów. Oficyna Wydawnicza PW, Warszawa 1998.
36. Sztarski M.: Niezawodność i eksploatacja urządzeń elektronicznych. WKŁ, Warszawa 1972.

Monograph Conclusion

The process of operation of objects is a complex interconnection of many activities: technical, social, organisational, and economic, that occur in machines, organisms, and communities [per Norbert Wiener—the founder of cybernetics]. Correct (optimal) execution of this process requires precise and unambiguous information about the machine and its environment. The communication between the machine and the environment, as well as the links within the machine, are provided by various channels of information. Of particular importance are the information relations between the environment and the quality of the object's operating process. Here, the importance of interference and the role of the decision-maker (Figures 1.2 and 1.3) in different conflicting relations (interference is a negative action, and the decision-maker is a positive action) are stressed.

The foundation of analysis of operating processes is a system model, which can be deterministic or probabilistic. The analysis deals with various problems, such as the study of the reliability of systems, the essence of regulation and control, the establishment of a basic regulation formula, the study of the equilibrium of systems, the dating of signals, the study of the proprietary and feed components of systems, the role of the Keynes multiplier in economic systems, the study of systems under mutual conflict, the study of systems with substitute methods (the Monte Carlo method), operational testing network models, and the study of the relations between information and energy for which a model in the form of Maxwell's demon was used.

In operating systems, the following are present: regulation, diagnostics, and reliability of the machine. They are in a close relationship and can only be optimally executed within the cybernetic operating system of the object. Information about the regulation status, technical status, and reliability status (Figure 2.2) is transmitted to the maintenance staff of the object (to improve the quality of maintenance activities), to the object's user (to adapt the conditions of use to the operating capacities of the object), and to the decision-maker (to continuously improve the system order), and finally converted according to Maxwell's formula:

$\Delta E = 10^{-16} \Delta l$ [erg/K] to conserve (save) time, energy, and material. Information management is the development of optimal decisions in machine regulation, diagnostics, and reliability.

The regulation of jet engines is carried out during the ground test from w. The dynamic quality of the engine "on the ground" is determined. During the test flight of the aircraft, which follows the ground test, the "in flight" engine dynamic quality from interference z is determined. Engine testing on the ground and in flight are complex, labour-intensive, and expensive processes, and they are not entirely safe. It appears that a jet engine that is very well regulated from w on the ground is not necessarily regulated so well from z in flight. It is mostly the case that when it is better from w on the ground, it is worse from z in flight (Tables 3.10 and 3.11). Therefore, the need exists to develop regulating decisions that ensure proper engine performance quality on the ground and in flight already during engine ground tests, with very limited and safe flight tests (Formula 3.18).

Fluid-flow machine blade/vane diagnostics are performed while the machine is running. Understanding the technical condition of the blade facilitates correct maintenance decisions to be made: to replace the blade, blend in the blade, or release for further safe operation. A number of methods have been developed to diagnose blades. The monograph presents a method based on diagnostic models with the elimination of the environment (Formulas 4.10 and 4.21). The technical condition of the blade was illustrated with the blade technical status portraits (Section 4.4).

In addition, the diagnostic models of the blade in motion (Formula 4.10 and 4.21), due to their formal form, can be reduced to spectral transmittance, where the output signal is the "airflow" from the blade and the input signal is the "airflow" to the blade. The spectral transmittances take the form of the inverses of Formulas 4.10 and 4.21. By determining the real part $P(\omega)$ from these transmittances, it is possible to determine the pulse and step responses of the blade (Formulas 4.24 and 4.25), which reduces the testing of the technical condition in motion to its testing during operation under determined conditions, and the quality of the blade operation is reduced to testing the regulation system (overshoot, $\chi < 20\%$ and regulation time t_r—short).

The reliability status of a single object is studied under the assumption that a sufficiently large set of objects of the same type is available. Since regulation and diagnosis are performed on every single (unitary) object at any arbitrary instance of its operation, reliability testing should also be performed according to the same convention. The transition from a set of objects to a single object and vice versa can be made by making appropriate use of the ergodicity of the stream of catastrophic failures, $m_a(t)$, parametric failures, $m_b(t)$, and transient failures, $m_c(t)$ (Formula 5.1). Since catastrophic failures are very dangerous, it was necessary for the reliability characteristics to be determined only by the number of parametric and transient failures. A method is specified for the identification of parametric and transient failures (Formulas 5.12 and 5.15) from diagnostic and utility (environment) signals reduced to point form (Tables 5.1 and 5.2). Next, estimators R_b^* and R_c^* (Formulas 1.129 to 1.135) of the reliability function $R(t)$ are determined, which is the basis for calculating the expected lifetime of the object $E(T)$ and the standard deviation of the object lifetime (Formulas 5.18 to 5.20). Tables 5.19 to 5.24 provide useful information about the reliability status of individual buses in the years of operation of interest.

The presented monograph is a compendium of knowledge for the synthetic study of any machine (a blade, a jet engine, or a bus) in any complex environment in order to determine the operational decisions that ensure the object's correct, safe, and reliable operation.

Index

A

acceleration, 110, 131
adaptive processes, 47
amplitude gain, 8, 28, 97, 147
autonomous system, 81, 82

B

balance of systems, 48–57
basic regulation pattern, 48–57, 89
baud, 86, 87, 89
Bergsonian time, xiii, 1, 92–96
bit, 84, 86
blade diagnostics, 146–174
blade, 100, 105, 146–153, 162–175
bus (object), 179–186

C

centralised system, 65, 66
chaos, 4, 86
closed system, 100, 101
complex signal, 147, 186
compressor, 105, 108, 127, 146, 147, 162
confidence level, 47
conflict situations, 58–61
control system, 10, 64, 65, 102, 103, 108–110, 119–122
control system sensitivity, 64
correlation coefficient, 27
coupling of systems, 41
critical graphs, 4, 52
critical path, 74–76
critical statistic, 18, 19
cross-correlation, 25, 27, 129, 133, 143, 151
cross-covariance, 27
cybernetic information, 80
cybernetic system, 65

D

deceleration, 109, 110, 112, 130, 131
decision-maker, xiv, 2, 3, 98, 104, 182, 191, 213
destruction, 94
deterministic system, 4–9, 29
diagnostic inference, 96–98, 175
diagnostic methods, 98
diagnostic model, 97, 99
diagnostic object, 98–100
diagnostic signal, 96, 97, 104, 147, 180, 184

diagnostic system, 95, 96, 98, 99
diagnostic testing, 96–99, 146
distribution function, 14–16, 20–22, 34

E

economic system, 57–58
elimination of environment, 149–153
engine, 98, 102, 108, 183–188
engine control system, 102–103, 109–110, 122–123
engine simulation testing, 113–119
engine test program, 110–112
environment, 1–3, 72, 96–98, 107–108, 120, 146–153
environment signal, 146–153
equations of interaction, 9, 179–183
equations of state, 9, 179, 182
ergodicity, 26, 201
essence of control, 47
estimation, 20, 22
estimator bias, 23
estimators, 20, 22–24, 33–34, 201
expected lifetime of the object, 32, 201, 207
expected time to failure value, 32
expected value, 22
expert weights, 186
exponential distribution, 36

F

failure, 29–40, 69, 71, 95, 98–99, 103–104, 178–183, 201
failure density function, 38
failure identification, 178–182
failure severity, 34–37
failure severity function, 32
fallibility, 29–31, 89
feed component, 48, 56, 89
follow-up transmittance, 7, 49
forming of signals, 97
Fourier transform, 28, 129, 149, 151
frequency response, 9, 87–88
fuel delivery and control system, 109–110

G

game, 58–61, 64
game theory, 58–59
ground and flight engine testing, 107, 112–113, 119

H

Hanning's window, 129, 133
hierarchical system, 2, 66, 67, 90

I

information, 66, 78–82, 85–87, 94–95, 113,
      183–184, 209
information/energy relations, 80–82
information entropy, 83–84
information quantity, 72, 84, 86
information–transmission, 82–89
information types, 79–80
in-service testing, 108, 112, 179, 183–201
interference transmittance, 7, 49

J

jet engine regulation, 100–103, 110

K

Keynes multiplier, 57–58
Kotielnikov's theorem, 88

L

Laplace transform, 5–6
large system, 63–67, 77
leading function, 32
limit values, 103–104
log-normal distribution, 34, 36–37
Lyapunov function, 9, 133, 143

M

maintenance system, 94
Markov's process, 26–17
mathematical models, 36, 67, 72, 97
maxmini strategy, 58–61
Maxwell, 86, 104
Maxwell's demon, 82–90
measurement of signals, 96
median, 32, 173
minimax strategy, 58–61
modified signals, 126–128
Monte Carlo method, 68–71

N

network model, 72–73
Newtonian time, 93–94
non-parametric diagnostics, 164–174
normal distribution, 16, 21, 26, 36

null and alternative hypothesis, 20–21
Nyquist interval, 9, 88

O

object fitness, 31, 94, 98–100,
      103–104, 151
open system, 100
operating systems, 99–100, 103–104
operational research, 72–78
operation-decision options, 76–78
operator transmittance, 8–9, 89, 164

P

phase model, 151
phase shift, 8, 28, 97, 147, 152–153
power of a test, 21
probabilistic systems, 9–29
probability, 10
probability density, 15–16, 21, 26
probability distribution functions, 16, 25–26,
      34, 36–37
proprietary component, 56, 58, 89

Q

quantile, 32

R

random signals–relationships, 27
redundant element, 29
regulation, 48–49, 56, 94, 100–103, 107–108,
      114, 126, 128, 142–143
regulation diagram, 114, 127
regulation essence, 45, 89
regulator power, 51
regulator transmittance, 6, 120, 122
relationships between random signals, 27
reliability, 29–34, 92, 95–96, 101–104,
      178–179, 201
reliability characteristics, 31–34, 102, 179,
      182–183, 196, 201
reliability function, 31, 34, 181, 206
reliability parameters, 201–208
risk, 61–63

S

self correlation, 25, 27, 129, 133, 143,
      149, 151
self covariance, 27
setting, 113
Shannon's formula, 89

shift of phase, 8, 28, 97, 147, 152–153
signal dating, 48, 89
signal flow graph, 2–4
signal transform, 5–6
significance level, 21, 47, 173
spectral power density, 28, 96–97, 128, 151
spectral transmittance, 8–9, 28–29, 89, 122–123, 125, 129–130, 143
stability of systems, 4, 9, 48–56
standard deviation, 16–18, 34, 47, 151, 182, 201, 207
standard deviation of time to failure, 32
statistical hypothesis, 20
statistical threshold, 182
statistics, 9–10, 17, 22–23
step and pulse response, 9, 121, 123, 165
stochastic process, 9–10, 25–27
structure matrix, 41–45
supervision, 98
system conflict, 58
system network, 72
system order, 84–85, 104

system quality, 65, 97
system redundancy, 84

T

technical status, 92–93, 95, 97–98–104, 150, 162, 164, 180–183
technical status parameter, 180–182
technical status portrait, 162–164
time reserve, 75
type 1 error and type 2 error, 21–22

V

variance, 15, 22, 24–25
variance of time to failure, 32

W

Weibull distribution, 36–37
weights of experts, 186
Wiener process, 26, 96

For Product Safety Concerns and Information please contact our EU
representative GPSR@taylorandfrancis.com
Taylor & Francis Verlag GmbH, Kaufingerstraße 24, 80331 München, Germany